Essentials of **Psychological Assessment** Series

Everything you need to know to administer, score, and interpret the major psychological tests.

I'd like to order the following *Essentials* titles:

- ☐ WAIS®-IV Assessment (w/CD-ROM) / 978-...
- ☐ WJ III™ Cognitive Abilities Assessment, Second Edition / 978-0-470-56664-0 • $38.95
- ☐ Cross-Battery Assessment, Second Edition (w/CD-ROM) / 978-0-471-75771-9 • $48.95
- ☐ Nonverbal Assessment / 978-0-471-38318-5 • $38.95
- ☐ PAI® Assessment / 978-0-471-08463-1 • $38.95
- ☐ CAS Assessment / 978-0-471-29015-5 • $38.95
- ☐ MMPI®-2 Assessment, Second Edition / 978-0-470-92323-8 • $38.95
- ☐ Myers-Briggs Type Indicator® Assessment, Second Edition / 978-0-470-34390-6 • $38.95
- ☐ Rorschach® Assessment / 978-0-471-33146-9 • $38.95
- ☐ Millon™ Inventories Assessment, Third Edition / 978-0-470-16862-2 • $38.95
- ☐ TAT and Other Storytelling Assessments, Second Edition / 978-0-470-28192-5 • $38.95
- ☐ MMPI-A™ Assessment / 978-0-471-39815-8 • $38.95
- ☐ NEPSY®-II Assessment / 978-0-470-43691-2 • $38.95
- ☐ Neuropsychological Assessment, Second Edition / 978-0-470-43747-6 • $38.95
- ☐ WJ III™ Tests of Achievement Assessment / 978-0-471-33059-2 • $38.95
- ☐ Evidence-Based Academic Interventions / 978-0-470-20632-4 • $38.95
- ☐ WRAML2 and TOMAL-2 Assessment / 978-0-470-17911-6 • $38.95
- ☐ WMS®-IV Assessment / 978-0-470-62196-7 • $38.95
- ☐ Behavioral Assessment / 978-0-471-35367-6 • $38.95
- ☐ Forensic Psychological Assessment, Second Edition / 978-0-470-55168-4 • $38.95
- ☐ Bayley Scales of Infant Development II Assessment / 978-0-471-32651-9 • $38.95
- ☐ Career Interest Assessment / 978-0-471-35365-2 • $38.95
- ☐ WPPSI™-III Assessment / 978-0-471-28895-4 • $38.95
- ☐ 16PF® Assessment / 978-0-471-23424-1 • $38.95
- ☐ Assessment Report Writing / 978-0-471-39487-7 • $38.95
- ☐ Stanford-Binet Intelligence Scales (SB5) Assessment / 978-0-471-22404-4 • $38.95
- ☐ WISC®-IV Assessment, Second Edition (w/CD-ROM) / 978-0-470-18915-3 • $48.95
- ☐ KABC-II Assessment / 978-0-471-66733-9 • $38.95
- ☐ WIAT®-III and KTEA-II Assessment (w/CD-ROM) / 978-0-470-55169-1 • $48.95
- ☐ Processing Assessment / 978-0-471-71925-0 • $38.95
- ☐ School Neuropsychological Assessment / 978-0-471-78372-5 • $38.95
- ☐ Cognitive Assessment with KAIT & Other Kaufman Measures / 978-0-471-38317-8 • $38.95
- ☐ Assessment with Brief Intelligence Tests / 978-0-471-26412-5 • $38.95
- ☐ Creativity Assessment / 978-0-470-13742-0 • $38.95
- ☐ WNV™ Assessment / 978-0-470-28467-4 • $38.95
- ☐ DAS-II® Assessment (w/CD-ROM) / 978-0-470-22520-2 • $48.95
- ☐ Executive Function Assessment (w/CD-ROM) / 978-0-470-42202-1 • $48.95
- ☐ Conners Behavior Assessments™ / 978-0-470-34633-4 • $38.95
- ☐ Temperament Assessment / 978-0-470-44447-4 • $38.95
- ☐ Response to Intervention / 978-0-470-56663-3 • $38.95
- ☐ Specific Learning Disability Identification / 978-0-470-58760-7 • $38.95
- ☐ IDEA for Assessment Professionals (w/CD-ROM) / 978-0-470-87392-2 • $48.95
- ☐ Dyslexia Assessment and Intervention / 978-0-470-92760-1 • $38.95
- ☐ Autism Spectrum Disorders Evaluation and Assessment / 978-0-470-62194-3 • $38.95

Please complete the order form on the back.
To order by phone, call toll free 1-877-762-2974
To order online: www.wiley.com/essentials
To order by mail: refer to order form on next page

Essentials

of **Psychological Assessment** Series

ORDER FORM

Please send this order form with your payment (credit card or check) to:
John Wiley & Sons, Attn: J. Knott, 111 River Street, Hoboken, NJ 07030-5774

QUANTITY	TITLE	ISBN	PRICE
___	___	___	___
___	___	___	___
___	___	___	___
___	___	___	___
___	___	___	___

Shipping Charges:	Surface	2-Day	1-Day
First item	$5.00	$10.50	$17.50
Each additional item	$3.00	$3.00	$4.00

For orders greater than 15 items,
please contact Customer Care at 1-877-762-2974.

ORDER AMOUNT _____
SHIPPING CHARGES _____
SALES TAX _____
TOTAL ENCLOSED _____

NAME_____

AFFILIATION_____

ADDRESS_____

CITY/STATE/ZIP _____

TELEPHONE _____

EMAIL_____

❑ Please add me to your e-mailing list

PAYMENT METHOD:

❑ Check/Money Order   ❑ Visa   ❑ Mastercard   ❑ AmEx

Card Number _____ Exp. Date _____

Cardholder Name *(Please print)* _____

Signature _____

*Make checks payable to **John Wiley & Sons**. Credit card orders invalid if not signed.*
All orders subject to credit approval. • Prices subject to change.

To order by phone, call toll free 1-877-762-2974
To order online: www.wiley.com/essentials

Essentials of
WRAML2 and
TOMAL-2 Assessment

Essentials of Psychological Assessment Series
Series Editors, Alan S. Kaufman and Nadeen L. Kaufman

Essentials

of WRAML2 and
TOMAL-2 Assessment

Wayne Adams

Cecil R. Reynolds

John Wiley & Sons, Inc.

Published by John Wiley & Sons, Inc., Hoboken, New Jersey.
Published simultaneously in Canada.

For general information on our other products and services please contact our Customer Care Department within the U.S. at (800) 762-2974, outside the United States at (317) 572-3993 or fax (317) 572-4002.

Wiley also publishes its books in a variety of electronic formats. Some content that appears in print may not be available in electronic books. For more information about Wiley products, visit our web site at www.wiley.com.

Library of Congress Cataloging-in-Publication Data:

Adams, Wayne.
    Essentials of WRAML2 and TOMAL-2 assessment / by Wayne Adams and Cecil R. Reynolds.
        p. cm. — (Essentials of psychological assessment series)
    Includes bibliographical references and index.
    ISBN 978-0-470-17911-6 (pbk.)
        1. Wide Range Assessment of Memory and Learning. 2. Test of Memory and Learning.
    I. Reynolds, Cecil R., 1952–   II. Title.
BF375.5.W53A32 2009
153.1028'7—dc22

                                                                                        2008017695

Printed in the United States of America

10 9 8 7 6 5 4 3

To you who mean so much to me
and have provided wonderful memories,
Nora, Jen, Elizabeth, Martha, Cana, Ellie, and Scott
Gratefully,
Wayne

And to Julia,
Cecil

CONTENTS

SERIES PREFACE

In the *Essentials of Psychological Assessment* series, we have attempted to provide the reader with books that will deliver key practical information in the most efficient and accessible style. The series features instruments in a variety of domains, such as cognition, personality, education, and neuropsychology. For the experienced clinician, books in the series will offer a concise yet thorough way to master utilization of the continuously evolving supply of new and revised instruments, as well as a convenient method for keeping up to date on the tried-and-true measures. The novice will find here a prioritized assembly of all the information and techniques that must be at one's fingertips to begin the complicated process of individual psychological diagnosis.

Wherever feasible, visual shortcuts to highlight key points are utilized alongside systematic, step-by-step guidelines. Chapters are focused and succinct. Topics are targeted for an easy understanding of the essentials of administration, scoring, interpretation, and clinical application. Theory and research are continually woven into the fabric of each book, but always to enhance clinical inference, never to sidetrack or overwhelm. We have long been advocates of what has been called *intelligent testing*— the notion that a profile of test scores is meaningless unless it is brought to life by the clinical observations and astute detective work of knowledgeable examiners. Test profiles must be used to make a difference in the child's or adult's life, or why bother to test? We want this series to help our readers become the best intelligent testers they can be.

In *Essentials of WRAML2 and TOMAL-2 Assessment*, Drs. Adams and Reynolds provide excellent insights into their respective tests. Both beginners and those familiar with each instrument will find useful material that goes beyond what is found in the test manuals. Following a historical and neurological overview of memory assessment, sections highlighting each instrument are presented. For each battery, specific discussions of test rationale, content, and format are provided. Building on that foundation, a more sophisticated discussion then follows that includes key topics such as common administration errors, interpretative guidelines, and clinical applications. Supplemental data are presented that are not found elsewhere, along with competency-building aides. There is a nice balance between clinically applicable material and conceptual issues. Whether the reader uses the WRAML2, TOMAL-2, or both instruments, this book offers a sound professional grounding to learn, expand, and refine a variety of skills related to the measurement of memory assessment.

Alan S. Kaufman, PhD, and Nadeen L. Kaufman, EdD, Series Editors
Yale University School of Medicine

Essentials of
WRAML2 and
TOMAL-2 Assessment

One

FOUNDATIONS: MEMORY AND ITS MEASUREMENT

Generating meaning from these words is an impressive memory feat. You have to first remember procedural aspects like where to start on the page and to use your eyes and to scan left to right. You also need to remember what the various letter and word combinations represent phonetically and holistically. Then you need to remember what meaning to assign those many phonetic and visual combinations. You also need to remember the meaning at the beginning of a sentence until the end of the sentence, and the beginning of the paragraph until its end. Obviously, without memory, reading would be impossible. And actually, without memory, life as we know it would be impossible.

Memory is a central feature of human intelligence and is represented in nearly all day-to-day functions, be they intellectual, academic, social, vocational, or recreational. Memory makes us who we are and preserves our identity. Without the ability to recall our own personal history, we would be in a near state of confusion and constant dilemma. Indeed, the greatest tragedy of the dementias is that they eventually take from us who we are and what we know of ourselves. Memory allows us to acquire skills and knowledge, to perform our jobs, and to recognize and respond appropriately to our loved ones. Simply stated, memory is ubiquitous in daily life. *Memory,* as the term is used here, will reflect this commonsense understanding (i.e., the ability to recall an event, an object, or a behavior—to remember something).

While memory is a central cognitive process, it also is a very vulnerable brain function. Various trauma, minor or devastating, can affect the efficiency of the brain laying down new memories and/or retrieving those already stored. Generally speaking, if there is going to be some cognitive compromise resulting from a brain insult, it is most likely that memory will be among those processes negatively affected. Difficulties with memory and attention are the two most common complaints following even mild head trauma. Further, it seems that memory is susceptible to congenital vagaries as well. Therefore, memory, like intelligence, can be demonstrated to range widely across individuals, from very impaired to quite impressive, starting in early childhood. And like intelligence, there is developmental change associated with age. Therefore, it should not be surprising that psychologists, neuropsychologists, and neuroscientists have devoted and continue to devote much attention to memory and its measurement.

This book features the two major comprehensive memory batteries currently available for assessment of memory functions in children and adults—the *Wide Range Assessment of Memory and Learning–Second Edition* (WRAML2; Sheslow & Adams, 2003) and the *Test of Memory and Learning–Second Edition* (TOMAL-2; Reynolds & Voress, 2007). Each of these batteries is intended to sample reliably a variety of memory functions that are of clinical and theoretical interest for children, adolescents, and adults.

Memory can be broken down into a multitude of forms, or *types,* each of which has a seemingly endless number of variations of task, process, and stimuli. Depending upon one's theoretical orientation, distinctions among memory processes may carry such labels as abstract, meaningful, verbal, figural, spatial, associative, free recall, sequential, recognition, retrieval, procedural, episodic, working, and semantic, among others. There is no uniformly accepted terminology used to describe memory function. This diversity in memory terminology is rivaled only by the hundreds of terms designed to reflect specific aptitudes and personality characteristics.

A single task may carry multiple classifications legitimately because theories of memory and their terminology often overlap. Some have even considered this classic definition of learning as also defining memory (e.g., see

> **DON'T FORGET**
>
> The WRAML2 and the TOMAL-2 distinguish memory and learning by providing subtests that assess both immediate memory as well as new learning over multiple trials, and subsequent recall of that newly acquired information.

Kolb & Whishaw, 2003). However, although the distinction may be to some degree artificial (anything recalled must have been *learned*), the WRAML2 and the TOMAL-2 distinguish memory and learning by providing subtests that assess both immediate memory as well as new learning over multiple trials, and subsequent recall of that newly acquired information. Although clinical utility was emphasized in the development of the WRAML2 and the TOMAL-2 as well as throughout this volume, researchers will also find the tests valuable in that their content provides reliable coverage of more, different memory functions for this age range than is available in any other co-normed, standardized format.

HISTORICAL FOUNDATIONS

Unlike some domains of psychological testing, memory assessment had a relatively strong empirical base upon which to build. That foundation has had many contributors. Hans Ebbinghaus is generally recognized as among the first to study memory. His now classic "forgetting curve" was published as part of numerous findings related to more than a decade of research on memory and forgetting (Ebbinghaus, 1885). Ebbinghaus operationalized what we now think of as *immediate memory* using a digit span task and nonsense syllables. He showed that the amount to be remembered affects performance and having a way to *chunk* information increased performance. The meaningfulness of the information to the learner was shown to affect retention too.

A contemporary of Ebbinghaus was Alfred Binet, famous for creating the first measures of intellectual ability. Less known is Binet's interest in many facets of memory. This focus is perhaps one reason that 20% of his first intelligence test (the 1905 Binet-Simon Scale) consisted of questions directly assessing immediate verbal and visual memory abilities.

While Sigmund Freud did not investigate memory per se, his revolutionary theory was heavily reliant on diverse memory mechanisms. Later, Karl Lashley (long-term memory) (1950), George Miller (and his "7 ± 2" rule) (1956), Alexander Luria (the case of S and his unlimited long-term memory) (2006), and many others contributed an enormous amount of research that help us better understand memory. A lengthier treatment of research "pioneers" who contributed both directly and indirectly to memory assessment can be found in comprehensive sources like Haberlandt (1999), Squire and Schacter (2002), and Kolb and Wishaw (2003). Memory research continues, embracing new technologies and focusing on such contemporary and applied topics as the impact of blast injuries on the memories of soldiers serving in Iraq using fMRI imaging techniques along with formal memory testing.

Yet, despite over a century of research on the topic of memory, the clinical assessment of normal and disordered memory has been fraught with problems (Fuster, 1995; Miller, Bigler, & Adams, 2003; Prigatano, 1978; Riccio & Reynolds, 1998), many of which stem from difficulties separating attention and memory as well as immediate memory from short-

DON'T FORGET

The two most common complaints of individuals following a closed head injury are difficulties with attention and memory.

term and longer-term memory (see especially Fuster, 1995; Miller et al., 2003; Riccio & Reynolds, 1998; and Riccio, Reynolds, & Lowe, 2001).

We have known for a long time that certain neurological disorders of adulthood that tend to occur in the elderly (but also may appear as early as 40 years of age—e.g., Alzheimer's Disease, Binswanger's Disease, Huntington's Chorea, Korsakoff's Syndrome, Pick's Disease) have a profound impact on memory, and the type of memory loss that a person displays may have diagnostic implications for that disorder. Numerous neurological disorders of children and adolescents (including epilepsy, head trauma, most of the more than 600 known degenerative neurological disorders, and neoplasms) also have implications for memory, but they have less predictable and more global or generalized effects on memory than with adults. Children diagnosed as learning disabled, whether one views this as a neuropsychological disorder or not, commonly show a variety of memory problems (Reynolds & Fletcher-Janzen, 1997; Riccio & Reynolds, 1998; Riccio & Wolfe, 2003). When these conditions are chronic, related memory problems persist into adulthood (e.g., Goldstein & Reynolds, 2005).

As part of the standard neurological exam dating back to the beginning of the last century, neurologists have always asked the patient questions concerning "today's date," current news items, and some recitation of letters, words, or sentences as a crude attempt to establish whether memory was "normal." Such a screening assumed that individuals free of neurological disease or disorder would have no difficulty recalling such simple items, in contrast to neurologically compromised individuals who would display some type of impairment. However, it became evident that neurological disorders impacted memory with such variability that more elaborate assessment methods were necessary. Neuropsychiatric and psychological problems (e.g., de-

> **DON'T FORGET**
> ....
> Children diagnosed as learning disabled commonly show a variety of memory problems.

pression) also are known to affect memory subsystems differentially across the age range; therefore psychiatrists, among others, also routinely include informal memory tasks within their *mental status exam* of children, adolescents, and adults. With children and adolescents, the variability of normal development further complicates this type of informal assessment practice, and often demands more sophisticated evaluation. Regardless of the age or presenting complaints, memory assessment is paradoxical in certain regards: Memory is both fragile and robust. While even slight, seemingly inconsequential blows to the head can cause substantial memory problems (Levin, Eisenberg, & Benton, 1989), some individuals with massive neoplasms or even hydrocephalic children with greatly reduced neural tissue will sometimes exhibit little memory compromise. Systematic evaluation of memory is required to understand learning and behavioral functions, and their normal range of variability seems to dictate standardized procedures such as those represented on the WRAML2 and the TOMAL-2.

Recognizing the need to go beyond the common neurological and psychiatric memory "exam," Luria (1966) devised a more thorough and insightful evaluation, but he continued in a clinical tradition that was difficult to subject to quantification. Similar to neurologists of his day, Luria would often employ impromptu methods to assess a particular patient suspected of impaired memory. Again, the diagnostic assumption was that the patient would either be "impaired" or "not impaired." Such a dichotomous and idiosyncratic approach in clinical practice, while sometimes creative, did not provide an approach that would lead to quantifiable procedures. While qualitative approaches provided a certain richness and flexibility diagnostically, they did not easily provide nuanced evaluation of milder deficit or identification of areas of memory strength. Further, qualitative approaches require many, many years of experience, supervision, and exposure to a wide range of pathology, not to mention the immense creativity and careful theoretical reflection required in the clinician. In contrast, Western psychology, with its legacy of quantification, strongly influenced neuropsychological and other forms of assessment to proceed in a more psychometrically exacting direction.

Much of the evolution in modern neuropsychology in the United States can be attributed to events associated with World War II. With dramatically improved emergency medicine in field hospitals, for the first time in the history of warfare many soldiers survived brain injury. Many of these victims had accompanying deficits in memory function. During this era the need for some type of standardization or *battery* of tests that could assess memory became obvious. Such a battery would depend on quantification so that useful information concerning the nature of the deficit could be reliably relayed from one health specialist to another. With the success of the *Wechsler-Bellevue Intelligence Test* in 1939, David Wechsler developed the *Wechsler Memory Scale* (WMS) as a "rapid, simple, and practical" measure of memory (Wechsler, 1945, p. 16). The *Wechsler Memory Scale* was rapidly incorporated into clinical practice and by the 1950s and 1960s was entrenched as the *only* measure of adult memory that could be compared with an intelligence quotient. The WMS and its revisions, WMS-R and WMS-III, however, are primarily adult measures, beginning at the upper ranges of adolescence. Memory problems in children and their impact on development, learning, and behavior simply were not emphasized or even recognized to the same extent that adult memory symptoms were.

During this same period of time (1940–1960), other tests of memory were being developed, most notably, *Rey-Osterrieth Complex Figure Design* (Rey, 1941), the *Rey Auditory Verbal Learning Test* (Rey, 1958), and the *Benton Visual Retention Test* (Benton, 1946). The *Rey Auditory Verbal Learning Test* was a list-learning task in which 15 words were presented to the patient over five trials. This would permit creation of a learning curve; and by using an interference procedure one could examine forgetting— a factor particularly important in certain neurological disorders (Lezak, 1983). Additionally, the words could be embedded in a paragraph so that recognition memory could be assessed. Although widely used as a clinical test, it was never fully standardized or normed. Additionally, the Rey auditory verbal learning approach did not permit a detailed evaluation of storage and retrieval of information. To examine these principles of memory more fully, and to apply them to a clinical procedure, Buschke and Fuld (1974) developed the *Selective Reminding Test*. With this procedure, the individual is told only the words that are "failed" on the previous trial, thereby allowing another method of studying long- and short-term retrieval from storage.

Visual memory has been typically assessed by the *Benton Visual Retention Test* (Benton, 1974) or the *Rey-Osterrieth Complex Figure Task* (Rey, 1941). Both have the confound of requiring the examinee to use graphomotor abilities; and if there is any disturbance in perceptual-motor functioning, this can affect performance on either one of these tasks adversely. The *Benton Visual Retention Test* has sound psychometric properties for older children and adolescents. Unfortunately, it has not been fully standardized in the lower age ranges. The Rey-Osterrieth figure is complicated and somewhat difficult to score, and this has presented obstacles in its use and clinical utility. Also, the delayed recall feature of the Rey-Osterrieth has never been fully standardized and normed, and numerous methods for assessing delayed recall have been suggested. Both of these measures have also been criticized because there is an element of verbal categorization that can be used so that the tasks may also tap verbal memory as well as the intended domain of visual memory.

As they developed over the years since the late 1930s, memory testing efforts continued to be focused primarily on adults. Nevertheless, some pediatric focus was evident. The various versions of the *Halstead* (and *Halstead-Reitan*) *Neuropsychological Test Batteries* (e.g., Reitan & Wolfson, 1985) routinely included several brief memory measures for children 6 to 14 years of age. However, psychologists engaged in the assessment of memory in children were often forced to use informal techniques (such as a *recall* segment following administration of Bender's 1938 *Bender-Gestalt Test*) as follow-up to any suspected memory problems arising from the few memory procedures included on formal intelligence batteries. Dorothea McCarthy (1972), a developmental psycholinguist, placed a Memory Index on the *McCarthy Scales of Children's Abilities,* but even this scale overlapped other scales and was spare in its coverage. It was not until the 1990s that the first comprehensive, pediatrically focused memory measures appeared—specifically the original versions of the WRAML (Sheslow & Adams, 1990) and TOMAL (Reynolds & Bigler, 1994b).

It is of interest to note that by the late 1980s, 80% of a sample of various testing experts noted memory as an important aspect of a cognitive assessment (Snyderman & Rothman, 1987). Yet, despite the recognized importance of memory assessment and the inclusion as brief recall tasks on most popular IQ tests since the early 1900s, widespread adoption of comprehensive memory batteries was not seen until the beginning of the 21st century.

Rapid Reference 1.1 lists the evolution of instruments used in clinical memory testing, and Rapid Reference 1.2 lists memory phenomena identified by various researchers over the last 130 years. Most terms in Rapid Reference 1.2 are recognized by psychologists, and many of these research *products* have been formative in defining the content of contemporary memory tests. Those memory phenomena found within the subtests of both the WRAML2 and TOMAL-2 are also noted in Rapid Reference 1.2. The meaning of the terms can be found in almost any introductory psychology or cognitive psychology text.

You will note that neither the WRAML2 nor the TOMAL-2 include long-term memory tasks.

DON'T FORGET

It was near the mid-20th century when the first comprehensive memory measures appeared, but widespread use of comprehensive memory batteries, like the WRAML2 and TOMAL-2, was not common until the beginning of the 21st century.

≡ *Rapid Reference 1.1*

A Short Chronology of Memory Tests

1941. Rey-Osterrieth Complex Figure Task

1945. Wechsler Memory Scale (1987, Second Edition; 1997, Third Edition; 2009, Fourth Edition)

1946. Benton Visual Retention Test

1958. Rey Verbal Learning Task

1974. Selective Reminding Task

1987. California Verbal Learning Test

1990. Wide Range Assessment of Memory and Learning

1994. Test of Memory and Learning

1997. Children's Memory Scale

2003. Wide Range Assessment of Memory and Learning—Second Edition

2007. Test of Memory and Learning—Second Edition

In fact, there are no normed, psychometrically sound measures of long-term memory. This, obviously, is not because long-term memory is not an important aspect of our memory systems, but rather due to the difficulty of creating such a scale. In part, this is because everyone's background is different and so creating a scale not biased to one or more cultural backgrounds would be challenging. Further, item difficulties of a long-term memory scale likely would change frequently. Questions like, who is Catherine the Great? or what country has the largest Muslim population? can change in difficulty if a movie, video game, or breaking news story happens to highlight this information. A scale made up of such questions would have questionable validity. Therefore, because of a number of practical dilemmas, long-term memory,

≡ *Rapid Reference 1.2*

Memory phenomena from past research found on the WRAML2 and TOMAL-2

Included in WRAML2?	Memory Phenomena	Included in TOMAL-2?
Yes	Anterograde amnesia	Yes
No	Retrograde amnesia	No
No	Episodic memory	No
Yes	Semantic memory	Yes
Yes	Explicit memory	Yes
Yes	Short-term (Immediate) memory	Yes
Yes	Longer-term (Delayed) memory	Yes
Yes	Recognition memory vs. retrieval	Yes
Yes	Meaningful vs. rote information	Yes
yes	Developmental changes with age	Yes
Yes	Working memory	Yes
Yes	Visual memory contrasted with verbal memory	Yes
Yes	New learning over trials, resulting in a learning curve	Yes
Yes	Eidetic memory	Yes
Yes	Meaningful vs. nonmeaningful memory comparisons	Yes

while important, is a domain of memory not measured in memory batteries. While there is evidence showing delayed memory, as assessed in the WRAML2 and TOMAL-2, is moderately to highly correlated with various types of longer term memory (Lezak et al., 2004), there are scant data showing this is true in clinical populations.

ANATOMY OF MEMORY

Another avenue of investigation that contributed significantly to our understanding of memory is neuroanatomical research. Although a comprehensive review of the neurobiology of memory is beyond the scope of this chapter, a brief discussion of the neural substrates of memory systems will provide an important backdrop to a discussion of memory assessment. For a more in-depth discussion, excellent reviews are provided by Squire and Schacter (2002), Kolb and Whishaw (2003), and Zillmer, Spiers, and Culbertson (2008). Knowledge of the neurological aspects of memory and its pathology are important in guiding understanding and interpretation of clinical observations and test findings.

For memories to be formed the individual must experience internal or environmental sensations; awareness is not necessary. While memories can be formed and retrieved within any of our sense modalities, within our culture, visual and auditory systems are central. Therefore, historically, assessment of memory focused on these two modalities, with a greater emphasis placed on verbal processing. The verbal versus visual memory distinction provides an important heuristic for the clinician in that the left hemisphere is more oriented toward processing language-based memory and the right toward visuospatial memory (Zillmer et al., 2008). It follows then, that bilateral damage often affects both verbal and visual memory.

Regardless of the sensory modality, several critical brain structures are involved in the development of memories, including the hippocampus, fornix, mamillary bodies, diverse thalamic nuclei, and distributed regions of the neocortex (see Figures 1.1, 1.2, and 1.3). Briefly, neural impulses travel from the sensory organs, primary cortex, and association neocortex to the medial temporal lobe regions including the hippocampal formation (Figure 1.1). The hippocampus and nearby structures (e.g., fornix, mamillary body, anterior thalamus) seem to be the

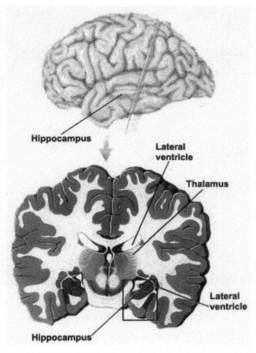

Figure 1.1. A coronal section of the brain showing the location of the hippocampus and related structures of both hemispheres.

(Used by permission, Bruno Dubuc, www.thebrain.mcgill.ca)

location where associations are formed between new incoming information and previously processed information. (Figures 1.2 and 1.3 show increasingly greater detail of this important area of the brain. Contemporary research of neuroscientists is examining functions of smaller and smaller areas within this region [e.g., the dendate gyrus, subiculum] and discovering yet greater complexity of memory storage and retrieval functions.) Damage to the hippocampal region can result in a person's being able to recall immediately a brief stimulus such as a picture or short sentence, but seconds later that information is no longer available to the person because the damaged region cannot help in storing new

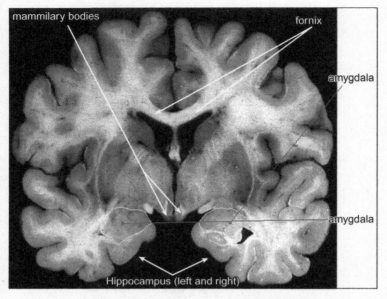

Figure 1.2 Hippocampus, fornix, and amygdala: bilateral, medial temporal lobe structures of the brain–coronal presentation.

(Used by permission, BrainInfo [2007], Neuroscience Division, National Primate Research Center, U. Washington, http://www.braininfo.org)

information. This was dramatically discovered from a client who in the mid-1950s underwent the surgical removal of much of the hippocampal structures in both hemispheres in order to remedy his intractable seizures (Corkin, 2002). While the surgery successfully eliminated most of the seizures, unfortunately it rendered the man, known as HM, mostly unable to lay down any new memories. HM's old memories remained available, but despite a normal IQ he was unable to function in contemporary society because his "conscious life" never progressed beyond the day of his surgery. Interestingly, *implicit* memory (memory not dependent on conscious learning) was much less impaired for HM. Subsequent research showed that unilateral lesions seldom produce severe global memory impairment. But dominant hemisphere (usually the left hemi-

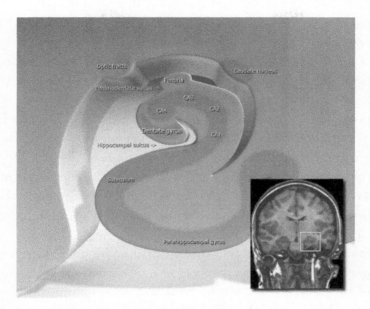

Figure 1.3 Some of the important hippocampal structures that are essential for laying down new memories.

(Image courtesy of Dr. Frank Gaillard, www.en.wikipedia.org/wiki/Image: Hipppocampus _(brain).jpg).

sphere) lesions in the hippocampal region can cause more noticeable deficits in laying down new verbal memories, whereas unilateral lesions of the nondominant (usually right) hemisphere tend to cause deficits in laying down new visual memories (Corkin, 2002). Further, Blumenfeld (2002) describes different cellular mechanisms (electrical and chemical) as well as anatomical structures that are also involved at different points within the time sequence associated with memory storage.

Examiners should have some basic knowledge of the neurobiology of memory because insult to various parts of the brain resulting from accident or disease or even genetic malfunctions may well disrupt memory function in a variety of ways and via more than one mechanism. In a discussion of the neurobiology of memory, two levels need to be considered: One is the cellular level; the other is the *system* level—that is, the synergistic interaction of nerve cells. At the cellular level, we know that a variety of changes may occur in an individual neuron, including alterations in its membrane and synaptic physiology. At the systems level, two critical regions mediate memory: the medial aspect of the temporal lobe (hippocampus and its connecting fibers, as with HM) and the midline structures of the diencephalon. Damage to either of these regions typically renders the individual impaired in establishing new memories (anterograde amnesia). An inability to recall past memories (retrograde amnesia) is commonly thought of as the definition of the term *amnesia,* and it can also be associated with hippocampal damage.

Research also demonstrates that the brain as a whole participates in memory functioning. Thus, patients with damage to the brain, regardless of its side or location, may be at risk for having diminished memory performance in a variety of domains. Accordingly, there seems to be a nonspecific lowering of memory performance associated with neurological dysfunction in general. It is not always clear whether this is attributable to pure memory systems or declines in attention and concentration, and assessing both is necessary. Attention is a precursor to memory (e.g., see Riccio et al., 2001). Damage to temporal and temporo-limbic structures will also disturb attention and concentration, as will frontal lobe damage—all of which may masquerade as memory deficiencies.

However, for intact brains, following new information entering the hippocampal circuit, long-term storage occurs as this structure seems to distribute the

DON'T FORGET

Anterograde amnesia refers to an inability or difficulty in establishing new memories.

DON'T FORGET

Retrograde amnesia refers to an inability or difficulty recalling previously learned information

information via various neural pathways to the cerebral cortex, where memories have received the most extensive processing and are the least vulnerable to injury. *Long-term memory,* the recall of well-established information or events, tends to be one of the most robust of neural functions, while sustained attention, concentration, and the formation of new memories tend to be the most fragile and subsequently the most sensitive to neural insult.

Along with these information-laden *memory circuits,* a secondary emotional memory function is also stored with long-term memories. The amygdala and its surrounding structures are responsible for *coloring* informational memories with feeling. This emotional component has not been a focus of formal memory assessment, although it serves as an important cue when memories are retrieved. However, it is thought that the binding of emotion to informational aspects of memory is an ongoing part of memory that allows us to recognize whether positive, negative, or neutral affect is associated with a past occurrence and to act accordingly.

DON'T FORGET

Patients with damage to any region of the brain may be at risk for having diminished memory performance.

DON'T FORGET

Memory can be fragile or robust! Old established memories are the last to be disturbed in most forms of trauma and even in degenerative neurological diseases, but the ability to form and acquire new memories can be disrupted by even mild head injuries and such a disruption is often the first detected symptom of a degenerative central nervous system disease such as dementia of the Alzheimer's type.

IN THE PAGES THAT FOLLOW

Using this impressive research legacy, a number of memory measures have been developed. This book is intended to introduce a variety of professionals to two widely used memory measurement batteries: the *Wide Range Assessment of Memory and Learning–Second Edition* (WRAML2) and the *Test of Memory and Learning–Second Edition* (TOMAL-2). The reader will be provided with a detailed presentation of the WRAML2 in the first half of the book, followed by a TOMAL-2 presentation in the latter half. Each test will be introduced with an overview of its format and test content. Then administration guidelines are discussed, including procedural suggestions and solutions for common problems examiners may encounter, most of which are beyond what will be found in each test's *Examiner's Manual*. Each test discussion concludes with extensive interpretive commentary based, in part, on recently completed research, as well as extensive clinical familiarity with the instrument. Each discussion of the instruments is written by a co-author of the instrument, and therefore, some bias undoubtedly slipped into the narrative. However, the authors tried to be objective and forthright in their treatment of the material, and it is hoped that the considerable familiarity each has with his instrument will provide a great amount of timely, authoritative, and useful information, and that will outweigh the potential of a less critical consideration. We hope you will find what follows of help clinically as you develop proficiency in the administration and interpretation of one or both instruments.

SOME CAUTIONS

Memory assessment is a particularly complex task requiring knowledge of lifespan developmental aspects, individual differences, psychometrics, individual assessment skills, and clinical acumen and experience not only with the tools of assessment. Evaluation of the pediatric and senior populations, as well as individuals with central nervous system trauma or disease, poses special challenges as well and requires far more than technical literacy with a test and its accurate administration. Memory is a complex phenomenon that, as we discussed earlier in this chapter, can be broken into numerous subcomponents, not all of which can be assessed with the WRAML2, TOMAL-2, or any one scale of memory. Further, and as mentioned earlier, many conditions other than memory deficits can mimic memory impairment. This is especially true for older clients whose medications may be taken improperly, younger adults who may be involved in recreational drug use, and in clients who are medically ill, such as those having hypothyroidism or undiagnosed renal problems. Even something as obvious as poor eyesight or hearing loss can be overlooked and misinterpreted as a memory deficit. A recently completed medical evaluation may be an important appointment for a *high risk* client prior to his/her assessment of memory functioning. Also, motivation can play a greater role in memory assessment, especially since tasks can seem less inherently interesting and feel more demanding of sustained effort. Therefore, significant fatigue or resentment from mandated testing can result in lower scores. In addition, one needs to be concerned about motivation to appear more impaired because of pending legal settlement.

Neither long-term memory nor incidental memory are assessed on the WRAML2 or TOMAL-2, although the delayed recall tasks of the two batteries are likely related to these components of memory. Distortions of initial perception and of retrieval processes are also relevant to understanding memory at all age levels, and the context of events and their recall may also strongly influence memory for day-to-day events. Complaints of everyday memory or learning problems re-

CAUTION

Some Memory Deficit Mimes

- Medical Illness (e.g., hypothyroidism)
- Hearing or Vision loss
- Fatigue
- Motivation
- Attention problems
- Emotional factors (e.g., depression)
- Medication mismanagement

DON'T FORGET

A thorough knowledge of client history and current physical status is crucial to memory test interpretation and the generation of useful recommendations.

quire additional information and investigation, particularly in the face of average or better WRAML2 or TOMAL-2 performance. Regardless, a careful and comprehensive history of the client is essential for targeting and understanding the nature of memory deficits and how they are impacting a given client's everyday functioning. A thorough knowledge of client history and current status is crucial to memory test interpretation and the generation of useful recommendations.

When viewed in the context of a thorough individual assessment, the WRAML2 and the TOMAL-2 should answer most questions regarding the nature and level of memory functions for a particular individual. However, these test results must be viewed in context. Anxiety and other psychiatric symptoms may interfere with memory processes, and while the WRAML2 and the TOMAL-2 are sensitive to such functional interference, they cannot reveal the source on their own. Thus some knowledge of personality and related matters will be useful at times, and instruments such as the *Revised Children's Manifest Anxiety Scale–Second Edition* (Reynolds & Richmond, 2008), the *Self-Report of Personality, Child and Adolescent Forms* (Reynolds & Kamphaus, 2004), the *MMPI-A* (Butcher et al., 1992), the *MMPI-2* (Butcher, et al., 1989), the *Adult Manifest Anxiety Scale* (Reynolds, Richmond, & Lowe, 2003a), the *Elderly Anxiety Scale* (Reynolds, Richmond, & Lowe, 2003b), and the *Clinical Assessment Scales for the Elderly* (Reynolds & Bigler, 2001) might prove useful as adjuncts in particular cases.

Clinicians should also be aware of the psychometric limitations of any scale chosen for use. Although carefully and broadly standardized in the United States, the verbal sections of the WRAML2 and the TOMAL-2 would not be appropriate for non-English–speaking populations. Floor and ceiling effects are evident at some ages and these are discussed in the following chapters in the context of each respective memory battery. These are important considerations and should not be overlooked. Attention to error in test scores is also important. The WRAML2 and the TOMAL-2 have very high reliability coefficients, but the scores continue to contain error variance, and rigid cutoffs or major alterations in interpretation based on slight score variations should be avoided. Additionally, although the collection of items on any one subtest or composite is highly reliable, individual test items tend not to be, and examiners should avoid attaching too much significance to individual item performance. Examiners who practice *intelligent testing* (e.g., see Kaufman, 1979; Reynolds, 1987) should avoid such problems in test interpretation. However, no caution can substitute for good psychometric sense, good history taking, a working knowledge of the appropriate psychological literature, and experience working with persons of the developmental level as one's client. When examiners proceed carefully, comprehensive memory assessments have considerable value and offer rich clinical and research information that should benefit our clients as well as our understanding of memory processes.

🐟 TEST YOURSELF 🐟

1. **The major domains covered in most memory tests are short-term and long-term memory.** True or False?

2. **Many memory researchers consider learning to subsume the construct of memory.** True or False?

3. **Among the most common complaints of individuals following mild head injury are difficulties with memory and attention.** True or False?

4. **The first Binet-Simon intelligence scale included an emphasis on memory skills.** True or False?

(continued)

5. **Children diagnosed with a learning disability tend to have a "typical" profile of memory deficits.** True or False?

6. **Memory evaluation is nearly always included by psychiatrists and other physicians when conducting a mental status exam.** True or False?

7. **Hippocampal formations play a major role in distributing information into long-term storage.** True or False?

8. **The amygdala, a component of the limbic system, deals primarily with affect and plays a minor or no role in memory formation.** True or False?

9. *Anterograde amnesia* **is a term related to difficulties establishing new memories.** True or False?

10. **Attention is a precursor to memory formation.** True or False?

11. **Poor performance on multiple sections of a comprehensive memory battery such as the WRAML2 or TOMAL-2 proves some kind of memory impairment in the client.** True or False?

12. **Adding supplemental assessment of personality components often "muddies the water" when attempting to interpret memory test performance and so is discouraged in most adult cases.** True or False?

13. **Both the WRAML2 and the TOMAL-2 emphasize assessment of retrograde amnesia.** True or False?

14. **Alexander Luria was a principal force in the development of psychometrically sound memory assessment measures.** True or False?

15. **The case of HM provided support for the notion that the long-term memory of past events could be erased if certain parts of the cortex were damaged.** True or False?

Answers: 1. False; 2. True; 3. True; 4. True; 5. False; 6. True; 7. True; 8. True; 9. True; 10. True; 11. False; 12. False; 13. False; 14. False; 15. False

Two

OVERVIEW OF THE WRAML2

The *Wide Range Assessment of Memory and Learning–Second Edition* (WRAML2) is an individually administered test battery designed to assess memory ability in children and adults. The battery is for clinical assessment of immediate and delayed recall of verbal and visual memory, and provides a global memory performance estimate. Comparisons between visual and verbal memory as well as between memory of meaningful versus rote information are also possible. Consequently, the battery can prove useful in many of the assessment contexts mentioned in Chapter 1.

FROM WRAML TO WRAML2

When the *Wide Range Assessment of Memory and Learning* (WRAML) was released in 1990, it was the first well-normed and standardized test battery that could be used to assess memory abilities in children. However, a number of revisions were introduced with the WRAML2, and Rapid Reference 2.1 outlines the major changes. Generally speaking, a clinician familiar with the WRAML can easily learn to administer the WRAML2 because of considerable format similarity. One of the major test changes is the expansion of the age range so that the battery can now be used with adults as well as children and teens. Another significant change is the inclusion of more than two dozen supplemental data sets that allow interested clinicians to ask more questions of the subtest

≡ *Rapid Reference 2.1*

Major modifications made in the revision of WRAML

WRAML	Modification	WRAML2
5–17 years	Age range	5–85+ years
9	Number of core subtests	6
4	Number of delay memory tasks	7
0	Number of working memory subtests	2
1	Number of recognition memory subtests	4
0	Qualitative analyses data	>25 data sets
3 factors: moderate support	Factor structure	3 factors: strong support

results as they try to piece together what may be contributing to the deficits being detected. While the WRAML2's core battery has fewer subtests and is therefore quicker to administer overall, more subtests are available but many are included as optional tasks whose uses are dependent upon idiosyncrasies that may characterize a given client's performance. Two subtests that evaluate working memory skills are examples of new optional additions.

In the WRAML2, the Verbal Memory and Visual Memory Indexes remain, but an Attention/Concentration Index replaced the WRAML's Learning Memory Index, which was the battery's weakest component from a factor-analytic perspective. The subtests of the WRAML's Learning Index experienced different fates. The Verbal Learning subtest remains unchanged in the WRAML2, although it is incorporated as part of the Verbal Memory Index. Sound-Symbol Learning also continues to be included in the WRAML2, but as an optional subtest whose use is limited to ages 5 to 8 years. Finally, Visual Learning was not included in the WRAML2, primarily because it was the weakest component of the factor-analytic structure in the WRAML, was

> **DON'T FORGET**
> ....
> Test kits and forms should never be left in unsecured areas!

the most time-consuming subtest to administer, and had the most pieces and parts, which could be lost and added significantly to the overall cost of the test kit. Some WRAML users will be disappointed with this exclusion, but there is no reason a WRAML veteran cannot continue to use the Visual Learning subtest as a procedure with children, even though it is not part of the WRAML2. Since the child norms for the WRAML2 Verbal Learning differ little from those shown for the same subtest in the WRAML manual, one might extrapolate that the norms for the Visual Learning subtest are probably still usable. However, that stance presupposes that, like Verbal Learning performance, no changes occurred in visual memory performance since the first norms were gathered. It is a reasonable position but waits to be demonstrated empirically.

USER QUALIFICATIONS AND RESPONSIBILITIES

As indicated in its *Administration and Technical Manual,* the WRAML2 should only be used by trained clinicians and/or researchers experienced in (a) the administration of psychological tests, (b) the domain of memory, and (c) the age group of the participant being examined. Although a teacher or certified technician may learn with supervised practice how to administer and score the battery appropriately, the interpretation of the results should be restricted to those with graduate professional training and supervised clinical experience in the area of cognitive assessment, including memory. In addition, examiners should be familiar with *Standards for Educational and Psychological Testing* (American Educational Research Association, 1999). Licensed or certified psychologists, speech and language pathologists, or LD specialists, including educational diagnosticians, are among those who traditionally have such training and may find the battery especially useful.

Those trained in the use of psychological tests know to take precautions to preserve the security of test materials. These materials should, at all times, be considered similar to other clinical information and treated in a confidential and protected manner. For example, test kits or forms should not be left or stored in unsecured areas, nor should test materials or the test manual be made available to nonprofessionals or others with inappropriate training or motive.

THE STRUCTURE OF THE WRAML2

The structure of the *core* components of WRAML2 is graphically represented in Figure 2.1. As can be seen, the basic or core battery is comprised of six subtests that yield three indexes: a Verbal Memory Index, a Visual Memory Index, and an Attention/Concentration Index. Com-

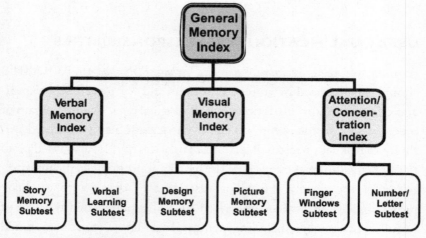

Figure 2.1. WRAML2 Core Subtests and Indexes

bined, these three core indexes form the General Memory Index. A description of each of the core subtests follows in the next section. The WRAML2 especially focuses on visual and auditory memory because of the prominence these two sense systems have in successfully functioning within our society.

There are no time limits imposed on clients' response times; however, there are a few subtests for which the examiner must observe time constraints to achieve a standardized administration (those are noted in the following). The typical administration of the six core subtests by an experienced examiner takes less than 40 minutes. All core subtests observe the customary test item progression from easy to harder. Tables for all indexes include standard scores (M = 100, SD = 15) and confidence intervals; tables are also provided for all subtests and allow conversion of raw scores to scaled scores (M = 10, SD = 3). Percentile and stanine conversion tables are also provided. Age equivalents are also given for clients, but only up to age 14 years, since, as descriptors, age equivalent scores become increasingly less meaningful after childhood. Intrabattery subtest and index discrepancy tables are also provided for determining differences that constitute statistical significance as well as prevalence data for those differences.

In addition to the core subtests, there are several optional subtests that are available to further evaluate various aspects of memory dysfunction suggested by core subtest findings (see Figure 2.2). Also available for investigative use are more than a dozen "Qualitative Analyses," which also are data sets provided for aiding diagnostic clarity. More will be said of core and optional subtests and the qualitative analyses in the sections that follow.

While the WRAML2 was standardized assuming all core subtests would be administered, because of examiner time pressures and limited stamina in clients it is common for clinicians to administer only portions of this or other tests. While clinically there does not seem to be any noticeable difference when this is done with the WRAML2, the

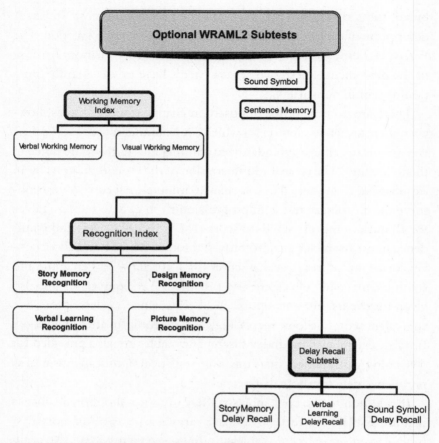

Figure 2.2. Optional Subtests of the WRAML2

reader is reminded that empirically, it is unknown how a partial administration may impact a client's scores. For example, the core subtests alternate between auditory and visual memory demands. A change in this sequence could conceivably increase the fatigue in a client by confronting her/him with multiple tasks that make extended memory demands of verbal or visual skills. Therefore, the clinician should always be reluctant to deviate from a standardized administration, and when that occurs, he or she should approach findings with greater caution.

A brief description of each subtest and its contents follows. In each discussion there is a description of the principal *Domain Assessed*. Obviously, any test procedure taps multiple domains,

> ## CAUTION
>
> The clinician should always be reluctant to deviate from the standardized subtest sequence, and when that occurs, he or she should approach findings with greater caution.

and the reader should eventually think more broadly than these somewhat narrow initial subtest descriptions. However, for heuristic purposes, in this chapter we will emphasize the central intended focus of each subtest, and additional nuances will be added in the next two chapters.

The *Subtest Procedure* associated with each core subtest is also included so the reader can begin to understand what is required of the examiner and client in the administration of each subtest. Specific suggestions related to administering these subtests (beyond those included in the WRAML2 *Manual*) will be left until the next chapter.

CORE INDEXES AND CORE SUBTESTS

Verbal Memory Index

Story Memory Subtest

Domain Assessed   This subtest evaluates auditory memory of extended meaningful verbal material such as is associated with listening to a conversation or a lecture, as well as reading text in newspapers or books.

Subtest Procedure   Two short stories are read to the participant who, following each, is asked to orally recall as many parts of the story as can be remembered. Three stories are included with the subtest, but only two stories are ever used with a given client. The stories are intentionally constructed with differing developmental levels of interest and linguistic complexity, and so the client's age determines which pair of stories to utilize. Some information within each story must be remembered exactly (*verbatim*) to receive credit, and other information need only be paraphrased (*gist*). A rationale and applications for this distinction are included in the Interpretation chapter (chapter 4). For now, it is sufficient to say that two stories are administered in order to obtain a substantial sampling of verbal memory ability that has especially important ecological significance. Story content ranges from 26 to 40 elements.

Verbal Learning Subtest

Domain Assessed   This subtest evaluates auditory memory of meaningful verbal information that is without context (or language structure). The task evaluates a client's ability to actively learn new, relatively unrelated verbal information, such as might be tapped when first trying to learn the colors of the spectrum or the names of the 13 original U.S. colonies. Since four learning episodes or *trials* are administered, a learning acquisition curve is obtained.

Subtest Procedure   The Verbal Learning subtest is a list-learning task adapted from Rey (1958). The evaluator reads the participant a list of common, single-syllable words followed by an immediate free-recall trial. Three identical word-list presentation and immediate recall trials follow. For participants 8 years and younger, 13 words are used; for participants 9 years and older, 16 words make up this list-learning task. The total number of words accurately reported over the four learning trials constitutes the subtest raw score.

Visual Memory Index

Design Memory Subtest

Domain Assessed   This subtest evaluates short-term visual retention of quasi-meaningful visual information by using a brief exposure to simple geometric shapes and then having the client redraw them in their proper locations. The task evaluates a client's ability to remember new, relatively unrelated visual information, such as might be tapped by a first grader copying from the board or a workbook, or an adult trying to redraw a diagram found in a text or on a computer screen.

Subtest Procedure   One at a time, five 4 × 6–inch cards with multiple, simple geometric forms are each presented for a 5-second exposure. Following each card's exposure and a 10-second delay, the participant is asked to draw what he/she remembers of the card's content. Because motor difficulties are sometimes experienced by the WRAML2's youngest and oldest participants, a brief warm-up copying task is provided so that the examiner can score memory output relatively independent of the client's graphic skills. Therefore, deficits in perceptual-motor skills play a minimal role in performance on this subtest. Since the drawings of the five cards are done on a separate drawing form, a permanent record is created and may be scored later. An easily accessible and abbreviated scoring guide is provided on the Examiner Record Form. This is the most subjective scoring procedure on the battery; yet, the test manual reports interrater reliabilities on scoring this subtest to be around .98. The number of correctly recalled shapes and their relative positions across the five cards contributes to the total raw score achieved on this subtest.

Picture Memory Subtest

Domain Assessed   This subtest evaluates visual memory using skill to detect changes in specific features or details within meaningful visual arrays—specifically, four different "familiar" scenes. The task evaluates a client's ability to remember new, contextually related visual information, such as might be tapped in remembering visual content from a billboard just passed or in a room just visited.

Subtest Procedure   The participant is briefly shown a colorful, everyday scene that he/she is asked to scan for 10 seconds, before it is removed.

Then, a similar, alternate scene is immediately presented and the participant is asked to identify those pictured elements that have "been moved, changed or added" (WRAML2 Manual, p. 40). The participant marks the remembered changes right on the altered scene, which is found in a separate response form, making a permanent record of the client's response that may be scored later. Training is allowed just on the first card to ensure the client understands the nature of the task before proceeding with three additional scenes. The client uses a special marker (provided in the kit) to help the examiner easily spot what has been marked, since pen or pencil marks can sometimes be hard to detect on the four-color response form. The total number of correctly identified changes across all four cards constitutes the client's total raw score. If the client seems to be guessing or marking haphazardly, she/he is asked to mark only those details she/he is sure of.

Attention/Concentration Index

Finger Windows Subtest

Domain assessed   This subtest evaluates short-term memory of rote, visual sequential pattern. The task evaluates a client's ability to actively remember rote and sequential visual information, such as might be tapped when trying to remember a route found on a map.

Subtest Procedure   The participant shows memory of a demonstrated visual pattern using a 8×11–inch plastic template containing nine asymmetrically located holes, or *windows*. The examiner, sitting behind the template that is held horizontally perpendicular to the work surface, models a given sequence of windows and asks the participant to imitate the sequence by placing her/his finger through the same windows in the correct

> ## CAUTION
> ....
> The Finger Windows subtest is often the most challenging WRAML2 subtest to learn to administer.

order. The total number of correct sequences achieved determines the level of performance. Series length ranges from one window to nine windows. Among psychology graduate students, this is often the most challenging of the WRAML2 subtests to learn to administer.

Number Letter Subtest

Domain Assessed   This subtest evaluates a client's ability to remember sequential, rote auditory information using the familiar *digit-span* format, although this task uses letters as well as digits. Such memory demands are made when an acquaintance provides a new phone number and you try to remember it until it gets written down.

Subtest Procedure   The Number Letter subtest requires the participant to repeat a sequence of single digits and letters orally presented by the examiner. It is a bit more difficult than a digit-recall task because the inclusion of letters requires the use of two symbol systems. This format is especially demanding for clients whose memory for symbolic material may be impaired. However, inclusion of letters also automatically decreases possible chances of success by guessing. Use of letters also minimizes success sometimes achieved by spontaneously chunking number patterns, such as "three-hundred-sixty-two." Importantly, this subtest's format does not confound forward and backward recall tasks, because different (although overlapping) memory systems have been shown to be involved in forward versus backward rote recall. Items range from one symbolic element to ten.

Optional Subtests and Qualitative Analyses Descriptions

In addition to the six core subtests, there are several optional subtests provided and conormed with the core subtests, allowing a more comprehensive assessment of memory functions. As with the core subtests, the optional subtests provide examiner's with scaled scores and, where appropriate, additional descriptive data such as means, standard deviations, and percentile cut-off scores for qualitative analyses. Figure 2.2 illustrates the optional subtests available on the WRAML2, as well as how they are organized. Their use for diagnostic and interpretive purposes is discussed in Chapter 4. Among the optional subtests are two that are similar to their namesakes on the WRAML, namely Sentence Memory and Sound Symbol.

Sentence Memory Subtest

Domain Assessed   This subtest measures verbal short-term memory for words in context. That is, in contrast to the Number Letter subtest or the first trial of the Verbal Learning subtest, Sentence Memory assesses immediate auditory memory when the memory system is using the "linguistic glue" provided by the structure of language, allowing memory span to exceed the customary 7 + 2 limitation (Miller, 1956). The ability assessed in the Sentence Memory subtest may be observed in everyday tasks such as accurately relating a short message just taken on the phone, or following verbal directions in a classroom or job setting.

Subtest Procedure   In administering the Sentence Memory subtest, the examiner asks the client to repeat one sentence immediately after it is read. Sentences vary in length from 2 to 26 words; the subtest's starting point is determined by the client's age. Sentences are each read at a normal conversational pace, and only once.

Sound Symbol Subtest

Domain Assessed   This subtest is a paired-associate task challenging the learner to remember what unique sound is associated with a unique nonsense shape. The task is similar to one that confronts children being taught phonics (i.e., what sound does this nonsense shape [i.e., letter(s)] make?). Administration of the Sound Symbol subtest is reserved for children 5 to 8 years of age because of the subtest's relevance to early reading competence (Alvord et al., 2001).

Subtest Procedure   The subtest uses a small easel booklet that has a simple, presumably meaningless abstract symbol on each page. The examiner shows a symbol appearing on a page of the easel booklet, and then identifies its sound that the child repeats. The child is asked to try to recall that same sound when she/he again sees the same symbol. The examiner then proceeds to the next easel page. There are eight different sound and symbol pairs. If the child is wrong or cannot remember, she/he is told the correct sound and the examiner proceeds to the next symbol. Four such learning trials are administered, each trial presenting the symbols in a different order. The total score achieved across the four trials is the variable translated into a scaled score and, similar to the Verbal Learning subtest, a learning curve can be constructed using the child's performance over the four trials.

Working Memory Index and Subtests

Two new subtests have been added to the WRAML2 in order to evaluate Working Memory, an area that has attracted increased research and clinical interest since the 1990s (Baddeley, 1992; Miyake & Shah, 1999). What is meant by *working memory* is a rote, short-term memory process in which the participant also *works* with the information while trying to preserve the original information and continue to draw upon it, as needed. Both working memory subtests may be administered to those 9 years of age and older. Scores from each of the working memory subtests can be combined to yield a Working Memory Index.

Verbal Working Memory Subtest

Domain Assessed   This subtest assesses verbal working memory using fairly simple vocabulary and conceptual demands. Verbal working memory tasks are common in the everyday world. For example, a radio announcer says, "It was a close game between the Colts and Sea Hawks. At the beginning of the fourth quarter the score was 11 to 12." Once the listener hears the scores, she/he then has to *attach* them to the correct teams to know who had the edge. Similarly, if the following math problem is dictated, verbal working memory is essential in order to answer it correctly, assuming the listener has the necessary math skills (and is not allowed to write anything): "John had 20 quarters. If pens were 3 for a dollar and John bought 9 pens, how many quarters would he still have after the purchase?" The listener would have to hold all of the numbers in a short-term memory *buffer* until the end of the problem makes clear what information is being asked for, and continue to preserve what is in the buffer as various parts of the multi-stepped problem are completed.

Subtest Procedure The Verbal Working Memory subtest has two difficulty levels, Tasks A and B constituting the first set, and reserved for those 9 to 13 years of age. Tasks B and C make up the second set, to be administered to those older than 13 years. For Task A, the examiner reads a list of nouns, some of which are animals, such as *dog* and *cat,* and others are nonanimals, such as *spoon* and *table.* The client is asked to listen and restate the string, always first reporting the animals before including the nonanimal words. Items range from strings of two words (one animal and one nonanimal) to five words. Task B is similar, although more challenging; the client is additionally asked to repeat the animal words according to animal's size, smallest to largest. Task B item strings range from three to seven words. Task C introduces yet another level of difficulty—that of recalling the nonanimal words in order of their sizes. Task C items range from four to six words. Scoring is based upon the total number of correct subgroupings recalled.

Symbolic Working Memory Subtest

Domain Assessed This subtest assesses a combination of verbal and visual working memory using the common symbol systems of numbers and letters.

Subtest Procedure Unlike the Verbal Working Memory task, the Symbolic Working Memory subtest is completed by the client using a nonverbal response (pointing). The subtest has two parts. For the first level, the examiner dictates a random series of numbers and asks the client to point out the numbers dictated but in the correct numerical order, using a laminated stimulus card containing the numbers one through eight. For the second level, a randomly interspersed number and letter series is dictated and the client is asked to point out the numbers first in numerical order and then the letters in alphabetical order. Series range from two to seven symbolic elements. Scoring is based upon the number of complete subgroupings correctly reported.

Delay Recall and Recognition Subtests

Domains Assessed   All of the core subtests assess immediate memory—that is, immediate recall after an initial exposure to visual or auditory information. If this immediate memory system is defective, obviously, longer term memory for the same information will also suffer. However, as discussed in Chapter 1, it is possible to have an intact immediate memory system but an inability to access that information minutes, hours, or days later. Therefore, it is critical that a memory assessment tool allow an assessment of longer term memory. The "grandfather" of memory research, Hans Ebbinghaus (1885), long ago demonstrated that for most people the greatest amount of memory loss (i.e., forgetting) occurs within the first 20 to 30 minutes following its being learned—so some memory loss is normal. But, for some persons, the amount of information lost becomes abnormally large and is a major handicapping condition. Therefore, it is important to assess retention beyond short-term memory span. The WRAML2 allows evaluation of this kind of longer-term storage capacity. Three Delay Recall subtests are provided for the assessment of forgetting: Story Memory Delay Recall, Verbal Learning Delay Recall, and Sound Symbol Delay Recall. Comparing relative levels of performance between immediate and delay recall formats allows the examiner to evaluate the extent of this kind of forgetting.

DON'T FORGET

The greatest amount of memory loss occurs within the first 20 to 30 minutes of the information being learned, and so measuring that decrement is important.

Putting It Into Practice

Clients in the early stages of dementia or who recently sustained a brain injury may especially struggle with retrieval of information that is stored but appears forgotten.

In addition, clients will occasionally present with concerning levels of forgetting (that is, delay memory), yet when given the information using a nonretrieval format, they demonstrate well-above chance levels of performance. That is, these clients struggle with retrieval of information, although some or much of the information remains stored as evidenced by relatively age-appropriate levels of recognition performance. Clients in the early stages of dementia or immediately following brain injury may demonstrate such patterns. Therefore, to distinguish between retrieval versus storage deficits, four Recognition subtests and a Recognition Index are provided on the WRAML2.

Story Memory Recall and Story Memory Recognition Subtests

Subtest Procedure   Approximately 20 minutes (i.e., three subtests) after administration of the original Story Memory subtest, and without forewarning, the client is asked to retell as much of each story as possible. For those parts of the story that were omitted, it is unknown whether the information is stored but cannot be retrieved or is no longer stored. Therefore, to help determine which, the WRAML2 provides the Story Memory Recognition subtest, which consists of questions focusing on specific details of the story. A multiple-choice format is used and three possible answers are offered. The client is to select the correct alternative. Only those items not just recalled during the Story Memory Recall trial need to be queried. Obviously, if the client did well on Story Memory Recall, administration of the Recognition component would have little value and may prove frustrating for the client because of its obvious simplicity. Accordingly, few errors using this recognition format are made by those in a nonclinical population.

Verbal Learning Recall and Verbal Learning Recognition subtests

Subtest Procedure Approximately 20 minutes (and three subtests) after administration of the Verbal Learning subtest, and without forewarning, the client is asked to again recite the list of isolated words. Generally, performance drops by one word compared to Trial 4 of the immediate memory phase used with the core subtest administration. As noted previously, distinguishing between memory retrieval deficits and storage process deficits has clinical utility. Accordingly, there is also a Verbal Learning Recognition subtest provided. The examiner reads single words and to each the client responds "Yes" (verbally or by head movement) if the word was on the list, or "No" if he/she thinks the word was not on the list. Some of the incorrect words are semantically similar to words on the list (e.g., *comb* versus *brush*), and other incorrect words are phonologically similar (e.g., *map* versus *tap*). Depending on the client's age, 34 or 40 items are queried. More than a few recognition errors is rare for those from a nonclinical population.

Design Memory Recognition Subtest

In addition to the two verbal recognition tasks just described, there are two additional visual recognition subtests. About 20 minutes after performing the Design Memory subtest, the Design Memory Recognition subtest may be administered. The client is shown successive pages on which appear numerous designs and she/he is asked to decide whether each option was or was not on the cards she/he saw earlier in the session. This forced-choice format is used over four pages containing 46 designs, 23 of which were on the original cards.

Picture Memory Recognition Subtest

Similar to the core Design Memory subtest, the core Picture Memory subtest also has an optional recognition component. Once again, 15 to

20 minutes following the original presentation, the client inspects mini-pictures and is asked to decide for each whether the picture was part of a scene viewed earlier in the session. No distinction between scenes in the stimulus cards or response pages is made for this recall procedure. There are 44 items, half of which were seen earlier.

Recognition Memory Index

The scaled scores of the four subtests using a recognition format (Story Memory Recognition, Design Memory Recognition, Picture Memory Recognition, and Verbal Learning Recognition) can be combined to yield a General Recognition Index (Mean = 100, SD = 15), which can be compared to the recall and/or immediate memory subtest performance. More will be said of this in Chapter 4, which deals with test interpretation.

QUALITATIVE ANALYSES

The term *Qualitative Analysis* is used in the WRAML2 manual to signal the clinician that standardization data are available for testing diagnostic impressions or otherwise for digging deeper into how the participant performed the task to earn the points achieved. That is, there are many ways in which a client can earn any given scaled score. Therefore, reasonable amounts of quantitative data are provided to evaluate many of the clinician's suspicions. For example, for Story Memory, a client might do well on the first story but rather poorly on the second, but earn the same score as a client scoring just the opposite on two stories, or earn the same score by performing equally when recalling each story. If the clinician wonders what the most common pattern of scoring is, the average raw scores for both stories are provided in the WRAML2 *Manual,* according to client age (Table A.1). Therefore, the clinician can *test* her/his subjective hunch using the standardization data. Consequently, think *quantita-*

tive basis or *process* analysis when you see the WRAML2 phrase *Qualitative Analyses*. In a sense, all subtests are a quantitative analysis of a qualitative impression. The scores provided for WRAML2 Qualitative Analyses are scaled scores whenever psychometrically justified. Otherwise, or in addition, cut-off scores are provided based on prevalence rates. All of the more than 20 qualitative analyses are related directly to the four Visual and Verbal Memory Core subtests, or to an optional subtest that itself relates to one of these four core subtests. The good news is that few of the Qualitative Analyses require more work with the client. In most cases, the work has already been done and can be harvested, if the clinician is so inclined. All Qualitative Analyses will be discussed in the next chapter within the context of the respective core subtests they complement.

MEMORY SCREENING OPTION

Because of time constraints, sometimes a clinician may want to *screen* a client in order to decide if more in-depth assessment is indicated. On such occasions, the examiner may choose to administer the first four WRAML2 subtests comprising the Screening Memory Index: Story Memory, Picture Memory, Design Memory, and Verbal Learning. These subtests sample verbal and visual memory skills as well as provide an opportunity to assess new learning over trials. Further, a Verbal and Visual Memory Index can be obtained. Administration of the subtests comprising the Memory Screening Index requires approximately 20 to 25 minutes, saving about 10 minutes by not administering the Attention/Concentration Index subtests. The cost for the 10-minute savings is not being able to generate the General Memory Index. However, the psychometric integrity of its substitute, the Memory Screening Index, is strong since the entire standardization sample was used in its development (the first four subtests of a complete core WRAML2 administration are used). A correlation of .92 is found between the Memory

Screening Index (MSI) and the General Memory Index (GMI). The average mean difference between the GMI and the MSI is less than one standard score point (99.98 GMI versus 100.01 MSI). The variability associated with each index is also nearly identical (GMI SD = 14.95 versus MSI SD = 14.93).

WRAML2 PSYCHOMETRIC PROPERTIES

The usual technical information test developers are expected to provide is found in Chapter 7 of the WRAML2 *Manual*. A sample of those data typically of greatest interest to test users is found in Rapid Reference 2.2 and Rapid Reference 2.3. While it is beyond the scope of this book to review the various psychometric components reported in the Technical chapter of the WRAML2 *Manual*, it seems fair to say that the data reported document for users reasonable to strong psychometric integrity for the instrument.

READMINISTRATION OF THE WRAML2

Often examiners wonder how soon a readministration of a test can be completed following the initial testing. Although, a 6- to 12-month estimate is often suggested for many tests, such an interval has no empirical basis that we can discover. Instead, it would be sounder to look at the data reported for test-retest results in order to make this determination for any test. The WRAML2 reports a test-retest median interval of 49 days, and test-retest data are provided for subtests and indexes. The median change of the WRAML2's subtest and index scores are increases of .85 scaled score and 5.5 standard score points, respectively. Design Memory showed the greatest practice effect for a subtest (+ 1.6 scaled score points) and Finger Windows the least (.2 points). The Verbal and Visual Indexes each show about a 6.5-point gain, but the Attention/Concentration Indexes showed remarkable stability (1.7-point

≋ Rapid Reference 2.2

WRAML2: A sampling of reliability data provided in the manual

| Core Subtest (N ≥ 1,426) | RASCH statistics | |
	Person Separation Reliabilities	Item Separation Reliabilities
Story Memory	.94	.99
Design Memory	.92	1.00
Verbal Learning	.88	.99
Picture Memory	.85	1.00
Finger Windows	.91	1.00
Number Letter	.90	1.00

Median Coefficient Alpha (N = 1,200)

Verbal Memory Index	Visual Memory Index	Attention/ Concentration Index	General Memory Index	Screening Memory Index
.92	.89	.86	.93	.93

Used by permission.

gain). Therefore, one can say that repeating the WRAML2 after about 7 weeks will create some increases in scores, although not dramatic increases even though the content of memory tests, by their nature, is especially vulnerable to practice effects. Therefore, a readministration of the WRAML2 even earlier than the often-quoted 6-month guideline seems acceptable, realizing that some modest practice effects are normal. It is likely that in a clinical population, such as TBI, finding such practical effects might be thought of as an indirect way of demonstrating encouraging recovery.

☰ Rapid Reference 2.3

WRAML2: A sampling of validity data provided in the manual

Factor Loadings (Validity) for the Standardization Sample (N = 1,200)

	Factor 1 Attention/ Concentration	Factor 2 Visual Memory	Factor 3 Verbal Memory
Eigenvalues	2.4	1.0	.76
% variance	40.3	17.3	12.6

Also provided:

- Intercorrelations of WRAML2 Indexes and Subtests
- Goodness of Fit Statistics for Core Subtests
- Item Bias Analyses (DIF) on gender and ethnic groups (Hispanic, African-American versus Caucasian)
- Correlations with other memory measures (WMS-III, CMS, TOMAL, CVLT-II, WAIS-III, WISC-III, WRAT3,WJ-III)
- Preliminary Data on Clinical Groups, including Alzheimer's Disease, Learning Disabilities, Traumatic Brain Injury, Parkinson's Disease, and Alcohol Abuse

Used by permission.

TEST FORMS

There are five different forms associated with the WRAML2. The most extensive is the 22-page Examiner Form, designed to assist the examiner in administering and scoring the test in a manner that promotes accuracy. Reminders of important procedural rules associated with each subtest's administration are provided. The content of each subtest appears on the Examiner Form as well, eliminating the need to be looking in the manual for this material. For example, for the Story Memory subtest, the stories as well as abbreviated scoring criteria are provided all in one place on the Examiner Form along with the Delay Recall and Gist-Verbatim components for this subtest.

The Picture Memory Response Form and the Design Memory Response Form each provides a permanent record of the client's responses for each of these core subtests. Each of these forms has four pages. The Picture Memory scenes are in full color.

Two additional response forms are associated with administration of two optional subtests—namely, the Picture Memory Recognition Form and the Design Memory Recognition Form. Each is four pages long. These two forms are probably utilized less than the other three simply because, as noted earlier, in most cases their use would be predicated upon discovering deficits in performance on their respective core subtest counterparts. If no deficits are noted, the recognition forms would likely not be used.

Rapid Reference 2.4 lists the contents of a WRAML2 testing kit. Rapid Reference 2.5 lists relevant publication information of the WRAML2.

≋ Rapid Reference 2.4

WRAML2 Test Kit Components

The WRAML2 Test Kit includes the following materials:
- WRAML2 Administration and Technical Manual
- 25 Examiner Forms
- 25 Picture Memory Response Forms
- 2 red grease pencils (for use with the Picture Memory Response Form)
- 25 Picture Memory Recognition Forms

(continued)

- 25 Design Memory Response Forms
- 25 Design Memory Recognition Forms
- 4 laminated, full-color 8 x 10–inch Picture Memory stimulus scenes
- 5 Design Memory stimulus cards, laminated (black and white)
- 1 Finger Windows Board (8 x 10 inch, hard plastic)
- 2 laminated, 8 x 10–inch Symbolic Working Memory pages (Levels A and B)
- Sound Symbol subtest easel booklet for displaying subtest's visual symbols used for the four learning trials
- 1 soft-canvas briefcase with removable strap

⩵ *Rapid Reference 2.5*

Publication Information for the WRAML2

Authors: David Sheslow and Wayne Adams

Publication Date: December, 2003

Age Range: 5–85+

Administration Time: Core subtests: 30–40 minutes
Memory Screener subtests: 20–30 minutes
Scoring and Interpretive software available

Publisher: Psychological Assessment Resources (PAR)
16204 N. Florida Avenue
Lutz, FL 33549
1-800-331-8378
www.parinc.com

Price: Complete test kit price = $499 (as of June, 2008)

TEST YOURSELF

1. **Which of the following estimates is not part of the WRAML2?**
   (a) General Memory Index
   (b) Working Memory Index
   (c) Verbal Memory Index
   (d) Delay Memory Index
   (e) Recognition Memory Index

2. **The age range for the WRAML2 is**
   (a) 5 to 17 years.
   (b) 6 to 21 years.
   (c) 16 to 79 years.
   (d) 21 to 90 years.
   (e) 5 to 85+ years.

3. **Recognition Memory subtests are provided on the WRAML2 in order to compare recognition memory ability with**
   (a) immediate recall.
   (b) delay recall.
   (c) immediate and delay recall.
   (d) a learning curve.
   (e) working memory.

4. **General Memory Index subtests is to Memory Screening Index subtests as**
   (a) 2:1.
   (b) 4:2.
   (c) 6:4.
   (d) 8:4.
   (e) 9:6.

(continued)

5. The WRAML2 consists of all the following except

(a) rote learning measures.

(b) procedural memory measures.

(c) visual memory measures.

(d) working memory measures.

(e) new learning (over trials) measures.

Answers: 1d; 2e; 3c; 4c; 5b

Three

ADMINISTRATION AND SCORING OF THE WRAML2

The *WRAML2 Administration and Technical Manual* should be consulted for step-by-step administration instructions for all WRAML2 procedures. What follows is intended to supplement that important information. We will use the standardized sequence of subtest administration to guide the order of this chapter's administration and scoring commentary. A part of the information provided includes subtest administration times, but it should be noted that the administration times listed will vary depending on the client's age, memory ability, and idiosyncratic test-taking characteristics. And, as with most tests, examiner familiarity with the instrument will directly impact administration time. Therefore, expect younger adults with good memory skills to take longer than children on subtests for which a discontinue rule applies (i.e., the Finger Windows, Number Letter, Sentence Memory, and the Working Memory subtests). In addition, older adults often are more reflective and slower moving, so they may take the longest. Some perfectionist, anxious, or compulsive clients will need encouragement to move along. However, the majority of clients will perform within the administration time intervals provided. These time approximations may be especially useful in estimating appropriate elapsed time intervals to use before administering Delay Recall subtests when undertaking a partial administration of the WRAML2.

There are three subtests with timing requirements: Design Memory,

Picture Memory, and Sound Symbol. For these subtests, having a stop-watch or some other means of precisely determining 5 or 10 seconds of elapsed time is necessary. A wall clock with a second hand can be made to work satisfactorily. However, keeping track of how long a client takes to complete a task is unnecessary for the entire WRAML2; obviously, then, there are no "bonus points" or other scoring adjustments based upon time. The only time constraints that exist are related to test administration (and relevant only to the three subtests mentioned at the beginning of this paragraph).

Found in the following is WRAML2 commentary organized by subtest; for each, there are three subsections: an estimated time range likely needed for administration, subtest-specific observations worth noting, and a listing of the most commonly made examiner errors for that subtest. Regarding the subsection entitled "Interesting Observations," most examiners are aware of the many generic happenings that are important to observe whenever conducting any assessment, such as consistency of response, cooperation, quality of speech and language, frustration tolerance, persistence when encouraged, distractibility, body language, and so on. These important domains of observation are not mentioned in the commentary that follows because it is assumed that examiners will already be vigilant observers of the spontaneous behaviors, reactions, and mannerisms important in any evaluation. Instead, what is listed within "Interesting Observations" are those that are specific to the subtest or, in some cases, unique to the WRAML2 overall.

Similarly, within the concluding subsection entitled "Common Examiner Administration Errors," generic mistakes that examiners commonly make are not included (e.g., not following standardized procedures, using a noisy or poorly lit room). Again, basic examiner test administration skills are assumed (Rapid Reference 3.1 lists these basic examiner considerations). Instead, highlighted are those errors that have often been noted during teaching the WRAML2 to graduate students or that are commonly encountered during professional workshop presenta-

≡ Rapid Reference 3.1

General Test Administration Considerations

	Yes	No
1. Room well lit.		
2. Furniture comfortable and size appropriate.		
3. Room relatively free from distractions.		
4. Participant seated and positioned appropriately at table.		
5. Examiner sits across table from participant.		
6. Attempts to establish/maintain rapport evident.		
7. Participant told breaks are okay.		
8. Avoids use of words "test" and "pass/fail."		
9. All test forms available but not observable by client.		
10. Test materials available (e.g., pencils, timer).		
11. Preliminary questions asked by participant answered.		
12. Sequence of subtests followed accurately.		
13. Examiner speaks loudly and clearly.		
14. Response encouraged if hesitant or unsure.		
15. Responses recorded immediately and accurately.		
16. Efforts to maintain motivation evident and appropriate.		

tions. The number associated with each subtest that follows corresponds to the order of subtest administration and the subtest numbering found on the Examiner Form.

Each subtest ends with a checklist that can be used by those learning or teaching the WRAML2 to check accuracy of test administration. Ideally, after video-recording her/his subtest administration with a practice client, the checklist can be used to help establish the level of accuracy achieved.

SUBTEST DURATION, UNIQUE OBSERVATIONS, AND ERRORS TO AVOID

1. Story Memory (Core subtest)

Approximate administration time: 7 to 10 minutes.

Interesting Observations
There is adequate space on the Examiner Record form to record client responses. This information is especially important to capture for possible use in subsequent diagnostic exploration. Be alert for the following:

- Retelling the story in a disorganized manner (possible organizational—frontal lobe—deficits). Clients typically recall the story in the order it was read. To examine this characteristic, the *Manual* suggests numbering the content in the order it is recalled rather than just making a check mark next to each correctly remembered item. Earning credit does not depend upon retelling story content in the correct sequence, but a disjointed recall style is unusual and may have clinical significance. Those new to the subtest may find it helpful to record the client's response and score it later.
- Recency and primacy effects. It is unusual for a client to tell

only the beginning (or end) of the story (i.e., demonstrating only a primacy or a recency effect). It is even rarer to have only the middle content reported. Be sure to encourage the client to tell more of the story in order to help determine if you are observing an oversight, impulsiveness, or a real recall deficit (this kind of encouragement is consistent with the administration guidelines found in the WRAML2 *Manual*).

- Confabulations (that is, renditions of parts of or the entire story that contain distortions or inventions). These should be recorded verbatim when possible. Omitting small "chunks" throughout a story is a more typical recall pattern, and this is especially characteristic for details found in the middle of a story. Distorting or embellishing the gist of the story is atypical, whereas omitting or distorting a detail is more common.

- Incorrect renditions of any portion of a story. Like confabulations, these smaller errors can be helpful in understanding the nature of the memory deficit. Affective attributions to characters in the story are sometimes interesting. Occasionally, you may need to request the client to slow down the pace of his/her responding so you can keep up. Doing so with this subtest is consistent with the directions in the WRAML2 *Manual* and should not negatively impact the score earned since short-term memory of meaningful information tends to be robust (i.e., 5-second delay versus 20-second delay scores are equivalent).

- Blending portions of the content of the first story with that of the second story is atypical and suggestive of a significant information processing deficit.

- Behaviors triggered by differential difficulty levels between the stories. The second story is usually experienced by the client as being harder than the first. Therefore, note if the client seems to give up prematurely with the increased work demand. If so, will examiner encouragement re-elicit client involvement? Sometimes, the little bit of extra difficulty causes a fragile memory system to become overloaded, resulting in very poor performance with the second story. Age-based norms are provided in the WRAML2 *Manual* to compare performance on the first versus second stories (Table A.1).

Common Examiner Administration Errors

- Not first establishing rapport with a shy or anxious child or adult. This is especially important with this WRAML2 subtest since it is the first one administered. So, if the participant is not responding easily to informal chit-chat, delay starting memory testing and invest more time getting the client at ease, or administer an alternate procedure tapping the client's likely strengths.
- Stories are read too quickly, too slowly, or robotically. The WRAML2 *Manual* suggests a "speed and inflection appropriate to reading a story in an interesting manner to someone at the Participant's developmental level" (p. 25).
- Not encouraging the anxious or reluctant client sufficiently. "Take a guess" or "What else do you remember about the story?" are two examples provided in the WRAML2 *Manual* (p. 25).
- Client's responses are not correctly recorded because of client speed of response or examiner's unfamiliarity with the story content. Developing beforehand some kind of shorthand recording system will be helpful. Taping the client's responses (and subsequently recording and scoring them) is noted in the WRAML2 *Manual* as an acceptable practice for beginning examiners, although be cautious using this approach with more paranoid or anxious clients.
- Reading only one story.
- Reading a story not appropriate for the participant's age.

- Not observing "verbatim" and "gist" scoring guidelines (avoid scoring in the colored blocks within the Verbatim and Gist columns in the Examiner Form; use only the white spaces). Rapid Reference 3.2 provides a checklist to use to avoid common administration errors for the Story Memory subtest.

≡ Rapid Reference 3.2

Story Memory Subtest

	Yes	No
1. Instructions read verbatim.		
2. All instructions included.		
3. Instructions read clearly.		
4. Two age-appropriate stories are read.		
5. Stories read with appropriate pace, inflection, and clarity.		
6. Story recall requested after each story.		
7. Participant asked to slow down or repeat if recall too rapid.		
8. Items scored correctly for each story (guides in Manual consulted).		
9. Item scoring is accurate.		
10. Total Raw Score is accurate.		
11. Correct Scaled Score obtained.		
12. Verbatim and Gist Responses scored accurately.		

2. Design Memory (Core subtest)

Approximate administration time: 6 to 8 minutes.

Interesting Observations
Be alert for the following:

- Portions of the stimulus cards that may seem to be ignored in the client's reproduction. This is especially true for those "ignoring" most of the right or left side (or top or bottom) of the cards, since this may be suggestive of a field cut (resulting from injury to the retina or optic nerve) or visual neglect.
- Spatial placement of elements, especially on the easier cards (Cards 1 and 3). For example, with Card 1, if the client correctly draws the stimuli but places them in quadrants 1 and 4 rather than where they appear on the stimulus card (quadrants 2 and 3), a spatial deficit may accompany or mimic a memory deficit.
- Negative responses to the ostensibly more difficult cards (Cards 2 and 4) may suggest motivation is affected by level of difficulty.
- Pattern of eye movements. Examine whether the client looks at all parts of the card, as directed.
- The client waiting for significant periods seemingly expecting that "a solution will come to me." This is an ineffective strategy in a short-term memory task and should not be used—or if initially used, ultimately abandoned. Otherwise, one would wonder about perseverative tendencies and/or deficient executive functioning. Of course, a poor visual memory can cause such behavior, too.
- Squinting or moving his/her face noticeably close to the stimulus card or off to one side may indicate visual acuity problems. Be sure to always ask if the client wears glasses at the

outset of the evaluation, and uses them if glasses are typically used for reading or other close-up work.

Common Examiner Administration Errors

- Not strictly adhering to the 5-second stimulus card exposure, and/or the 10-second delay imposed once the stimulus card is removed. The required 10-second delay can easily be achieved if the examiner appropriately paces what should be done following stimulus card removal—that is, supplying the Response Form, giving the directions, and then providing a pencil should be made to comfortably fill the requisite 10-second delay.

- Not orienting the cards correctly (e.g., rotated 90 or 180 degrees). There is an arrow on the nondesign side of the stimulus cards. It should be pointing at the examiner when the card is placed on the table in front of the client (centered on the midline).

- Inadvertently displaying stimulus cards other than during their administration (e.g., leaving them face-up on the side of the table). This should be avoided even after a card is administered, since it may interfere (or assist) with the drawing of other cards, or inappropriately influence performance on the Recognition trial.

- The scoring guidelines are not consulted by examiners new to giving the WRAML2 (only the abbreviated "hints" on the Examiner Form are used). Additional guidelines are provided in the *Manual* (pp. 32–37) and should be consulted, especially while the scoring system is being learned.

- Failing a "sequence item" (e.g., Card #5, Item 8) because one of the elements is rotated. Note General Scoring Guideline 3 on page 33 of the *Manual:* "an incorrect rotation of any shape contained within the sequence should **not** cause the sequence to be scored as incorrect."

- Failing an item because of the client's inability to draw, rather than using the client's reproduction from the preliminary copy procedure to define *correctness*. Rapid Reference 3.3 provides a

 *Rapid Reference 3.3*

Design Memory Subtest

	Yes	No
1. Drawing area cleared for participant.		
2. Preliminary drawing task completed as appropriate.		
3. All instructions included and read verbatim and clearly.		
4. Examiner points to record form area with verbal instructions.		
5. Cards placed about 18 inches from edge of table.		
6. Cards all exposed exactly 5 seconds.		
7. Exactly 10-second delay imposed.		
8. Response Form and pencil immediately available after 10-second delay.		
9. Pencil removed after each card is drawn.		
10. Participant prompted following 10 seconds of nonresponsiveness.		
11. Preliminary drawings used for scoring criteria when appropriate.		
12. All five cards presented and in proper order.		
13. All cards oriented correctly.		

	Yes	No
14. Expanded scoring criteria in *Manual* consulted as needed.		
15. Scoring for card 1 correct.		
16. Scoring for card 2 correct.		
17. Scoring for card 3 correct.		
18. Scoring for card 4 correct.		
19. Scoring for card 5 correct.		
20. Raw score computed accurately.		
21. Scaled Score accurately obtained.		

checklist to use to avoid common administration errors for the Design Memory subtest.

3. Verbal Learning (Core subtest)

Approximate administration time: 6 to 8 minutes.

Interesting Observations
Be alert for the following:

- A discrepancy between Trial 1 performance and the number of elements recalled on another verbal rote memory task. They should be roughly equivalent. Anxiety may play a role when noting a lower Verbal Learning Trial 1 level of performance, since giving all the words at once (versus a more gradual procedure as with most digit span formats) may emotionally overwhelm a client ("I can't do this!"). Alternatively, or consistent with this finding, such behavior may denote a true input capacity deficit (i.e., the amount of material to be learned must be carefully controlled; otherwise, the input system *caves in* when confronted with too much information).

- The order of recall. The examiner should record the client's recall by numbering the words in the order they are recalled (rather than just checking the items off). As with Story Memory, numbering response can allow the examiner to better explore various performance aspects (e.g., are primacy and recency effects apparent at least within Trials 1 and 2?).
- If a client recalls a word on one trial, is that word recalled on subsequent trials? This is generally the pattern with most nonclinical clients.
- Does the client introduce an intrusion error on Trial 1 or 2, and retain it for Trials 3 and 4 (and Recall)? Such performance questions the client's ability to monitor verbal input and/or output, or hints at extreme perseverative tendencies.
- Are semantic clusters apparent by the third and/or fourth trials? For example, with older children and adults, it is common to hear *door* and *wood* or *boat* and *lake* or *wood* and *nail* reported together by Trial 3 or 4. It is sometimes valuable, at the conclusion of all parts of this subtest, to ask the client "How did you do it?" Improved performance over trials is usually attributable to increased informational organization (executive function), not increased rote memory capacity.
- Does the client ask or use his/her fingers to determine the total number of words administered? Gaining such knowledge is a reasonable strategy and suggests productive (and independent) problem-solving ability. This may be more common

in a capable person with a relatively weak short-term verbal memory.

- Does the examiner cup his/her hand by his/her ear or lean forward when the examiner recites the words, possibly signifying a peripheral hearing loss?

Common Examiner Administration Errors

- Administering the words too slowly or too quickly. (When learning the test, record your administration of the subtest, and then check its accuracy.)
- Not enunciating words clearly (e.g., Is *boe* a client's intrusion error, or the correct recall of what the examiner said when he/she omitted the ending sound in *boat*?)
- Incomplete recording of the client's performance because of the client's fast word recall. This is a common problem for examiners new to the test. Solutions: (a) use a tape recorder and score the subtest later, or (b) write only the first letter of each correct word recalled. Since each word on the list starts with a unique letter, the examiner can subsequently recreate and score the client's performance as well as examine the order of word recall.
- Not noticing that most words given on Trial X are not also provided in Trial X + 1? When this occurs, be sure to use the prompt found in the WRAML2 *Manual,* "Be sure to tell me all the words you remember—the words you told me last time as well as any new words you remember" (p. 38).
- Telling the client how many words make up the list.
- If the client is nonresponsive or hesitant, neglecting to give the prompt, as indicated in the manual, "How did the list begin?" or something similar in order to encourage responding (p. 38). Rapid Reference 3.4 provides a checklist to use to avoid common administration errors for the Verbal Learning subtest.

≡ Rapid Reference 3.4

Verbal Learning Subtest

	Yes	No
1. All instructions included and read verbatim.		
2. Words pronounced clearly, especially final consonants.		
3. Exactly 1 second between list words.		
4. Correct number of words used, determined by client age.		
5. Prompt provided if client hesitant at outset.		
6. Prompt to report "old" and "new" provided, if indicated Trials 2–4.		
7. Examiner asks client to "slow down" or repeat, as appropriate.		
8. Waits ≥ 5 seconds after client stops reporting before starting next trial.		
9. Four trials administered.		
10. Raw score obtained accurately.		
11. Accurate Scaled Score obtained.		
12. Intrusion errors accurately recorded and counted each trial.		

4. Picture Memory (Core subtest)

Approximate administration time: 5 to 8 minutes.

Interesting Observations

- *Ignored* portions of the Response Form (i.e., no marks are placed), possibly suggesting a visual field cut (resulting from injury to the retina or optic nerve) or visual neglect.
- The client marks numerous Response Form items, most of which are incorrect *guesses,* even after the examiner reminds the client to "mark only those items you are sure of" (p.40). Possibly the client is very impulsive and/or has such a significant visual memory deficit that he/she is trying to respond as best he/she can, which is by guessing. Alternatively, oppositional or perseverative tendencies can be evoked by the response format of this subtest.
- The client is initially nonresponsive when asked to respond, as if strategizing that "it will come to me if I just think about it." This is an ineffective strategy in a short-term memory task, and should not be used, or if initially used, quickly abandoned. Otherwise, one would wonder about perseverative tendencies, deficient executive functioning, and/or a significant visual memory deficit.
- Squinting or moving his/her face noticeably closer to the stimulus scenes and Response Form alternatives may indicate visual acuity problems. Is the client wearing his/her glasses?
- Note eye movements to examine whether the client is looking at all parts of the scene during the 10-second exposure, as the directions encourage.
- The client does not seem to understand the task even with the prescribed teaching component associated with the first scene. With an older child or adult this may suggest low intellectual

ability and/or poor executive functioning (*intuiting* the nature of the task).

- The Picture Memory subtest score is higher than other subtest scores. This can happen simply because of scoring artifact. That is, there is no scoring penalty associated with guessing, and therefore a score can be spuriously high because of excessive random marking. Remember that the typical total number of Commission Errors is about four across the four scenes (total average commission error range = 2.6 to 4.4, with 5-year-olds making the most—4.4 errors). Children with ADHD have been shown *not* to perform differently from matched controls on this subtest (Weniger & Adams, 2006); more is said of this clinical group in Chapter 4.

Common Examiner Administration Errors

- Stimulus scenes are not displayed for exactly 10 seconds.
- Examiner does not provide Response Form and grease pencil immediately after the 10-second stimulus scene exposure.
- The teaching component is omitted for Scene 1.
- Stimulus or record form scenes are visible before or following item administration. Rapid Reference 3.5 provides a checklist to use to avoid common administration errors for the Picture Memory subtest.

5. Story Memory Delay Recall (Optional subtest)

Approximate administration time: 2 minutes.

Picture Memory Subtest

	Yes	No
1. Drawing area cleared for participant.		
2. All instructions included, read verbatim and clearly.		
3. Scenes exposed for exactly 10 seconds and then removed.		
4. Response Form altered scenes immediately presented.		
5. Grease marker provided with marking directions.		
6. Errors in Scene 1 pointed out using original laminated scene.		
7. No additional training done beyond the first scene.		
8. Participant instructed not to guess, as appropriate.		
9. All four pictures administered and in proper order.		
10. Scoring for card 1 correct.		
11. Scoring for card 2 correct.		
12. Scoring for card 3 correct.		
13. Scoring for card 4 correct.		
14. Subtest raw score computed accurately.		
15. Scaled Score accurately obtained.		
16. Commission errors accurately detected and recorded.		
17. Scenes not viewable before or after their administration.		

Interesting Observations
- Normally, little of the original reported story recall content is forgotten for the delay recall trial; therefore, Delay Recall raw scores tend to be slightly lower than those obtained for the immediate recall trial. Usually the story order and initial recall errors are preserved in the retelling.
- Occasionally, the story is recalled better compared to the immediate memory administration of this subtest. This is seen more often in children than adults, but is still an unusual finding. Check other delay recall results to see if this is routine for the client. If so, a unique consolidation of memory seems to be occurring, and that has implications for recommendations.

Common Examiner Administration Errors

Administration errors for this brief procedure are rare. Occasionally, the examiner will not use the printed directions and give more information than is appropriate in order to "help" the client, especially if the client does not seem to recognize the material being requested (e.g., "What story?"). While no story recollection is rare, nonetheless, the standardized procedure found in the WRAML2 *Manual* should be the only procedure employed. Forgetting an entire story is noteworthy, and similar performance should be evident elsewhere in the testing and in informal interaction, as well as in any recent history that has been gathered. Contrasting the Delay score with the Recognition score usually allows focus on memory retrieval versus storage components.

6. Story Memory Recognition (Optional subtest)

Approximate administration time: 2 to 3 minutes.

Interesting Observations
- Contrasting this score with the Story Recall score provides comparison of memory retrieval versus storage processes.

- Story A Recognition has 20% of the correct choices as the third option; Stories B and C Recognition have 33% and 23%, respectively. Therefore, less than one third of items for Stories A and C have the third (and final) option as the correct answer. This was intentional, with the test authors assuming the third choice would be the most frequent if the client had poor immediate recall skills (i.e., a Recency Effect). Consequently, if a third or more of the client's selections are the third option, this may suggest guessing (i.e., poor recall) since the third option would be the easiest to remember and reproduce. This might also slightly elevate performance on Story B compared to the other story being recalled, providing a corroborating check if you expect very poor memory. Also, check Sentence Memory performance to evaluate the short-term verbal memory capacity needed to perform the Story Memory Recognition task.

While it is not mentioned in the WRAML2 *Manual,* Stories B and C recognition subtests were administered to college students who had not been read the stories, thereby examining random recognition subtest responding (such as would be the case with a client with very poor retention, severe inattentiveness, or a desire to perform poorly). Obtained Recognition scores were found at about chance levels, viz., 29% accuracy. Normally, 33% accuracy would have been expected, given three options being available. However, since there is a slightly higher proportion of correct answers in the first and second positions, a somewhat lower accuracy rate seems right on the mark, assuming random selection of three options by participants.

Common Examiner Administration Errors
- The most common administration "error" is asking all subtest items rather than only asking the items omitted or missed by the client during the Story Delay Recall subtest, which immediately precedes the recognition component. Actually, the

Manual indicates that the administrator *may* omit and automatically credit a recognition item if the information was just provided during the Story Memory Recall subtest. However, in our experience, asking for this information after just hearing it recalled creates client impatience. Stick with omitting the unnecessary repetition unless you think the client was confabulating and got lucky.

- Reading the alternatives too fast (or too slow) would compound the difficulty level for a client with poor immediate memory, possibly overestimating a recognition memory weakness. Therefore, noticeably pause between each option (but do not dawdle, since that extreme also taxes short-term memory).
- If the client is hesitant, be sure to get him/her to guess since by chance some items will be passed. Otherwise, no response will likely *cost* the client total points, possibly overestimating his/her verbal storage deficit. Rapid Reference 3.6 provides a checklist to use to avoid common administration errors for the Story Memory Recall and Recognition subtests.

7. Finger Windows (Core subtest)

Approximate administration time: 5 to 8 minutes.

Interesting Observations
- Can the client learn (be willing) to wait until you say "Begin" before initiating a response? If not, impulsivity, poor visual memory skills, and/or oppositional tendencies may be responsible. Corroborate with history and other behaviors observed.
- It is common for clients to do better on those parts of an item that are found at the periphery of the board and make more errors with holes near the center of the board. This normally holds unless a client has a field cut or inconsistent attention.

≡ *Rapid Reference 3.6*

Story Memory Recall and Recognition Subtests

	Yes	No
1. Story Memory Recall directions read verbatim and clearly.		
2. Proper two stories used for recall.		
3. Both Story Memory Recall raw scores accurately computed.		
4. Story Recognition given immediately after each story.		
5. Recognition directions read verbatim and clearly.		
6. Guessing is encouraged on Recognition subtests.		
7. Recognition items not administered if corresponding Recall item correct (optional unless client frustrated with needless repetition).		
8. Accurate Recognition raw scores computed.		
9. Accurate Recall and Recognition Scaled Scores obtained.		

- On items of moderate difficulty for the client, note whether the correct holes are all included but the sequence is wrong, or whether holes are omitted or incorrectly identified. If the former, note whether there are sequencing errors noted elsewhere on the WRAML2, other test measures, and in the client's history.

Common Examiner Administration Errors

- Not starting with Item 4 when administering the subtest to those 9 years and older.
- Be sure to determine the total raw score including items A, B, and C. Therefore, if the client answers all items correctly up through Item 10 and then fails subsequent items, the total raw score would be 10 (Items 1 through 10) plus 3 (Items A–C), or 13 points. Neglecting Items A, B, and C is among the most common scoring errors made on the WRAML2.
- Exposing the back of the Finger Windows board to the client. This will likely suggest to the client to use a numbering (verbal) strategy.
- Because the examiner has not practiced adequately, administering a more difficult item in a confusing manner is likely increasing an item's difficulty. In our experience, the Finger Windows subtest is the most difficult for graduate psychology students to learn (possibly because psychologists generally tend to have stronger verbal than spatial abilities). We often recommend that a new examiner practice this subtest more, and if competency is still shaky, use colored, erasable markers on the examiner side of the board beforehand to draw "paths" for a few of the harder items likely to be administered. However, after drawing four or five such paths, the value of color coding the paths decreases as the multiple intersections make things visually confusing. Using multiple window boards is an alternative. Rapid Reference 3.7 provides a checklist to use to avoid common administration errors for the Finger Windows subtest.

≡ Rapid Reference 3.7

Finger Windows Subtest

	Yes	No
1. Work area cleared for participant.		
2. Instructions read verbatim and clearly.		
3. Correct starting item selected, based on age.		
4. Plastic card placed about 12 inches from edge of table.		
5. Card held perpendicular to the table in front of client.		
6. Examiner's fingers near edge, not blocking any "windows."		
7. Printed side of card never seen by participant.		
8. Eraser end of a pencil used to touch through "windows."		
9. Half-inch of pencil eraser passes through bottom edge of each window.		
10. Pencil insertion and removal lasts 1 second per window.		
11. Slight pause exists between window insertions using pencil.		
12. "Begin" direction follows examiner's demonstration.		
13. Examiner "teaches" procedure on items A–C if needed; no other help is given.		

(continued)

	Yes	No
14. If 9-year or older participant fails the first item (#4), Items A–C administered but no second administration of Item 4.		
15. Participant verbalization discouraged if present.		
16. Discontinue rule observed (3 consecutive errors).		
17. Raw score computed accurately, including Items A–C in total.		
18. Scaled Score accurately obtained.		

8. Verbal Learning Delay Recall (Optional subtest)

Approximate administration time: 1 to 2 minutes.

Interesting Observations

- Compared to Trial 4, usually about one word is forgotten on the Delay Recall trial and, as expected, it tends to be one from the middle of the list.
- Occasionally, especially with children, one will see evidence of memory consolidation, that is, the words being given in the correct order for the Delay trial, even though the words were not presented in the correct order in Trials 1 through 4. It is an interesting phenomenon to witness and is suggestive of intact and interactive memory and organizational systems operating outside of awareness.
- Note whether intrusion errors are retained and reported during Delay recall. This is not a good memory characteristic; good memories should be able to distinguish between actual versus related verbal input.

≡ Rapid Reference 3.8

Verbal Learning Delay Recall Subtest

	Yes	No
1. Instructions read verbatim and clearly.		
2. Examiner does not read word list again.		
3. Items scored using final column of Verbal Learning subtest on Examiner Form.		
4. Total raw score correctly summed.		
5. Scaled Score accurately obtained.		

- Are the words reported in Trials 3 and 4 also reported for the Delay Recall trial? This is typical. Unusual is a tendency to report words from Trials 1 and 2 that were not reported on Trials 3 and 4. While this could mean many things, one wonders about the client's understanding of the immediate recall component of the verbal learning task (i.e., ". . . tell me the words you remember—the words you have already said *as well as any new ones* you can remember").

Common Examiner Administration Errors

Errors with this brief subtest will tend to be similar to those made on the immediate recall administration administered earlier. Rapid Reference 3.8 provides a checklist to use to avoid common administration errors for the Verbal Learning Delay Recall subtest.

9. Number Letter (Core subtest)

Approximate administration time: 4 to 6 minutes.

Interesting Observations

- There are differences in accurately recalling letters versus numbers—usually the numbers are easier. If so, beyond memory difficulties, one should also wonder if there might be an auditory discrimination problem or peripheral hearing impairment.

- String length (number of elements recalled) should be similar to other rote auditory short-term memory tasks performed by the client, such as Trial 1 of Verbal Learning, or a digit span forwards task from another test battery. The scaled score should be similar to other tasks of immediate rote verbal memory.

- Note whether an item is failed because most of the elements are wrong, or only one or two are incorrect. Note if the error is an omission or transposition of item elements. A series of *close passes* may temper one's interpretation of a mediocre score, versus a failed item in which most of the elements are missing or wrong. Transpositions may signal sequencing problems (compare with other verbal sequential tasks like following sequential directions, or with a visual sequential task such as Finger Windows).

- Note if an item is failed because elements from the previous item are incorporated into the subsequent item. *Leaky* rote verbal memory skills have clinical implications (e.g., confusing which details are associated with which steps in a set of directions).

Common Examiner Administration Errors

- Numbers/letters are read too quickly or too slowly (versus one per second).
- The examiner's voice does not fall with the last element of an item (in order to signal the end of the series).
- Elements are not enunciated well or not loudly enough by the

≡ Rapid Reference 3.9

Number Letter Subtest

	Yes	No
1. Instructions read verbatim and clearly.		
2. Letters and numbers read one per second.		
3. Examiner voice drops slightly with last element of each item.		
4. All other elements of items are read with equal inflection.		
5. If Items 1 or 2 incorrect, indicated training ensues.		
6. Discontinue rule observed (3 consecutive failed items).		
7. Raw score computed accurately.		
8. Scaled Score accurately obtained.		

examiner (e.g., possibly signaled when the client says "two" when the examiner says "Q"). Rapid Reference 3.9 provides a checklist to use to avoid common administration errors for the Number Letter subtest.

10. Design Memory Recognition (Optional subtest)

Approximate administration time: 4 to 6 minutes.

Interesting Observations

- Note if the client obsesses over most items on the Design Recognition Response Form. Typically, clients respond within seconds of each item's presentation, probably since one immediately recognizes an item or does not. Additional thinking or reasoning about an item is not a productive strategy.

- The client should be willing to comply with your request not to return to a prior page. If not, oppositional or impulsive behavior may characterize everyday life.
- Note how much assistance the client seeks for this challenging task whose format is quite simple. Most nonclinical clients understand the procedure within the first few items and want to proceed independently.

Common Examiner Administration Errors

- More than one page of the Response Form is exposed to the client (this most often occurs with exposing both pages 2 and 3 together).
- The examiner neglects to prevent the client returning to earlier pages of the Response Form and changing answers.
- Guessing is not encouraged.
- The examiner does not review the form carefully to be sure the client has not omitted any items before the session ends. Rapid Reference 3.10 provides a checklist to use to avoid common administration errors for the Design Memory Recognition subtest.

II. Picture Memory Recognition (Optional subtest)

Approximate administration time: 4 to 6 minutes.

Interesting Observations and Common Examiner Administration Errors

See listing under Design Memory Recognition, immediately preceding; those observations and examiner errors are also associated with the Picture Memory Recognition subtest, which is very similar in for-

≡ Rapid Reference 3.10

Design Memory Recognition Subtest

	Yes	No
1. Clear work surface provided.		
2. Instructions read verbatim and clearly.		
3. Clarifies the task if the participant has questions.		
4. Positions participant correctly at work surface.		
5. Response Booklet flat on the table, page correctly oriented.		
6. Examiner provides the examinee with a pencil or marker.		
7. Examiner points at designated items while reading directions.		
8. Only one page of the booklet is ever exposed.		
9. Examiner proceeds item to item until client understands task.		
10. Examiner only repeats directions when responding to client questions.		
11. Client not allowed to return to a previously completed page.		
12. When client finishes, examiner reviews form for completeness.		
13. Raw score accurately computed.		
14. Scaled Score accurately obtained.		

mat. Rapid Reference 3.11 provides a checklist to use to avoid common administration errors for the Picture Memory Recognition subtest.

⟰ Rapid Reference 3.11

Picture Memory Recognition Subtest

	Yes	No
1. Clears work surface.		
2. Instructions read verbatim and clearly.		
3. Examiner positions client correctly.		
4. Response Booklet flat on table, page properly oriented.		
5. Pencil or marker provided.		
6. Examiner points at designated items while reading directions.		
7. Only one page of the booklet is ever exposed.		
8. Examiner proceeds item to item until client understands task.		
9. Examiner only repeats directions when responding to client questions.		
10. Client not permitted to return to a previous completed page.		
11. When client finishes, examiner reviews form for completeness.		
12. Raw score accurately computed.		
13. Scaled Score accurately obtained.		

12. Verbal Learning Recognition: (Optional subtest)

Approximate administration time: 3 to 5 minutes.

Interesting Observations
- Note if most errors are semantically or phonologically based, using the Examiner Form.
- If more than a few errors are made, note if the client is aware of his/her faulty knowledge about items (i.e., "I think it is something like this . . ."). Obviously, unawareness is qualitatively a worse characteristic than being unsure of one's recall.
- Note if the client remains focused right to the end of this task, which can seem monotonous after the halfway point.

Common Examiner Administration Errors
- Disregarding the client's age, the examiner uses the wrong list.
- The examiner's enunciation is poor and therefore the number of phonological errors is spuriously increased.
- Guessing is not encouraged in clients who are hesitant or claim they remember no words (the WRAML2 *Manual* says guessing should be encouraged). Rapid Reference 3.12 provides a

≡ Rapid Reference 3.12

Verbal Learning Recognition Subtest

	Yes	No
1. Instructions read verbatim and clearly.		
2. Subtest only administered after Recall subtest administered.		

(continued)

	Yes	No
3. Examiner administers age-appropriate list.		
4. Examiner enunciates each word clearly.		
5. Guessing is encouraged, as appropriate.		
6. Words, head movements, or other response indicators allowed.		
7. Raw and scaled scores computed accurately.		
8. Phonological/Semantic scoring completed accurately.		

checklist to use to avoid common administration errors for the Verbal Learning Recognition subtest.

13. Sound Symbol (Optional subtest for 5- through 8-year-olds)

Approximate administration time: 5 to 8 minutes.

Interesting Observations
- Note if the errors the child makes are phonologically similar or quite different. For example, confusing *kye* and *lex* is a much better error than responding with a sound that resembles no syllable in the *family* of eight subtest responses. The latter kind of error may suggest some kind of basic auditory processing deficit, such that the child is unable to distinguish between or recall sounds recently heard and unique sounds. Learning phonics in reading and spelling requires such skill in order for the child to be successful.
- Is there a difference between ease of learning the association between the visual stimuli that resemble the sounds (i.e., *tabe,*

wa, and *ha*) versus those for which there is no visual-auditory correspondence (i.e., the remainder of the sounds). It is common for children to readily learn the *pictographs,* that is, the shapes that evoke a similar sound (e.g., *tabe* and *table*). Therefore, if a child learns pictograph items and continues to noticeably struggle with the rote sound-visual symbol pairings, it seems reasonable to dismiss motivation or lack of task understanding as causes for the difficulty.

- Normally, the typical, gradually increasing learning curve is observed. Note that the *Manual* provides an average number of pairings achieved per trial for each age group, and cut-offs for helping identify atypical learning rates. Trial 1 versus Trial 4 comparison (i.e., slope) and retention (Trial 4 versus Recall trial) analyses are also possible using data provided in the *Manual.*

- Note if the child is focused on the booklet or distracted when the examiner is providing relevant information. If this is a rare show of inattentiveness, the problem may be more related to task demands than to an attention deficit.

- If a child recalls a sound-symbol association on one trial, is that pairing recalled on subsequent trials? That is generally the pattern with most nonclinical clients.

Common Examiner Administration Errors

- The examiner proceeds too fast for the initial presentation trial, neglecting the 5 seconds per item standard specified in the WRAML2 *Manual.*

- The examiner does not tell the child the correct sound when the child is unresponsive or says "don't know" on any item in Trials 1 through 3; or mispronunciations are not corrected.

- The examiner waits beyond the 5 seconds per item guideline when the child is unresponsive, or credits a response given by the child after the 5-second time limit.

- The examiner mistakenly corrects the child's errors during learning Trial 4. Rapid Reference 3.13 provides a checklist to

≡ Rapid Reference 3.13

Sound Symbol Subtest

	Yes	No
1. Clear work surface provided.		
2. Instructions read verbatim and clearly; all instructions included.		
3. Examiner clarifies the task if the child has any questions.		
4. Positions child correctly at work space.		
5. Examiner uses spiral notebook in an easel format.		
6. Child shown each card and told proper sound for learning trial.		
7. Presentation rate for learning trial is 5 seconds per item.		
8. Child asked to repeat sound after each card of learning trial.		
9. The examiner corrects the child's pronunciation, if necessary.		
10. Exactly 4 recall trials administered.		
11. Examiner allows up to 5 seconds to respond.		

	Yes	No
12. Response errors are corrected on recall Trials 1–3.		
13. After 5 seconds, correct sound provided if child gives no response.		
14. No examinee feedback given during the fourth recall trial.		
15. Spontaneous self-correction met with appropriate examiner query.		
16. Total raw scores computed correctly.		
17. Accurate Scaled Score obtained.		

use to avoid common administration errors for the Sound Symbol subtest.

14. Verbal Working Memory (Optional subtest for those over 8 years of age)

Approximate administration time: 7 to 11 minutes.

Interesting Observations

- Client is able to provide the animal or nonanimal listing, but not both. Clearly the client is trying, but the task taxes his/her working memory and correspondingly important elements in the short-term memory store are lost.
- Compare performance on this subtest to that achieved with Number Letter or a rote verbal memory task from another measure. Sometimes the more demanding working memory

task overwhelms the short-term memory store, resulting in a much lower working memory score than rote memory score. When this occurs, one would wonder about the client's ability to perform when rote memory demands increase (e.g., being able to accurately record a phone number versus accurately remembering more involved directions).

Common Examiner Administration Errors

- Examiner administers the wrong levels to the client, or administers only one level.
- Examiner discontinues prematurely by misinterpreting the Discontinue scoring criterion, "2 consecutive 0-point items." Examples of "items" are A-1, B-3, or C-2. That is, each item consists of two-word series (animal and nonanimal) and a bonus point possibility. Scoring 0 on both word series (also resulting in no bonus point) yields 0-points earned for the *item*. Two such consecutive failed items results in discontinuing that level of the subtest. Two levels are always administered.
- The only way 2 points can be earned for an item is if the animal and nonanimal components are correct (with no intrusions), but the nonanimals are reported before the animals. Rapid Reference 3.14 provides a checklist to use to avoid common administration errors for the Verbal Working Memory subtest.

15. Sentence Memory (Optional subtest)

Approximate administration time: 3 to 5 minutes.

Interesting Observations

- Be sure to write down the client's response verbatim so that the error analyses (see following) are possible. Space is available on the Response Form. It will probably be easiest to

Rapid Reference 3.14

Verbal Working Memory Subtest

	Yes	No
1. Not administered to participants under 9 years of age.		
2. Reads instructions verbatim and clearly; all instructions included.		
3. Clarifies the task if the participant has questions (*training items only*).		
4. One-second pause between words.		
5. Examiner uses the same intonation for each word other than last word.		
6. Examiner's voice drops slightly for last item of a word series.		
7. Training items used when appropriate (*A = Items 1 & 2; B = Item 1; C = none*).		
8. Discontinue rule (2, 0-point items) followed for both levels administered.		
9. Proper two levels used for client's age.		
10. Sequence of client response recorded for each grouping.		
11. "Intrusion responses" noted and recorded.		
12. Correct word groupings scored +1 each.		
13. Bonus point awarded for two correct groupings given in proper order.		
14. Total raw score correctly calculated.		
15. Accurate Scaled Score obtained.		

record errors above the words that were changed. Omitted words can be noted by simply crossing them out or putting a slash line through them.

- Once the client starts making errors, is most of the meaning of a sentence preserved (despite the errors), or do important aspects of the meaning get distorted or lost? Encourage guessing (as suggested in the WRAML2 *Manual*) so this qualitative information can be captured. While a paraphrased sentence probably earns 0 points, such an item failure is a much "better failure" than remembering only the first and last few words. The interpretation of the score should reflect these features in addition to the total score earned.

- Note if errors are predominantly semantic (e.g., substituting *gray* for *black*), phonological (e.g., substituting *Terry* for *Gary*), or verbatim (e.g., not remembering names or numbers). Compare the type of errors made to those noted in Story Memory and/or Verbal Learning.

Common Examiner Administration Errors

- The incorrect starting place is used for those 9 years of age and older (Item 8 rather than Item 1).
- If an older client fails the starting Item 8, the examiner fails to then go to Item 1.
- Sentences are read too quickly or slowly, rather than with a "relaxed 'story reading' rate, rhythm, and inflection" (*Manual*, p. 58).
- Items are scored too leniently. The scoring guidelines in the test *Manual* say to score items strictly while ignoring local accents or colloquialisms. Therefore, in most cases, tense changes, word additions, word omissions, or even partial word changes (e.g., plural to singular) are errors. Rapid Reference 3.15 provides a checklist to use to avoid common administration errors for the Sentence Memory subtest.

≡ Rapid Reference 3.15

Sentence Memory Subtest

	Yes	No
1. Reads instructions verbatim and clearly.		
2. Correct starting item used (based on age).		
3. If starting Item 1 is not correct, training is extended.		
4. If starting Item 8 is not correct, examiner proceeds to Item 1.		
5. Relaxed, "story reading" style is used.		
6. Scoring follows 2, 1, 0 criteria specified.		
7. Accurate raw score computed.		
8. Accurate Scaled Score obtained.		

16. Symbolic Working Memory (Optional subtest for those over 8 years of age)

Approximate administration time: 6 to 10 minutes.

Interesting Observations

- Note if numbers are more easily reported than letters (or vise versa). It is typical to have more difficulty when numbers and letters are combined (i.e., level B versus Level A); nonetheless, are most of the numbers but few of the letters (or most of the letters and few of the numbers) reported accurately?
- Note if difficulties encountered are related to sequencing weaknesses as much as or more than memory difficulties.

- Is working in dual symbol systems (Level B versus Level A) noticeably more difficult (and evident in the early *easy* items)?

Common Examiner Administration Errors
- Training items are omitted.
- Sequences are read too quickly or slowly (one number/letter per second).
- Neglecting to remove the Stimulus Card between items.
- Neglecting to move the Stimulus Card to the table immediately after reading the item. Rapid Reference 3.16 provides a checklist to use to avoid common administration errors for the Symbolic Working Memory subtest.

≡ *Rapid Reference 3.16*

Symbolic Working Memory Subtest

	Yes	No
1. The participant is older than 8 years of age.		
2. Clear work surface provided.		
3. Instructions read verbatim and clearly.		
4. Examiner administers training items T1 and T2 for Level A.		
5. Help is extended on Level A training items, as needed.		
6. No help is given with subsequent Level A items.		
7. Sequence read at one number per second.		
8. Examiner's voice drops slightly for last number of an item.		

	Yes	No
9. Number Stimulus Card presented immediately following oral number sequence.		
10. Number Stimulus Card removed before administering next item.		
11. Discontinue rule (3 failed items) observed for Level A.		
12. Level B administration follows Level A.		
13. Examiner administers training items T1 and T2 for Level B.		
14. Help is extended on Level B training items, as needed.		
15. Client verbalizing responses discouraged throughout subtest.		
16. Number-letter sequence read at the rate of one per second; voice falls at end.		
17. Number Letter Card presented immediately following oral number sequence.		
18. Number Letter Card removed before administering next item.		
19. Discontinue rule (3 failed items) observed for Level B.		
20. Total raw score computed correctly.		
21. Scaled Score correctly obtained.		

17. Sound Symbol Delay Recall (Optional subtest for 5- to 8-year-olds)

Approximate administration time: 1 to 2 minutes.

Interesting Observations

Most of the observations listed under the immediate memory component of this subtest (Trials 1– 4) are also relevant for this Recall component.

Common Examiner Administration Errors

- Failing to again use the first administration trial sequence for this final recall trial.
- Scoring the item as failed (i.e., 0 points) if the child's response time exceeds 5 seconds.
- For this Delay trial, the *Manual* leaves it up to the examiner whether or not to provide the correct answer if the child misses an item. I recommend not providing the answer if the examiner thinks it is possible the subtest may be readministered in the near future (e.g., to assess medication effects, document recovery from head injury). Rapid Reference 3.17 provides a checklist to use to avoid common administration errors for the Sound Symbol Delay Recall subtest.

≡ Rapid Reference 3.17

Sound Symbol Delay Recall Subtests

	Yes	No
1. Only administered to child younger than 9 years of age.		
2. Work surface clear.		
3. Reads instructions verbatim and clearly.		
4. No learning trial administered.		
5. Proper Recall Trial items used from easel (Trial 1).		
6. Client allowed up to 5 seconds to respond.		
7. No examiner response necessary to a client response (right or wrong).		
8. Spontaneously changed response is queried for which response should be scored.		
9. Total raw score is accurately computed.		
10. Prevalence rate is accurately obtained.		

🐿 TEST YOURSELF 🐿

. . . .

1. **All the following are mistakes in administering the Verbal Learning subtest, except**
   - (a) recording the order in which the words were recalled in a given recall trial.
   - (b) waiting quietly if the client is nonresponsive after the examiner reads the list.
   - (c) telling the client how many words are in the list.
   - (d) reading the words at the rate of one every 2 seconds.
   - (e) informing the client of the words that had been omitted at the end of each trial.

2. **Recording the speed at which a task is completed is an examiner's responsibility for which subtest?**
   - (a) Story Memory
   - (b) Design Memory
   - (c) Verbal Learning
   - (d) Picture Memory
   - (e) none of the above

3. **Using a colored grease marker might be helpful to increase the examiner's scoring accuracy on which subtest?**
   - (a) Design Memory
   - (b) Picture Memory
   - (c) Finger Windows
   - (d) Sound Symbol
   - (e) Visual Working Memory

4. **The subtest thought to be most difficult for many psychologists to learn to administer properly is**
   - (a) Design Memory
   - (b) Picture Memory
   - (c) Finger Windows
   - (d) Sound Symbol
   - (e) Verbal Working Memory

5. **Which memory phenomenon is not associated with the Story Memory subtest?**

   (a) primacy effect

   (b) recency effect

   (c) commission errors

   (d) forgetting verbatim but remembering gist features

   (e) recognition memory

Answers: 1a; 2e; 3b; 4c; 5c

Four

INTERPRETATION OF THE WRAML2

Before we begin a discussion surrounding interpretation of WRAML2 results, a quick, general overview of interpretation of test scores seems in order. The question often is, with all the scores available, how does the clinician choose the *best* score(s)?

LEVELS OF ANALYSIS

As with other tests of cognitive ability, the WRAML2 may be interpreted using different levels of analysis; commonly included are (a) the combined index level (i.e., the General Memory Index), (b) the separate index level (the Visual, Verbal, and Attention/Concentration Indexes; Working Memory and Recognition Memory Indexes might also be included), (c) individual subtest level (some combination of the six core and possibly additional optional subtests), and (d) some combination of the prior three levels.

Test interpretation based upon multiple test findings is always the preferred basis of interpretation because, generally, more items (i.e., more sampling) provide stronger psychometric properties for the resultant estimate(s). Consequently, using the General Memory Index (GMI) provides the strongest psychometric basis for formulating a WRAML2 interpretation since the GMI is made up of three index or six subtest scores, which themselves are each made up of numerous memory items. Using a combined score is always preferred unless the component scores contributing to that summary score are found to be highly variable—that is, disagree among themselves.

As usual, index variability is related to the standard error of measurement (SEM) between the index scores. Index SEMs for various age ranges are found in Table 7.10 of the WRAML2 *Manual*. The SEMs have been plotted in Figure 4.1 by age. As can be observed, the SEMs are somewhat different for each of the core indexes, with the Verbal Memory Index generally showing the least variability. Attention/Concentration shows the most, especially for adults. While there are some changes with age, those changes are relatively small other than for the Visual Memory Index, which shows the greatest variability for the youngest participants, but shows variability comparable to the Verbal Memory Index by young adulthood. As would be expected, the score with the greatest number of items, the composite score known as the General Memory Index, has less variability than any of its contributors.

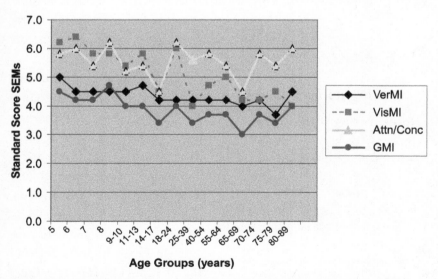

Figure 4.1 Standard Errors of Measurement for Verbal, Visual, and Attention/Concentration Indexes, as well as the composite, General Memory Index

GMI Versus Index Level of Analysis

To justify performing interpretive analyses at the GMI level, there should be relative consistency or sameness between the index scores. Just what constitutes indexes that are *consistent* or *different* is somewhat arbitrary, but generally, once index scores differ by more than 2 SEMs from each other, the summary index score (GMI) should be avoided. Discrepancy data found in Table A.8 of the WRAML2 *Manual* are based on the SEM data and provide the test user with the now-familiar information for determining statistical significance at both the .15 and .05 levels for each of the age groupings. Prevalence rates for differences between indexes are found in Table A.9 of the WRAML2 *Manual*. As with IQ measures, determining meaningful discrepancies between indexes can be based on statistical and/or clinical (i.e., prevalence) differences.

For precision, one should use the tabled values. However, as indicated in Rapid Reference 4.1, a convenient rule of thumb is to start suspecting that statistical differences exist once index differences exceed 10 points.

When a significant difference between core indexes is found, the composite score (i.e., the GMI) is likely a misleading summary statistic; and in such circumstances, the examiner should move to the next level of analysis, namely the core index level. Examples of this instance are provided in Tables 4.1 and 4.2. Using the WRAML2 *Manual*'s Table A.8, the mean difference between

Rapid Reference 4.1

Putting it into Practice

Interpreting Differences

Rules of Thumb:

- Suspect Index differences are interpretable if > 10 standard score points
- Suspect Subtest differences are interpretable if > 3 scaled score points

(*But use tabled values for actual decision making.*)

Table 4.1   A Misleading GMI for a 17-year-old Client Because of Significant Variability Among the Contributing Core Indexes

	Sum of Scaled Scores	Index Score	Discrepancy with GMI
Verbal Memory Index	21	102	+15
Visual Memory Index	20	100	+13
Attention/Concentration Index	10	70	−17
General Memory Index	51	87	

Table 4.2   Differences Between Index Scores, Associated Statistical Significance Levels, and Prevalence Rates (in parentheses) for Index Scores Found in Table 4.1

	Versus Verbal Memory Index	Versus Visual Memory Index
Visual Memory Index	Difference = 2 points *ns. (49%)*	
Attention/Concentration Index	Difference = 32 points *p < .05 (1%)*	Difference = 30 points *p < .05 (6%)*

Note: ns. = not significant. Index scores were obtained from Table A.2 of the *WRAML2 Manual*.

Using the WRAML2 Manual's Table A.2, the mean differences between index scores exceed 2 SEMs, and therefore the GMI summary statistic is suspect. In this case, the summary statistic (i.e., the GMI) suggests the client's general memory skills are within the low average range. Further, none of the three index scores falls within the low average range; two index scores are solidly average and one is within an impaired range.

the Attention/Concentration Index score and the other two index scores (Verbal and Visual) exceeds the .05 critical difference value (12.1) for a client of this age. Table A.9 further indicates that differences of this magnitude rarely occur (compared to the standardization sample). Therefore, the GMI summary statistic is suspect. In this case, the GMI suggests the client's general memory skills are within the low average range. As can been seen, none of the three index scores falls within the low average range; two index scares are solidly average and one is within an impaired range. Therefore, one can observe that if interpretation occurs at the GMI level of analysis, an erroneous generalization would be made, and one would miss a relative weakness (assuming this kind of weakness can be supported with additional test findings or history). When significant amounts of variability are noted among index scores, proceed to the next level of score analysis (i.e., move from GMI to individual core index scores) for interpretation. Some clinicians would argue that the GMI should not even be reported because of the risk of possible misinterpretation.

To restate the principle, if the GMI is made up of index scores that are fairly close to each other, the GMI is the preferred statistic for reporting and interpretation. However, if there is significant variability between any of the three core indexes, then the GMI should probably be avoided as a summary statistic. Instead, the examiner should move to the next level of analysis, namely to the Verbal, Visual, and Attention/Concentration Index scores, despite their somewhat lower reliabilities.

Index Versus Subtest Level of Analysis

Similarly, each of the core or optional indexes should be used for interpretation, provided that the two subtests contributing to an index score are fairly similar. However, once again, if the subtests contributing to an index score differ significantly, then the index is probably a misleading summary statistic. Discrepancy analysis results are not tabled for the many core subtest differences across the various age groups. Standard error of measurements (SEMs) for core subtests are provided in Table 7.11 of the WRAML2 *Manual*. The SEMs differ by subtest and age group, but generally are slightly more than 1 scaled score point. Therefore, as a rule of thumb, if subtests contributing to an index differ by more than 3 scaled score points (>2 SEMs), the index score is probably not a representative summary statistic and the subtest scores would provide a better level of analysis. (Again, the actual tabled subtest SEMs should be used rather than this rule of thumb, for actual decision-making situations.) To the degree that the subtest scores contributing to an index differ more than 3 scaled score points, it is to that degree you should be cautious about using that index for interpretive purposes. Note that SEMs for optional and Delay Recall and Recogni-

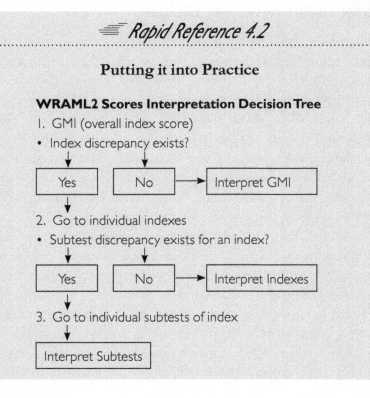

≡ *Rapid Reference 4.2*

Putting it into Practice

WRAML2 Scores Interpretation Decision Tree

1. GMI (overall index score)
• Index discrepancy exists?

| Yes | No | → | Interpret GMI |

2. Go to individual indexes
• Subtest discrepancy exists for an index?

| Yes | No | → | Interpret Indexes |

3. Go to individual subtests of index

Interpret Subtests

tion subtests are found in Table 7.12 of the WRAML2 *Manual*. Working Memory SEMs and several other optional subtests' SEMs are found in Table 7.13.

The best strategy for selecting the soundest score(s) for interpretation is to use the test score(s) consisting of the most items; however, as the contributing scores increasingly differ, their average (the summary score) will increasingly misrepresent the client's ability. The remedy is to move down one interpretive level, although the cost is decreased reliability. This strategy can be seen using a decision tree format in Rapid Reference 4.2. With this guideline in mind, we will turn to the topic of test interpretation of the various WRAML2 scores generated.

INDEX SCORE INTERPRETATION

Following the guidelines discussed in the preceding sections of this chapter, using the GMI score makes sense when the three indexes are generally in agreement. Therefore, a low GMI (with similarly low Verbal, low Visual, and low Attention/Concentration Indexes) would suggest that a client has general impairment in laying down new memories, regardless of content or sensory modality. This overall difficulty with immediate memory (and long-term) processes would be expected for a client with a severe congenital condition, such as overall developmental delay, or could result from a major generalized acute insult such as a sustained anoxic episode associated with drowning.

In addition, with clinical referrals, it is relatively common to find differences between Visual, Verbal, and/or Attention/Concentration Indexes. When this occurs, the interpretive picture usually involves subdomains of differential weaknesses. Therefore, a low Verbal Memory Index (compared to Visual or Attention/Concentration) would usually be made up of low Story Memory and Verbal Learning subtest scores. In such cases, laying down new verbal memories, especially with linguistic content, is likely difficult for the client. Remembering conversations, lectures, or the content of phone messages will likely be noticeably impaired. Similarly, a low Visual Memory Index would predict difficulty remembering new visual information, such as that related in correctly retracing one's route to a new office or classroom, or recalling a graph seen in the morning newspaper or in a textbook (as well as where on the page it was located). A low Attention/Concentration Index is usually associated with difficulty with rote learning tasks, possibly when proper sequence is important. Examples of such memory demands include correctly recording an advertised phone number just heard on a radio ad, remembering who sat where within the room when reflecting on a meeting that occured earlier in the day, or the correct spelling of an infrequently used phonetically irregular word.

The clinical meaning of differences between indexes needs to be qualified. A 20-point difference seems substantial, although whether it will be noticeable clinically will likely depend on what is the overall level of the client's memory functioning. For example, a person who achieves a Verbal Memory Index of 140 with a Visual Memory Index of 120 has differential memory ability on the test, but he/she may go through life unaware of the relative weakness in Visual Memory because his/her weakness is at a level far above the majority of age mates. Plus, that client may well use compensatory memory abilities from the formidable verbal memory domain to assist when encountering relative weaknesses in the visual. Conversely, a client with Verbal and Visual Index scores of 75 and 55 may perceive a difference in remembering verbal versus visual information, but the disparity may not be noticed by instructors or employers because of the marked degree of weakness that characterizes both domains. Plus, the area of relative strength is not strong enough to compensate for another area of marked weakness. Generally, differences between index scores have noticeable and ecologically meaningful effects the greater the differences are found away from the extremes of the performance distribution. Therefore, finding a Verbal Memory

Index of 100 and a Visual Memory Index of 80 should be quite noticeable by the client and by those living and/or working with the client, in addition to the psychologist who did the evaluation.

Qualitative Descriptors for WRAML2 Indexes

Descriptors common to many IQ measures can be used as qualitative descriptors when reporting index scores, especially to the lay public. The descriptors and cut-offs found in Table 7.1 in this volume's treatment of the TOMAL-2 should appear familiar to most examiners, and may be applied to interpretation of WRAML2 index scores.

Subtest Score Interpretation

As noted earlier, for all cognitive instruments, subtest interpretation is fraught with considerable risk of clinical error given the lower reliability of those scores. The literature and personal experience clearly show that psychologists are very prone to use subtest comparisons in order to form diagnostic impressions. While interpreting disparate subtest results should be only cautiously undertaken, their interpretation can have value, especially if such findings are extreme and are supported by other test results and/or history. Therefore, subtest diagnostic guidelines and interpretive suggestions are presented here; but as mentioned several times already, because of lower reliability, subtest interpretation must be conducted cautiously and advanced only within the context of other corroborative quantitative findings and qualitative (i.e., ecologically meaningful) supporting evidence. Interpretation of indexes by summing across the commonality of the respective subtests contributing to the index is also a legitimate use of the commentary that follows. Since clinical interest with memory tests tends to be deficit driven, the following comments focus on weaknesses; but note that ideas provided can be reversed and be relevant for focusing on strengths that have been discovered in an evaluation. The core subtest discussions that follow are listed in the typical order of subtest administration. The initial component of each section lists common weaknesses that can contribute to poor performance on the respective subtest. Obviously the listing should not be construed as comprehensive; the most common contributors do appear, however. The second component of each section includes ways to further corroborate diagnostic suspicions raised by an unusual subtest score.

Following possible interpretive meanings for individual subtest performance, additional remarks focus on how to use the WRAML2 to explore emerging diagnostic suspicions.

Core Subtests

Story Memory

Poor performance may be attributable to one or more of the following:

- Poor verbal memory
- Expressive Language Disorder
- Expressive/Receptive Language Disorder
- Low verbal intelligence or overall intelligence
- Hearing Impairment
- Anxiety (this is the first WRAML2 subtest administered, and so anxiety may be at its highest level)

Useful comparisons for diagnostic clarity:

- Compare Story Memory performance with Sentence Memory and Number Letter performance in order to compare relative levels of rote, somewhat meaningful, and very meaningful verbal memory demands. Language impairment will negatively affect Story Memory most, and Number Letter least, with

Sentences falling in the middle. Attention difficulties manifest themselves the opposite way (Number Letter most affected, Story Memory least affected).

- Compare Story Memory Recall performance with Story Memory Recognition in order to compare memory retrieval inefficiencies (that is, ability to retrieve specific information intentionally versus recognizing content previously provided—a much less intentional and effortful memory skill set).

- Compare the first and second story levels of performance with each other in order to evaluate consistency in verbal memory abilities and the impact of greater language demand (second story) upon performance.

- Compare the client's ability to recall the gist of meaningful verbal material versus ability to recall details nested within meaningful verbal material.

- Compare level of Story Memory performance with Reading Comprehension levels. If reading decoding skills are generally adequate, then reading comprehension will be greatly dependent upon language and verbal memory skills (this seems intuitively reasonable, especially as reading becomes less of a visual and verbal memory task [as it is in the early grades] and becomes more an automatic and cognitively demanding task in upper grades). Obviously, if a client struggles with Story Memory, he/she may also struggle with reading comprehension. That is, if the client has difficulty with story recall when the examiner reads the passages, the client will normally have even greater difficulty when he/she must independently read and recall written material. Sometimes, this is solved by the client's slowing down and rereading the material. When this is the case, reading fluency measures are usually found in the impaired range. While it would need to be empirically demonstrated, intuitively it makes sense to conceptually combine reading decoding performance and Story Memory performance and expect to have a reasonable estimate of reading comprehension.

- Try to obtain estimates of *listening skills* during informal conversation as well as for everyday tasks such as listening to lectures, job instructions, and interactive conversations. There should be correspondence between Story Memory performance and demonstrated skill levels in these real-world contexts. Language deficits as well as verbal memory deficits can affect such performance. As noted previously, language deficit will usually be more apparent with Story Memory than with Sentence Memory performance, and more apparent with Sentence Memory than with Letter Number performance.

Recommendations that could be helpful:

- Tape recording material may be helpful for the repetition of content it provides, but it is time consuming and not always practical or permitted.
- If visual memory skills are a relative strength, it can be helpful to encourage the listener to visualize the scene and *action* being described.
- For some contexts, it may be helpful for the listener to learn to say, "See if I got this right," and then try to paraphrase what has been said up to that point.
- If mostly verbatim aspects are weak, it may be helpful to keep a note pad handy to jot down details that can be subsequently reviewed.
- If there is an outline of what is to be said (e.g., a lecture, book chapter) it would be helpful to provide that ahead of time so the listener has a structure in which to "fit" information. Any strategy that allows the listener to organize information being delivered should improve retention of that information.

- Preferential seating near the source of information may be helpful by minimizing distractions.

Design Memory

Poor performance may be attributable to one or more of the following:

- Poor visual memory
- Spatial skills deficit (are there up/down and/or left/right confusions, especially with cards 1, 2, and 3?)
- Visual field cut or neglect (are there consistent locations on the stimulus cards that are poorly recalled?)
- Impairment in visual acuity

Useful comparisons for diagnostic clarity:

- If Design Memory Recognition performance is good compared to Design Memory recall, then visual retrieval and/or spatial difficulties may be operating. How well does the client perform with spatial tasks on traditional IQ tests or other spatially demanding procedures? Clients with spatial rather than visual memory deficits will often draw the correct shapes on the WRAML2 Response Form because of their spatial simplicity (and ease of labeling), but the shapes may be located incorrectly, thereby earning lower scores.
- Proficiency on other tasks of abstract but less meaningful visual memory should be related to Design Memory performance if the deficit is visual recall (e.g., WRAML2 Finger Windows, Rey Complex Figure Test).
- Examination of the optional introductory copy task of this subtest should provide an impression of perceptual motor skill and its possible impact on task performance. Generally, however, quality of perceptual motor skill plays a minimal role in overall performance on this subtest.
- Examining the client's history, explore the existence of dif-

ficulty with retention of visual details, such as would be involved with copying accuracy of novel material or remembering visual details from a diagram or map.

Recommendations that could be helpful:

- Encourage the client to verbalize the visual details and to creatively impose meaning on them in order to retain important features (e.g., "The map of China looks like a rooster looking to the right, and having one leg.").
- Minimize visual memory task demands. For example, rather than having the student copy unfamiliar material like math problems from a chalk/white board, provide a photocopy of that information. In a training group in which the presenter speaks quickly and those in the audience need to take notes (including diagrams), the person with weaknesses on the Design Memory subtest might try photocopying a seemingly skilled note-taker's materials, or ask the speaker for a copy of his/her notes.

Verbal Learning

Poor performance may be attributable to one or more of the following:

- Poor short-term verbal memory
- Poor long-term verbal memory storage
- Expressive and/or Language Disorder (semantic and/or phonological confusions may be present and therefore suggest language difficulties independent of or confounding memory deficits).
- Hearing Impairment (which will more likely be noted as phonological errors rather than semantic). Pay special attention to sounds in the high frequency range where hearing loss is more common; for example, the /s/ sound in the word *sand*, which might instead be rendered *and* or *hand*; or the /h/ sound in the word *hat*, which instead might be rendered *at* or *rat*.

- Anxiety (anxiety will normally be at its highest level on Trial 1 but abnormal levels of anxiety may negatively impact several or all learning trials). Severe anxiety and/or depression, among other possibilities, should be considered when encountering a relatively flat learning curve.
- Poor executive (frontal lobe) skills that are automatically engaged and allow the client to organize the list in some fashion, resulting in more words being memorized on Trials 3 and 4 (see the next section).

Useful comparisons for diagnostic clarity:

- As just noted, poor executive (frontal lobe) functioning could be contributing to a flat learning curve. On Trial 1, which is really a challenging rote memory task, performance usually conforms to the 7 ± 2 rule (at least for young adolescents and adults). However, frontal lobe strategies will usually be employed by the second or third trial, resulting in more than seven words to be recalled. When that is not found, compare client performance on other traditional frontal lobe measures (e.g., Wisconsin Card Sorting Task).
- Note the slope of the learning curve (slope is one of the qualitative measures provided in the manual). If learners show a relatively flat learning curve, it may be questionable to recommend more massed practice or review of verbal material. Sometimes after the formal evaluation is completed, it may be useful to add a fifth or sixth learning trial in order to discover if something eventually "clicks" with yet more practice. If little incremental learning is found, then additional review and rehearsal are probably not helpful recommendations. In fact, a recommendation against these common "interventions" should be considered.
- Note the amount of forgetting that occurs on the Delay Re-

call trial. One of the qualitative measures provided in the WRAML2 *Manual* is an age-based norm for the amount of loss that is typical following Trial 4 (i.e., for the Delay Recall trial). Generally, there is a loss of about one word. If you find several more than this, it would be of interest to note the existence of comments from teachers, family, or employer like, "The next day, it is like he never heard that material."

- In contrast to the learner just described, sometimes there is a slow but noticeable positive slope. Sometimes, additional Verbal Learning trials are necessary to demonstrate its existence (testing these limits after administering the Verbal Learning Recall and Recognition subtests). These are the kinds of learners who do benefit from review and overlearning strategies, although the amount of incremental learning may be less than is normally observed. For these learners, the recall trial shows that they retain what they learn, although the learning proceeds slowly. In these kinds of cases, practice makes for slow improvement, but the student and teacher will need to be patient and persistent. Frequent, although brief, computerized practice sessions may be part of the learning solution.

- Comparing Trial 1 of the Verbal Learning subtest and the overall results of Number Letter subtest should yield consistency in relative levels of auditory, rote learning. However, if Trial 1 performance is much lower than Number Letter performance, it may be that the amount of information to be recalled is a significant factor for the client's memory performance. There are clients who do reasonably well with five or six bits of information, but for whom the entire memory system seems to collapse when one or two additional bits of information are introduced. Such vulnerability may be seen with the *dumping* of 13 or 16 words, compared to the gradually increasing approach used with Number Letter. However, once the client's limit is approached, even Number Letter performance is dramatically affected. That is, the client does not provide a close approximation to the correct answer; instead, the numbers and letters reported are few or do not even approximate those administered. Sometimes the response may resemble the prior item more or the item just administered. *System collapse* is suggested when the numbers and letters no longer closely resemble the elements of the item just administered, in contrast with the prior item that may have been missed by a single element. Look for similar performance in a digit span task from an IQ measure, or in the Sentence Memory subtest, once near-ceiling levels are reached.

Recommendations that could be helpful:

- As noted in the previous section, all persons with verbal memory impairment do not benefit from rehearsal (that is, repeated learning trials, or "let's go over it again"). A recommendation for repetition (i.e., *review*) as an appropriate learning strategy should have empirical grounds for being made. If the learning curve from this subtest is relatively flat and history also has evidence that repetition does not seem to have much benefit, then dropping this time-consuming strategy may be a wiser way to proceed, likely reducing considerable frustration for the learner and teacher.
- When sets of terms need to be remembered, using some kind of verbal mnemonic (e.g., "Roy G. Biv" for the order of the colors of the spectrum) or musical mnemonic may be helpful. Visual mnemonics can also be created and useful, such as visualizing an absurd scene containing the six items one wants to remember to pick up at the grocery store.
- For individuals with a learning slope that is positive even if

slowly increasing, helping devise an efficient review system should be valuable. Something as simple as 3 x 5 cards (question on the front, answer on the back) can be quite worthwhile, as is something more elaborate that can be computerized.

Picture Memory

Poor performance may be attributable to one or more of the following:

- Poor visual memory, especially that which is often labeled *eidetic imagery* (which in part relates to recalling exact visual details of what one has recently seen).
- Spatial skills deficits (especially in figure-ground perception and spatial orientation).
- Visual field cut or neglect (are there consistent locations within the stimulus scenes that are poorly recalled?).
- Impairment in visual acuity (Is the client wearing his/her glasses?).
- Examining rates of commission errors allows an estimate of impulsiveness. Specific commission error rates by age are provided in the manual (p. 81 and Table A.7), although generally no more than three to four commission errors are made across all four cards. Depending on age, more than five commission errors is considered a statistically unusual occurrence and may have clinical significance, such as poor visual memory, as well as impulsiveness, or difficulty conforming to imposed rules.

Useful comparisons for diagnostic clarity:

- Comparison with Design Memory and Finger Windows allows contrasting memory for visually meaningful with less meaningful visual content.
- Picture Memory performance can be compared with Picture Memory Recognition performance to help decide if there is an

immediate and/or recognition memory problem (i.e., is visual information stored and therefore recognizable?).

- The client's history should at least hint at visual memory problems, such as "gets lost easily," "cannot find his/her way back to new locations recently visited," "often cannot find where he/she puts things," or "often spends time searching for his/her car in the parking lot."

Recommendations that could be helpful:

- Converting aspects of a visual task into a verbal task can be helpful. For example, teach the client to depend on written or verbal directions rather than looking at a map or navigating "from memory." Technology such as a (verbal) GPS system can be very valuable.
- Identify specific problem areas that arise from visual memory weaknesses then allow specific problem solving to occur. Sometimes clients do not connect a visual memory problem to a specific real-world deficit, such as finding their car in a parking lot. Obtaining a detailed history from the client and from at least one other person who knows the client well will often uncover these everyday memory deficits. Visually based deficits tend to be more subtle, but many lend themselves to simple but gratifying solutions, such as writing down the parking space identifier and putting it in one's pocket before leaving the car (or using the brief dictation memo feature on a cell phone).

Finger Windows
Poor performance may be attributable to one or more of the following:

- Poor visual, rote immediate recall
- Deficits in sequential processing
- Spatial skills deficits (note if the client's error pattern suggests

confusions with left-right or up-down reversals). Typically, the outer hole locations are easier to remember than the inner hole locations.

- Visual field cut or neglect (are there consistent locations on the Finger Windows board that are poorly recalled?)
- Impairment in visual acuity (including diplopia)
- Course tremor or other fine motor impairment

Useful comparisons for diagnostic clarity:

- Compare with other visual memory subtests in order to investigate sequential visual recall versus gestalt recall of whole visual arrays. Portions of reading and spelling require sequential memory aspects; compare performance on those tasks. For example, compare the spelling of phonetically regular words with phonetically irregular words; the latter make greater visual memory demands.
- Comparison with the WRAML2 Number Letter subtest allows a modality-specific comparison of sequential material (visual versus auditory).

Recommendations that could be helpful:

- Like with other visual memory suggestions, verbally based compensation can often aid visual memory weakness. Therefore, verbal mnemonics (e.g., "i before e except after c") can be very helpful.
- Drawing attention to a relevant location in a visual sequence may also help, such as first teaching a phonetically irregular word using a multiple choice format (using the client's misspelling or misreading as one of the alternatives) before using a free recall format (e.g., "Which is correct? *beleeve, beleave, believe, beleive, beelive*"). Start with two or three alternatives and gradually add more as the person demonstrated increasing success.

- Practicing rote sequential memory tasks (which often have both visual and verbal components) before having to demonstrate them in the real world can be helpful, such as practicing with a combination lock at home before having to go to school, to work, or to the fitness center to use one's newly assigned locker.

Number Letter

Poor performance may be attributable to one or more of the following:

- Poor auditory (and/or verbal) rote immediate recall
- Difficulty with sequential recall of rote auditory information
- Impaired hearing and/or auditory discrimination skills. If auditory discrimination is a problem it is usually noted more commonly with letters being incorrectly recalled versus numbers. This occurs, in part, because there is less ambiguity and therefore less difficulty identifying numbers (there are fewer numbers than letters, plus letters can sound more alike than numbers). Examine the subtest errors and note whether they are related to phonological confusions (e.g., 3 for C, X for S, Q for 2, K for A).
- Poorer performance on Sentence Memory versus Number Letter is often suggestive of language delay or disorder. Because of their differential language demands, the score of Verbal Learning Trial 1 often falls in between the relative levels of performance for Sentence and Number Letter subtests (Number Letter subtest > Verbal Learning Trial 1 recall > Sentence Memory subtest), and would provide support for a language versus verbal memory deficit.

Useful comparisons for diagnostic clarity:

- Compare to performance on the Sentence Memory or Trial 1 of Verbal Learning subtest, each of which is a rote memory task that has greater verbal meaningfulness than Number Letter. Similarly, requirements of the Sentence Memory and Trial 1 of Verbal Learning subtest makes less demand on rote sequential accuracy.

- Compare with Verbal Working Memory, which makes more demands on rote memory. Sometimes clients will do reasonably well with Number Letter and digit span tasks, but when the level of memory demand increases, requiring more organizational and short-term recall demand, the short-term system collapses, making for relatively poor performance on Verbal Working Memory as compared to Number Letter.

Recommendations that could be helpful:

- Teach the client to routinely reiterate rote information to the speaker when that is practical (e.g., "Let me try repeating your message you want me to give, just to be sure I got it all right.").
- Teach the client to routinely keep a small note pad or tape recorder handy to record important verbatim information.
- Encourage use of visual mnemonics such as associating the name of the new person just introduced (e.g., "Bill Newton") with a funny scene (such as a fig newton cookie with a "bill" dangling from it) for subsequent short-term retrieval ("I'd like to introduce you to Bill Newton.").

OPTIONAL SUBTESTS

Sentence Memory
Poor performance may be attributable to one or more of the following:

- Poor auditory (and/or verbal) immediate recall
- Poor expressive and/or receptive language ability
- Peripheral hearing impairment

Useful comparisons for diagnostic clarity:

- Compare the performance of Sentence Memory to that of Story Memory and Number Letter. When a language problem is operating, performance on Story Memory and Sentence Memory both seem more impaired compared to Number Letter. Those with language impairment tend to leave out nonessential elements with Sentence Memory recall—words like *of, the,* and *it.* The sentence meaning is often preserved. Contrast that to failing an item because the first or last several words of the sentence were omitted, which is associated more with an auditory memory deficit. A different failure might result from the client paraphrasing much of the sentence, which again may be more of an expressive language-based deficit and/or a memory deficit per se. Expect clients with language disorders to do better on the nonverbal memory tasks on the WRAML2. In addition, with more severe language disorders one would expect verbal memory performance to result in poorest client performance on the Story Memory subtest (which makes the greatest language demand), followed by Sentences, with Number Letter showing the highest score of these three auditory memory tasks.
- Weaknesses in Sentence Memory are often found in children and adults experiencing difficulties following oral directions. Consult history or explore this area during the diagnostic interview.

Recommendations that could be helpful:

- Depending on the kind of problem that makes for poor Sentence Memory performance, recommendations will vary. Since remembering a single or several brief sentences is often found in the common tasks of giving and receiving directions, such areas are often negatively impacted. Similarly, recording or delivering phone messages accurately is often impacted. Consequently, if the client's problem is primarily a short-term memory deficit, encourage the client to routinely and immediately reiterate the information the speaker provides (e.g., "Let me try repeating your directions: you first want me to go to the sales department to deliver these forms, then pick up a personnel file from Mrs. Elmo, and take it to Mr. Davis' office before returning here. Is that right?").

- A technological solution would be to encourage the client to use a small pocket tape recorder or cell phone recorder, and teach the client to quickly activate it when directions or messages are about to be provided. More low-tech, but useful, might be a simple note pad and pen being kept handy.
- Count the number of words found in the highest item earning full credit, and just before the client started scoring one or zero points. That number is a reasonable estimate to recommend for sentence length for those working with the client when giving directions or instructions.

Verbal Working Memory

Poor performance may be attributable to one or more of the following:

- Impaired verbal working memory
- Difficulty with sustained attention (possible with any memory task, but it is especially taxed in working memory tasks)
- Poor short-term rote memory
- Impaired hearing

Useful comparisons for diagnostic clarity:

- Inspect item performance on this subtest. Occasionally a client will perform adequately despite never being successful recalling both subgroupings (animal and nonanimal) in an item. While reciting both groupings in the correct order earns bonus points, if a person is capable in short-term verbal memory (e.g., they do well on Sentence Memory and Number Letter), they could earn a marginal score on this subtest (e.g., just reporting animal groupings). What the examiner should expect is client success on both subgroupings for simple items, success with either of the two subgroupings on middle items, and then failure on both. Persons who consistently perform well on only one subgrouping (usually animals), even with the easier items, may have more impaired working memory than implied by the Verbal Working Memory subtest scaled score. Be sure to compare client performance on other tasks demanding verbal working memory, such as answering orally dictated arithmetic word problems. The *single subgrouping client* just described would likely do well on Number Letter, which demands little working memory; however, performance on Story Memory would be relatively weaker because the task requires some working memory. (See Rapid Reference 4.3.)

- Learning a foreign language may be very difficult for persons with impaired verbal working memory because of the

≡ *Rapid Reference 4.3*

Putting It into Practice

Working memory demands can sometimes so overwhelm an otherwise adequately appearing short-term memory system that large differences can be noted between simple auditory short-term memory performance (e.g., Number Letter subtest) and auditory working memory (Verbal Working Memory subtest). For such clients, auditory memory task demands become especially important to consider.

processing demands in this domain (e.g., listening to a string of words, translating them, and imposing meaning and remembering it while listening for the next grouping of foreign words. The most taxing job for verbal working memory may be doing simultaneous translation.).

Recommendations that could be helpful:

- Compensating for poor verbal working memory is difficult since such demands tend to be fairly common, such as understanding a news broadcast or succeeding with an arithmetic word problem. Specifically, there is often extensive auditory information to juggle over time. While tape recorders can be helpful, listening again to a broadcast or lecture is time consuming and often not very practical. If an organizational structure can be provided before the memory demands are made, sometimes the person can perform adequately. For example, a student with poor working memory who is provided with a professor's outline before class could develop an organizational structure and likely follow along and participate in the class far better because working memory demands have been reduced.

Symbolic Working Memory

Poor performance may be attributable to one or more of the following:

- Impaired working memory
- Difficulty with sustained attention (possible with any memory task, but it is especially taxed in working memory tasks)
- Poor short-term rote memory
- Difficulties with sequencing, especially sequencing abstract elements (such as months of the year, letters of the alphabet, etc.)

- Impaired fine-motor skills (struggles with pointing)
- Impaired hearing or vision

Useful comparisons for diagnostic clarity:

- Comparing performance with other sequential tasks should allow testing the suspicion that the client has sequencing difficulties. The WRAML2 tests that stress sequencing include Finger Windows and Number Letter. For a client with this kind of weakness, examining errors on those subtests would likely reveal that often items are failed not for omitting item elements, but for missequencing the elements.
- For those reared in the United States, developing mastery of written, non-Romance languages is likely difficult for those with weak symbolic working memory.

Recommendations that could be helpful:

- Clients who wrestle with symbols, such as those who struggled learning the alphabet or copying an algebraic equation accurately, often continue making errors well after the traditional school years. However, many persons do figure out ways of compensating for difficult memory tasks involving symbols. Having *back-up* systems is common, such as having the sequential list (alphabet, numbers) taped to a child's school desk, asking for photocopied pages of board work, reading and reviewing the manual rather than listening to sequential computer programming instructions, and so on. These back-up systems can each allow a client to progress with reasonable success.

CEILING AND FLOOR CONSIDERATIONS IN INTERPRETATION

Whenever test examiners prepare to interpret a test result using norms, they should be aware of how well those norms cover the full range of ability. It is common for cognitive tests to have less rigorous norms *coverage* at the ability and age extremes. In part, this is related to lower reliability often found at ability extremes (very few persons are included that represent those extremes) as well as lower reliability at age extremes (i.e., very young children and very old adults tend to demonstrate more variability than other age groups). The easiest way for an examiner to check on adequacy of norm coverage is to simply examine the norms tables provided and look for dashes or blanks! Doing that using the WRAML2 *Manual,* one will notice for young 5-year-olds several dashes rather than numbers associated with some subtest scaled score listings, usually those at or below scaled scores of 3 or 4. For example, one can spot that Design Memory has minimal measurement precision when young children do poorly on this subtest. That is, a young 5-year-old cannot earn a scaled score below 5 on that subtest. Therefore, an examiner can conclude that a child with a raw score of 0 or 1 is performing nearly two standard deviations below average (a scaled score of 5), but this examiner is unable to determine the degree of weakness with much accuracy. Clinically, such precision in defining deficits may not have great importance (that is, does it matter if one can document a severe but not a very severe deficit?). However, if this is the case over several subtests, then the examiner needs to recognize that for a given age, poor performance may yield a score that may be an overestimate of a child's true ability because of a weak psychometric floor (i.e., less precision at that level). The same can happen in detecting strengths if so-called *ceiling* scores do not have full range on one or more subtests.

On the WRAML2, inspection of the norms shows that there are some floor limitations in interpreting results for 5-year-olds. For the most part, this floor inadequacy is not problematic from 6 years of age and older. However, examiners should be aware that they could overestimate a 5-year-old's memory ability if the child does very poorly. This sometimes surfaces in retesting situations when a child was evaluated at a young age, and then reevaluated a few years later. For example, with the WRAML2, a young 5-year-old who earned no points on all core subtests would generate a scaled score total of 12, which yields a General Memory Index of 55—the lowest score one can earn on the WRAML2. But that child may, in fact, be performing well below that estimated level of ability. The instrument, like many others, is simply unable to precisely measure extreme deficit at this age. For most clinicians, documenting a significant deficit is adequate and valuable, even if pinpointing the degree of extreme deficit is not possible.

To follow on with the example of our hypothetical 5-year-old, if that same child earned three raw score points on each subtest 12 months later, that may represent an impressive accomplishment qualitatively. However, the quantitative result would indicate little change had occurred in the child's position relative to his/her age mates because the child's GMI would remain at 55. Therefore, as with most psychological tests, caution needs to be observed when interpreting test results earned by the weakest performers on the age continuum—that is, the youngest and oldest persons for whom norms are provided.

However, limiting ceiling effects do not exist for the WRAML2. That is, the top-performance range for memory (which tends to be in the early to mid-twenties) has adequate raw score range at the upper levels of all subtests. Therefore, it is possible for scaled scores of 13 to 19 to be earned, and consequently, relative levels of *memory giftedness* can be legitimately determined with psychometric precision at all age ranges.

ITEM BIAS: GENDER AND MINORITY GROUPS

On pages 123 through 129 of the WRAML2 *Manual,* considerable data are presented that should provide confidence to examiners that there is evidence for no item bias between genders as well as across principal ethnic groups, specifically those with African American, Hispanic, and Caucasian backgrounds. This is shown for each of the core subtests, with 17 of 18 Differential Item Functioning statistics over those six subtests being well above .90.

CHILDREN WITH ADHD AND READING DISORDER

Since ADHD and reading problems are such common referrals, especially for those working with pediatric populations, we will now look closely at WRAML2 performance in children having these diagnoses. This discussion draws heavily on data obtained from dissertation research done by Robert Weniger (Weniger & Adams, 2006). Weniger compared WRAML2 performance of children diagnosed with ADHD, Combined Type, to that of three other subgroups. One of those subgroups of children had been diagnosed with a reading disorder but did not meet ADHD diagnostic criteria; another group had been diagnosed with a reading disorder and also met diagnostic criteria for having ADHD. The third contrast group was a nonclinical group, created using randomly chosen children from the standardization sample after being matched on gender and age. Diagnostic characteristics of each of the clinical groups are found in Table 4.3.

Note the moderate sizes of the subgroups, so the findings should be looked at cautiously, although the effect sizes are respectable. Table 4.4 shows index means and SDs for the four groups. Analyses at the index level revealed the following WRAML2 performance patterns for children with ADHD when contrasted with children with a reading disorder or children with both ADHD and a reading disorder. The results are shown graphically in Figure 4.2.

- Overall, children with ADHD show normal memory performance (that is, average GMI, Verbal Memory Index, and Visual Memory Index scores). However, children with ADHD have a lower Attention/Concentration Index, but so do children with reading disorder without ADHD. Likewise,

Table 4.3 Characteristics of Subgroups of Children with ADHD and Reading Disorder

Variable	ADHD Group (N = 23)		Reading Disorder Group (N = 24)		ADHD + Reading Disorder Group (N = 23)	
T-score Mean (and SD), Connors Rating Scale, Inattention Index	74.1	(11.2)	54.1	(5.6)	74.6	(8.1)
T-score Mean (and SD), Connors Rating Scale, ADHD Index	76.8	(10.9)	55.1	(5.3)	75.5	(8.8)
Reading standard score	88.1	(3.48)	78.9	(9.2)	70.8	(7.3)
Intelligence Quotient	95.6	(8.8)	95.9	(8.5)	92.5	(6.1)

Note: ADHD = Attention-Deficit/Hyperactivity Disorder.

children with ADHD have a lower Working Memory Index, as do children with reading disorder without ADHD. Therefore, while a lower Attention/Concentration Index is related to ADHD, that finding is not unique to ADHD. That is, the Attention/Concentration Index is sensitive but not specific to ADHD.

- In a related vein, the increased rote memory demands of working memory are a more robust expression of the Attention/Concentration Index. Specifically, analyses showed that if the Working Memory Index minus the General Memory Index was less than −10, a .75 sensitivity and .74 specificity resulted in differentiating children with ADHD from the nonclinical sample. A 74% hit rate was achieved between these two groups using that one criterion.

- Having a reading disorder seems to be related to lower vi-

Table 4.4 WRAML2 Scores of Children with ADHD, Reading Disorder, and Both Conditions

	ADHD Group	Reading Disorder Group	ADHD with Reading Disorder Group	Nonclinical Group
General Memory Index	97.4 (12.0) *bc*	89.2 (8.2) *ab*	84.3 (9.5) *a*	101.0 (13.0) *c*
Verbal Memory Index	102.5 (10.2) *b*	91.3 (8.0) *a*	89.2 (11.1) *a*	102.7 (12.7) *b*
Visual Memory Index	97.8 (13.9) *b*	91.4 (11.1) *a*	91.0 (10.9) *a*	100.3 (11.7) *b*
Attention/ Concentration Index	94.3 (11.6) *a*	94.1 (10.8) *a*	85.2 (10.6) *b*	99.5 (13.8) *a*
Working Memory Index	92.9 (13.6) *a*	89.8 (11.7) *a*	82.7 (12.0) *ab*	100.9 (14.0) *c*
General Recognition Index	106.0 (13.7) *b*	91.0 (12.6) *a*	89.7 (8.9) *a*	102.9 (15.3) *b*

Note: ADHD = Attention-Deficit/Hyperactivity Disorder. Group means within a given row with different italicized letter subscripts are statistically different, $p \leq .05$; likewise, within a given row, means that have the same italicized letter are not significantly different.

sual as well as verbal memory performance. Of interest, this seems true of recognition memory performance as well; that is, ADHD children and the nonclinical group score within normal limits on tasks requiring recognition memory, whereas those with a reading disorder (with or without ADHD), have

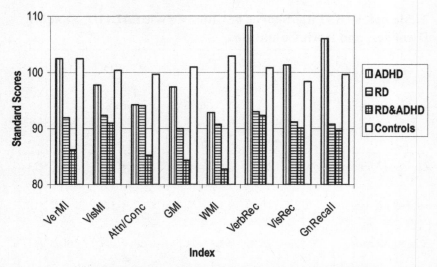

Figure 4.2 WRAML2 index scores for children with ADHD, Reading Disorder, and both disorders compared to a nonclinical contrast group

compromised recognition memory. This difference is apparent with both Verbal and Visual Recognition Index scores.

- Having both a reading disorder and ADHD is associated with greater memory deficit across the board, and especially on tasks making greater rote memory demands. Therefore, in most cases, children with both deficits scored worse than children with just one.

Moving to the subtest level of analysis, only one of the core subtests falls significantly below average for children with ADHD, namely the Number Letter subtest (ADHD group scaled score = 8.6). There is a trend for Design Memory to also be lower (scaled score = 8.9), but that difference only approaches significance ($p > .10$) and the effect size is relatively small.

Therefore, overall, lower Attention/Concentration Index and Working Memory Index are consistent with an ADHD diagnosis, but they can also be obtained in children with a reading disorder. However, having those deficits but average recognition was found only with children with ADHD. Having both ADHD and reading disorder is related to much worse memory performance in both rote and meaningful memory tasks, and for both verbal and visual memory systems. The core subtest showing the worst performance for children with reading disorder was Verbal Learning (scaled score = 8.0), and this one WRAML2 subtest discriminated between an ADHD and reading disorder diagnoses with reasonable accuracy.

The reader should not conclude from this discussion that the WRAML2 should be used as a means to diagnose ADHD. However, as part of a larger assessment, it seems that the above WRAML2 results can provide useful information in the overall formulation of that hypothesis. The battery also has utility in differential diagnosis among children who may also have reading disorder.

MALINGERING

Because motivation is known to play a significant role in test performance, estimating motivation is an important part of any evaluation. Often, estimates are obtained using *stand alone* tests designed to assess tendencies to malinger—that is, to be motivated to intentionally perform at a lower ability level for some external gain, such as financial reward from an insurance settlement. Recently, neuropsychologists and others using and interpreting cognitive and emotional test results have been encouraged to use measures that also provide a motivation estimate in addition to the cognitive and/or emotional estimates. While this is a sound aspiration, it is infrequently realized given the many traditional measures that were developed before motivational estimating was considered important. However, research has recently been completed that allows a motivational estimate to be obtained using the WRAML2. Shaver and Adams (2005) used a traditional simulation research paradigm in which clinically "normal" participants were encouraged to perform as if they had a head injury. They were provided general information about cognitive effects of head injury obtained from a number of Internet sites. Further, the simulation participants were reminded that "fooling the examiner" required careful strategizing, since, while some compromised cognitive performance was necessary, if deficits were *overdone,* they would likely be detected. Simulators were also told that if they succeeded in "fooling the examiner," they would receive a meaningful monetary reward. The research compared performance of actual brain injured clients and a nonclinical sample to that of the brain injury simulators. Participants ranged in age from 18 to 50.

The investigators found that the WRAML2 was sensitive in detecting simulators and added to the sensitivity of a commonly used malingering measure (the *Test of Memory Malingering* [TOMM] (Tombaugh, 1996). The WRAML2 simulation analogue that was offered as having clinical utility and clinical simplicity is found in Table 4.5. Using the

Table 4.5 Hit Rates Using Three Atypical WRAML2 Results for Evaluating Possible Malingering in Adult Participants

Decision Rule	Hit Rate Simulators vs. TBI	Hit Rate Simulators vs. TBI vs. Controls
Attention/Concentration Index < 66	80.7%	89.7%
Number Letter subtest scaled score < 5	71.9%	83.2%
5 or more subtests with scaled score < 5	70.2%	84.1%

Note: TBI = traumatic brain injury.

analogue shown, *hit rates* were around 85% when attempting to discriminate simulators from real brain injured clients or a nonclinical sample. When used simultaneously, the TOMM and the analogue correctly identified 90% of all simulators. Therefore, with adults, if one is administering the WRAML2 to assess memory abilities, one is also able to obtain an impression of motivation that can be combined with other estimates.

CASE STUDY

The following case was selected because it illustrates how a memory measure can enrich a traditional evaluation using intelligence and academic measures. In the evaluation reported, only the core WRAML2 subtests (and two related optional subtests) were administered. (The author thanks Dr. Trevor Hall for contributing this actual case.)

Psycho-Educational Evaluation
Confidential Report

Name: Susan   Gender: Female
Date of Evaluation: August 20, 2007   Grade: starting second
Date of Birth: xx/xx, 1999   Primary Language: English
Current Age: 7 years, 9 months   Handedness: Right

Reason for Referral

Susan was referred because of persistent academic difficulties. These were experienced across all academic areas and were identified as early as the second half of kindergarten. It was hoped that sources of cognitive weakness could be identified for purposes of remediation program planning.

Relevant History

Susan was diagnosed with a seizure disorder in August 2005, related to Sturge-Weber syndrome. Currently, her seizures are generally well controlled using an anticonvulsant (Lamictal). Seizures tend to be localized in her face, can last up to 8 minutes, and are thought to have a right-temporal origin. She experiences no loss of consciousness during the seizures. The post-ictal state involves fatigue. Developmentally, typical milestones were achieved within normal limits. Academically, Susan's parents think that she is somewhat behind in math, reading, spelling, and writing. Susan was described as having general organizational difficulties, including distractibility, disorganization, difficulty making decisions, forgetfulness, losing things, and not finishing tasks. No concerns were reported in motor or coordination areas. Her teacher reports that Susan is often quiet and shy in class, but has several friends. Also, at times she appears unmotivated and "overly emotional." The assessment results are found in Table 4.6.

Table 4.6. Tests Administered and Results
WECHSLER INTELLIGENCE SCALE FOR CHILDREN–
Fourth Edition

Index	Standard Score	Skill Level
Verbal Comprehension	93	Average
Perceptual Reasoning	98	Average
Working Memory	99	Average
Processing Speed	83	Low Average
Full Scale IQ	91	Average

Verbal Subtest	Scaled Score	Perceptual Subtest	Scaled Score	Working Memory Subtest	Scaled Score	Processing Speed Subtest	Scaled Score
Similarities	9	Block Design	9	Digit Span	9	Coding	4
Vocabulary	7	Picture Concepts	9	Letter-Number Sequencing	11	Symbol Search	10
Comprehension	10	Matrix Reasoning	11				

WIDE RANGE ASSESSMENT OF MEMORY AND LEARNING–Second Edition

Index/Subtest	Standard Score	Skill Level
Verbal Memory	72	Borderline Low
Story Memory	6	Low avg—Borderline
(Story Memory Delay)	(5)	Borderline
Verbal Learning	4	Impaired
Visual Memory	85	Low Average
Design Memory	3	Impaired
Picture Memory	12	Average
Attention/Concentration	94	Average
Finger Windows	10	Average
Number Letter	8	Avg—Low Average
General Memory	77	Borderline

WIDE RANGE ACHIEVEMENT TEST–Fourth Edition

Subtest	Standard Score	Skill Level
Word Reading	85	Low Average
Sentence Reading	not administered	
Spelling	90	Average
Math Computation	75	Borderline

CHILD BEHAVIOR CHECKLIST (*maternal report*)

Area	T-Score	Clinical Significance
Externalizing Problems	34	Age-typical
Internalizing Problems	48	Age-typical
Behavioral Symptom Index	47	Age-typical

Clinical Impressions

At first glance, Susan's intellectual evaluation would suggest that she is a child of overall average intellectual ability, but her "Processing Speed" is mildly impaired. The WRAML2 results importantly supplement and qualify this initial impression. Because the GMI consists of indexes that are discrepant with one another, the GMI is not the preferred level of interpretation. Likewise, because the Visual Memory Index consists of discrepant Visual Memory subtest scores, it too is not to be used as the estimate of overall visual memory ability. Therefore, using the Verbal Memory Index, Attention/Concentration Index, and the subtests of the Visual Memory Index, the following interpretation is generated.

Susan's immediate verbal memory skills are within the borderline range. In contrast with the expectation derived from her WISC-IV Verbal Comprehension Index (VCI = 93) and Working Memory Index (WMI = 99), Susan is experiencing significant weakness in immediate verbal memory, which is likely causing her difficulties in school. That is, despite near average verbal reasoning ability, Susan has considerable difficulty remembering a developmentally reasonable quantity of meaningful verbal information presented orally. For example, her ability to listen and report what she hears of meaningful verbal information (Story Memory subtest) is seriously compromised, not because she does not understand its meaning, but because she cannot remember all the pieces (likely contributing to her apparent inattention in class). This deficit will also likely impact her reading comprehension. In contrast, short-term rote aural memory (Number Letter subtest) is not noticeably impaired, suggesting that language does not provide as much memory "glue" as it does for the "typical" 7-year-old.

Likewise, Susan struggles to learn new verbal information, and even after several *learning trials* her recall shows no improvement. This deficit in learning elements of new verbal information will likely be evident in academic requirements such as learning math and history facts. Examining her learning curve (Figure 4.3), one wonders how much repetition (beyond the four trials) would be needed in order to show evidence of incremental learning. This was, in fact, assessed following the evaluation, with additional list learning trials administered. By what would be the sixth trial, incremental learning was apparent (4 words recalled) and sustained (5 words recalled on the seventh trial). It is likely that, for now, extended practice sessions involving large amounts of new verbal information should be avoided and, instead, Susan's assignments should be limited to a relatively small number of facts that would be learned, and then overlearned. (*This suggestion seems reasonable because Finger Windows and Number Letter are within normal limits for age, whereas Story Memory and Verbal Learning are well below average. Language deficits are unlikely given the WISC-IV and VCI subtest scores, and the Comprehension subtest score.*)

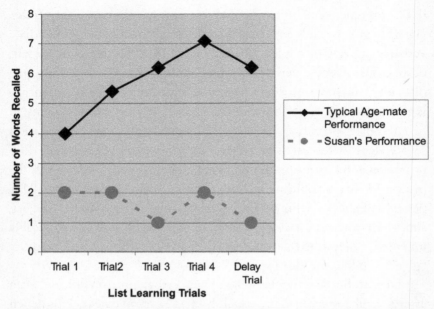

Figure 4.3 WRAML2 Verbal Learning subtest performance comparison between Susan and that of nonclinical age mates, across four learning trials and a delay trial

The WISC-IV Coding and WRAML2 Design Memory subtests together suggest that skills for remembering less meaningful visual information are impaired. (See Figure 4.4 for a qualitative illustration of Design Memory performance.) This weakness may be contributing to her apparent deficit in math computation and handwriting. One wonders whether this weakness is a function of having to write responses, and whether removing the writing/drawing requirement for demonstrating competency would result in performance being surprisingly "improved" (for example, compare Design Memory to Picture Memory). Sequencing visual information (see Finger Windows) does not seem to be a difficulty nor does remembering meaningful visual detail (see Picture Memory), but "remembering the overall gestalt" appears to be difficult

Figure 4.4 Susan's performance on the Design Memory Response Form's practice space (top) as well as her responses to Cards 1 and 3. Initially, notice the apparent perceptual motor delay reflected in her drawing of the rectangle in the practice space. Beyond this, though, Susan's response to the stimulus cards suggests that she is able to focus on a relatively small amount of visually abstract information at a time. This also seems to be the case verbally, given her Design Memory and the Verbal Learning subtest performance contrasted with Number Letter or Finger Windows. Both of the latter subtests make memory requests using formats that gradually make increasing retention demands, but start with relatively small amounts of memory demand, versus "dumping" a large amount of information that is more the format used with Design Memory, Verbal Learning, and Story Memory. Obviously, teaching implications follow from this observation.

for Susan. Therefore, handwriting and possibly organizing material on a page (e.g., writing out her math problems) is more problematic.

Susan's strengths are in areas of reasoning. Therefore, if rote memory can be less emphasized and reasoning about information can be highlighted, Susan will likely be more successful in school. Giving her convenient memory aides should prove worthwhile. (As an example, see

Recommendation 3.) Another recommendation would be to teach acronyms and use of imagery as other techniques of remembering factual verbal content. Teaching Susan how to use and access helpful memory *crutches* will be an important learning objective.

Recommendations:

1. Provide structure to Susan about what she is about to hear in a class presentation, discussion, or before a new routine is explained. This organization should help her better remember components of verbal exchanges going on in class. The same would be true for enhancing reading comprehension. That is, encourage Susan to get *the big picture* of what she is about to read so that as she encounters specific information she will be better able to store it in an organized fashion, thereby increasing its retention. She might do this by skimming the chapter looking at the pictures, figures, tables, and chapter subdivisions, or first looking at the chapter summary and the questions at the end of a chapter before she starts to read. At the end of each paragraph she should be encouraged to pause and ask herself if what she just read made sense with what went before and, if not, to reread that paragraph to resolve any apparent confusion.

2. An efficient review system will need to be developed since Susan's speed of new learning is likely very slow; but practice should lead to incremental improvement, although it will occur at a much slower rate than for many children. The system should be used on a daily and weekly basis, as well as the day before any end-of-term test over the material. The quantity of information she is expected to remember should be given to her in "helpings" at least half the size of what her age-mates

can normally handle, and content should be carefully selected and deemed especially important for future learning.

3. So that conceptual learning dependent on memory skills will not be slowed, provide help for Susan to move along in conceptual areas. For example, giving her a calculator when she is working on word problems would minimize the rote memory requirement, making performance on a word problem test a more accurate reflection of numerical reasoning once the rote memory demand of "math facts" is (temporarily) removed.

4. Because verbal rote memory skills are relative strengths for Susan, teachers and parents should be cautious that she is not just repeating material after she hears it, but actually is processing it so it is likely available later. For example, Susan may be able to repeat a verbal direction just given by a teacher but may not be able to paraphrase its meaning as she struggles to put all the short-term memory components into long-term memory storage. It is likely she will lose some of the components in this process.

5. Minimizing speeded written work seems indicated given her relatively slow written work style and perceptual motor struggles. For example, having Susan write each weekly spelling word 10 times is likely not the way Susan will best learn those words. Using a multiple-choice, recognition format may prove more helpful. Use of a word processor for certain in-class and homework assignments has promise and should be experimented with. Copying from the board or a workbook should be avoided.

6. It is anticipated that many of the apparent "distractibility, disorganization, forgetfulness, unmotivated, overly emotional, and shyness" concerns will lessen as accommodations similar to those recommended are implemented. However, review of

Susan's progress is also recommended by the end of the second marking period, and adaptations made as indicated.

7. The parents may have specific questions in dealing with Susan at home. This clinician would be available to discuss concerns using the previous findings to help brainstorm potential solutions. How to conduct "homework time" may be one domain of concern.

 TEST YOURSELF

1. **With which age group should WRAML2 examiners show greatest caution when interpreting very low scores?**
   (a) Any person from a minority group
   (b) 5-year-olds
   (c) 10- to 12-year-olds
   (d) 20- to 25-year-olds
   (e) low scores for all age groups should be interpreted with the same degree of caution

2. **WRAML2 performance for children with ADHD tends to show**
   (a) a lower Attention/Concentration Index than Visual or Verbal Memory Indexes.
   (b) overall, low average to borderline memory ability (i.e., GMI = 70–85).
   (c) lower scores than children with a reading disorder.
   (d) weaknesses in most memory domains.
   (e) none of the above

3. **A 29-year-old client who comes independently to your office earns subtest scaled scores of 4 or lower for all the core WRAML2 subtests. Which of the following diagnostic options would be most reasonable?**
   (a) ADHD
   (b) Traumatic Brain Injury from a motor vehicle accident
   (c) a and b
   (d) questionable motivation
   (e) depression

4. **Generally speaking, which WRAML2 estimate(s) would have the greatest psychometric soundness?**

   (a) GMI

   (b) Verbal Memory Index

   (c) Visual Memory Index

   (d) Attention/Concentration Index

   (e) The core subtests used individually

5. **The following WRAML2 Core Memory subtests scaled scores are achieved by a teenager: Story Memory = 5, Sentence Memory = 8, Number Letter = 11. Which of the following hypotheses would be best supported by just these subtest findings?**

   (a) The client has little motivation and so the results are highly suspect.

   (b) The client likely has a recent brain injury, and frontal areas are likely showing greatest impairment.

   (c) A congenital or acquired expressive language problem exists.

   (d) No diagnostic conjecturing is appropriate until a full neuropsychological battery has been completed.

   (e) Options a through c can be reasonably supported by these findings.

6. **The psychometrist generating the previous results (Question 5) brought them to his supervising psychologist. The best recommendation the supervisor could make is**

   (a) confront the client about his/her not trying and tell him/her to work harder.

   (b) see if there are other test findings and anything in the history supporting the working hypothesis just generated.

   (c) schedule the client for a subsequent appointment so these subtests could be repeated.

   (d) refer the client to a neurologist.

   (e) refer the client for an eye exam.

(continued)

7. **The following WRAML2 Core Memory subtests scaled scores are achieved by a teenager: Story Memory = 11, Sentence Memory = 8, Number Letter = 6. Which of the following is a reasonable expectation based only on these three WRAML2 subtest results?**

(a) Compared to age mates, this client likely has a general Verbal Memory deficit.

(b) This client likely has an IQ in the Low Average range of ability, or lower.

(c) Following verbal directions should generally pose little difficulty for this client.

(d) This client would likely have a higher gist than verbatim score on the WRAML2 Story Memory subtest.

(e) This client likely has good visual memory skills.

Answers: 1:b; 2:a; 3:d; 4:a; 5:c; 6:b; 7:d.

Five

OVERVIEW OF THE TOMAL-2*

The *Test of Memory and Learning–Second Edition* (TOMAL-2) is an individually administered test battery designed to provide a comprehensive assessment of memory skills in children and adults from ages 5 years 0 months through 59 years 11 months. For older adults, ages 55 years 0 months through 89 years 11 months, a shorter battery was devised to accommodate the special needs of assessing the senior population (Reynolds & Voress, in press). The TOMAL-2 is intended for clinical assessment of immediate verbal and nonverbal memory and delayed recall for verbal memory, as well as providing an overall or composite memory score. Comparisons between verbal and nonverbal memory as well as among a number of other memory variables including attention and concentration, associate memory, free recall, sequential recall, and learning over trials with common stimuli are also possible. Forward and backward recall are assessed separately based on a considerable body of research cautioning against combining these two forms of memory in clinical assessment (e.g., Ramsay & Reynolds, 1995; Reynolds, 1997).

The TOMAL-2 subtests systematically vary the mode of presenta-

---

*Portions of chapters 5 through 7 were adapted with permission of the copyright holder, PRO-ED Inc., from C. R. Reynolds and J. K. Voress (2007), *Test of Memory and Learning–Second Edition, examiner's manual*, PRO-ED, Inc., Austin, TX.

DON'T FORGET

TOMAL-2 is an individually administered test battery designed to provide a comprehensive assessment of memory skills in children and adults from ages 5 years 0 months through 59 years 11 months. For adults ages 55 years 0 months through 89 years 11 months, a shorter battery was devised to accommodate the special needs of assessing the senior population (Reynolds & Voress, in press).

DON'T FORGET

Forward recall and backward recall are assessed separately on the TOMAL-2.

DON'T FORGET

Selective reminding tasks allow a look at depth of processing and forgetting.

tion and response so as to sample verbal, visual, motoric, and combinations of these modalities in presentation and in response formats. Multiple trials to a criterion are provided on several subtests, including selective reminding, so that learning or acquisition curves may be derived. Multiple trials (at least five are necessary according to Kaplan, 1996) are provided on the selective reminding subtests to allow an analysis of the depth of processing. In the selective reminding format (wherein examinees are reminded only of stimuli forgotten or unrecalled), when items once recalled are unrecalled by the examinee on later trials, problems are revealed in the transference of stimuli from working memory and immediate memory to more long-term storage. Cueing is also provided at the end of the Word Selective Reminding Delayed recall task to add to the examiner's ability to probe depth of processing.

Subtests are included that sample sequential recall (which tends to be strongly mediated by the left hemisphere, especially temporal regions; e.g., see Hannay, Howieson, Loring, Fischer, and Lezak, 2004) and free recall in both verbal and visual formats to allow localization; purely

spatial memory tasks are included that are very difficult to
confound via verbal mediation
to assess more purely right-
hemisphere functions. Consequently, the battery can prove
useful in many of the assessment

> # DON'T FORGET
>
> The "easy pairs" on the Paired
> Recall subtest can be used to
> evaluate level of effort in many
> cases.

contexts mentioned in Chapter 1. It is particularly useful in forensic
evaluations and with examinees who may put forth questionable effort
during such cognitive assessments. The TOMAL-2 is one of few measures available that has items available to assess effort. For example, on
the paired recall subtest, examinees are presented with hard pairings of
words and very easy pairings of words (e.g., blue–sky). Examinees who
take the task seriously almost never miss the easy pairs of items. Other
subtests, such as Word Selective Reminding, allow evaluation of primacy and recency effects that also gives clues to level of effort.

Table 5.1 provides a listing of the various subtests and indexes (composite scores) available for the TOMAL-2. Scaling of each score is also
noted. Rapid References 5.1 and 5.2 provide information on availability
and ordering of the TOMAL-2 in addition to a listing of all the
TOMAL-2 test kit components. Additional information on the software is provided in Rapid Reference 5.3.

FROM TOMAL TO TOMAL-2

When the *Test of Memory and Learning* (TOMAL; Reynolds & Bigler,
1994a, 1994b) was released in 1994, it joined the WRAML as one of the
first well-normed and standardized test batteries that could be used to
assess memory abilities in children. Although successful as reflected in
widespread usage as well as a variety of research studies of its applications (e.g., Lowther & Mayfield, 2004), a number of revisions were introduced with the TOMAL-2. The major changes are outlined in

Table 5.1 Core and Supplementary Subtests and Indexes Available for the TOMAL-2

	M	SD
Core Subtests		
Verbal		
Memory for Stories	10	3
Word Selective Reminding	10	3
Object Recall	10	3
Paired Recall	10	3
Nonverbal		
Facial Memory	10	3
Abstract Visual Memory	10	3
Visual Sequential Memory	10	3
Memory for Location	10	3
Supplementary Subtests		
Verbal		
Digits Forward	10	3
Letters Forward	10	3
Digits Backward	10	3
Letters Backward	10	3
Nonverbal		
Visual Selective Reminding	10	3
Manual Imitation	10	3
Summary Scores		
Core Indexes		
Verbal Memory Index (VMI)	100	15
Nonverbal Memory Index (NMI)	100	15
Composite Memory Index (CMI)	100	15
Verbal Delayed Recall Index (VDRI)	100	15
Supplementary Indexes		
Sequential Recall Index (SRI)	100	15
Free Recall Index (FRI)	100	15
Associative Recall Index (ARI)	100	15
Learning Index (LI)	100	15
Attention/Concentration Index (ACI)	100	15

 *Rapid Reference 5.1*

Publication Information for the TOMAL-2

Authors: Cecil R. Reynolds & Judith K. Voress
Publication Date: December, 2007
Age Range: 5 years 0 months through 59 years 11 months
Administration Times
Core subtests: 30 minutes
Supplementary subtests: 20 to 30 minutes
Scoring software (unlimited use) available
Publisher: PRO-ED Inc.
8700 Shoal Creek Boulevard
Austin, TX 78757
1-800-897-3202
www.proedinc.com
Price: Complete test kit price = $376.00 (as of June, 2008)
Software (unlimited use) = $99.00
Combination test kit/software package price = $458.00

Rapid Reference 5.2

TOMAL-2 Test Kit Components

The TOMAL-2 Test Kit includes the following materials:
- TOMAL-2 Examiner's Manual
- 25 Examiner Record Booklets
- 25 Profile/Summary Forms
- 1 Deck of Delayed Recall Cue Cards
- TOMAL-2 Visual Selective Reminding Test Board
- TOMAL-2 Picture Book A
- TOMAL-2 Picture Book B

The kit may be ordered with the TOMAL-2 scoring software at a discounted price if ordered in the combination kit (see Rapid Reference 5.1).

≡ *Rapid Reference 5.3*

TOMAL-2 Scoring Software Description and System Requirements

The TOMAL-2 Scoring Software is a quick, efficient tool that (a) converts TOMAL-2 subtest raw scores into standard scores, percentile ranks, and age equivalents (if appropriate); (b) generates composite indexes; (c) compares subtest performance and composite performance to identify significant intraindividual differences; (d) computes and graphs learning curve analyses; and (e) provides a printed report of the examinee's identifying information and TOMAL-2 performance.

Minimum system requirements:

Windows System: Windows NT, 95, 98, or XP requires a minimum of

- 16 MB of RAM for Windows 95
- 32 MB of RAM for Windows 98
- 64 MB of RAM for Windows 2000
- 256 MB of RAM for Windows XP
- Minimum of 1024 × 764 screen resolution
- Minimum of 3 MB of hard disk space

Macintosh System: OS 10.2 or higher

- Minimum of 256 MB of RAM
- Minimum of 1024 × 764 screen resolution
- Minimum of 8 MB of hard disk space

Table 5.2. Generally speaking, an examiner familiar with the TOMAL can easily learn to administer the TOMAL-2. Most of the changes involve shortening the subtests, where this could be done with no tangible adverse affect on reliability of the subtest score, and moving particular tests from the core battery to the supplemental status. Basal and ceiling rules were tightened in several instances as well. These changes resulted in a significant reduction in administration time (long admin-

Table 5.2 Summary of Changes from TOMAL to the TOMAL-2

Consideration of published test reviews, personal observation (the first author was an active user of the TOMAL in his own clinical practice), and comments from individuals who used the TOMAL directed the TOMAL-2 authors in deciding upon changes to make in development of the TOMAL-2. The second edition of the TOMAL was changed in the following ways:

1. The age range was extended through 59 years 11 months. Individuals from 5 years through 59 years can now be assessed with a common set of subtests, as all subtests apply to all age levels.

2. Characteristics of the total normative sample were updated relative to socioeconomic factors, gender, disability, and other critical variables to be consistent with demographic data reported in the *Statistical Abstract of the United States* (U.S. Bureau of the Census, 2002, available at http://www.census.gov/) and are therefore representative of the current U.S. population.

3. Basal, ceiling, and discontinue rules were recalculated to improve accuracy. All of these rules and administration instructions were added to the Examiner Record Booklet and the manual. The Examiner Record Booklet now contains all of the information necessary to administer each subtest, easing the administration burden for the examiner.

4. The format of the picture books was revised. Picture Book A contains the items for Facial Memory and Memory for Location. Both subtests require that the book lay flat so that examinees may place chips on their responses. Picture Book B contains the items for the other subtests and is in an easel format. The pages in both picture books are now single-sided, to eliminate distraction when pages are turned and any issues with print bleeding through the pages.

5. The normative tables were reordered to follow the order of subtest presentation.

6. Visual Selective Reminding (the hardest and longest subtest to administer—it seemed MFL was the longest, but VSR was indeed the hardest to understand initially and to administer) and Digits Forward were moved from the core battery to supplementary subtest status. The core battery now consists of four verbal and four nonverbal subtests (as opposed to five core subtests on each scale in the TOMAL). For some subtests,

(continued)

Table 5.2 Continued

items were deleted and ceiling and discontinue rules were altered. Test administration for the core battery has been shortened to 30 minutes for the core subtests, and 20 to 30 minutes for the supplementary subtests.

7. Comparison to an additional memory measure was added to the validity chapter.

8. An additional story was added to Memory for Stories to accommodate adult examinees.

9. The overall size of the standardization sample was increased.

10. The TOMAL Delayed Recall Index (DRI) composition was altered to contain only two verbal subtests from the core battery, as one of the nonverbal tasks on the DRI was moved to supplemental status and there were concerns regarding the reliability of scores from a single nonverbal delayed recall task. This index was subsequently renamed the Verbal Delayed Recall Index.

---

istration time being the most frequent complaint to the authors and publisher about the TOMAL). The TOMAL-2 core battery can now be administered in 30 minutes or less to most examinees. While the TOMAL-2's core battery has fewer subtests and is therefore quicker to administer, all 14 of the original subtests are available, but many are included as supplemental tasks, whose use is dependent on the clinician's desire for a more in-depth look at memory skills and the need to make comparisons among the various supplementary indexes that are provided. A major change was the expansion of the age range, so that the battery can now be used with adults as well as children and teens.

> **CAUTION**
>
> Some of the ceiling or end rules have changed in the TOMAL-2, so if you were a TOMAL user and are switching to the TOMAL-2, be sure to review the end rules for each subtest. For ease of access, they appear in the manual and on the Examiner Record Booklet.

USER QUALIFICATIONS AND RESPONSIBILITIES

As indicated in the TOMAL-2 examiner's manual (Reynolds & Voress, 2007), examiners who give and interpret the TOMAL-2 should have formal training in individual assessment. This training should result in a basic understanding of testing statistics; general procedures governing test administration, scoring, and interpretation; and specific information about mental ability evaluation that includes memory assessment and applications of the results. Supervised practice in using mental ability tests is also desirable.

This special training can be obtained from numerous sources. Most often, the training can be acquired by enrolling in college courses devoted to assessment. Such courses are frequently found in departments of psychology, special education, adult education, speech pathology, reading, and counseling, among others. Workshops sponsored by local school agencies, state and national professional associations, or private consultants are other sources of training.

With such experience, examiners should have little difficulty in mastering the procedures necessary to give, score, and interpret the TOMAL-2 properly. Before actually giving the TOMAL-2, examiners should consult local school or agency policies, state regulations, and position statements of their respective professional organizations regarding the use of tests. This is especially the case when the purpose of testing is to diagnose disability conditions and to qualify individuals for special, remedial, or federally funded training programs. The TOMAL-2 authors do not give specific job or professional titles that qualify examiners for using the TOMAL-2 because there is so much variability within professions as to the training of individuals. However, individuals

> ### CAUTION
>
> Examiners who give and interpret the TOMAL-2 should have formal training in individual assessment.

must be appropriately licensed, certified, or otherwise credentialed in their state of practice for the use of individually administered tests of ability such as the TOMAL-2 and act in accordance with the applicable ethical codes of their profession in determining whether they are qualified to use the TOMAL-2.

THE TOMAL-2 STRUCTURE AND COMPONENTS

The TOMAL-2 is a comprehensive memory battery standardized for use with ages 5 years, 0 months, 0 days through 59 years, 11 months, 30 days. It is composed of a core battery of eight subtests (four verbal, four nonverbal) formally divided into a Verbal Memory Scale and a Nonverbal Memory Scale. A combination of these scales forms the Composite Memory Scale. Six supplementary subtests (four verbal, two nonverbal) are present for use when a broader, even more comprehensive assessment of memory is needed. Supplementary subtests may also be substituted for a core subtest when a core subtest cannot be given, is spoiled, or is inappropriate for a particular examinee. These subtests are also used in the derivation of certain supplementary scale indexes, to be noted in the following text. A delayed recall procedure is also available, which is based on recall of stimuli for two subtests of the core battery and yields a Verbal Delayed Recall Index.

Each TOMAL-2 subtest is scaled to a mean of 10 and a standard deviation of 3. Scale indexes are also scaled to a familiar metric, having a mean of 100 and a standard deviation of 15. Table 5.1 shows the various subtests and indexes available from the TOMAL-2, along with their respective standard score matrices.

Types of Normative Scores

Two primary types of normative scores are provided for interpretation of performance on the subtests and composite scales or indexes on the

TOMAL-2: standard scores and percentile ranks (several alternative score metrics are provided as well; see the following).

Standard Scores

TOMAL-2 standard scores are age-corrected, deviation-scaled scores of the same form used on the most popular intelligence scales—for example, the Wechsler series and the *Reynolds Intellectual Assessment Scales* (RIAS; Reynolds & Kamphaus, 2003). As noted, the subtests are scaled to a mean of 10 and a standard deviation of 3. Composite indexes have a mean of 100 and a standard deviation of 15. Standard scores indicate the distance of scores from the norm-group mean. A subtest scaled score of 13 and a composite index of 115 are both one standard deviation above the norm-group mean. TOMAL-2 standard scores are normalized scores derived using the method of continuous norming (see Chapter 4, Reynolds & Voress, 2007, for a more detailed explanation for derivation of TOMAL-2 scores and Roid, 1989, for a detailed explanation of the general procedures associated with continuous norming).

Percentiles

A *percentile* shows the percentage of the norm sample scoring at or below a specified score. A percentile of 98, for example, means the examinee's score equals or exceeds 98% of the norm sample and is in the top 2% (100 − 98) of scores.

Standard scores and percentiles provide different types of information. A TOMAL-2 standard score is an *equal interval metric* (Gordon, 1984) that describes the distance of a score from the mean. Standard scores are useful for additional calculations and can be manipulated arithmetically, as in discrepancy analyses, in viewing subtest scatter (Reyn-

DON'T FORGET

TOMAL-2 standard scores are age-corrected, deviation-scaled scores of the same form used on most popular intelligence scales and are on an equal interval metric.

olds, 1985, 1986), and in evaluating strengths and weaknesses within a profile of scores or comparing scores across test batteries. Percentiles do not allow for such manipulations. Percentiles reflect the rarity of a score in the distribution. Table 5.3 shows the comparability of selected TOMAL-2 scores. Various other score transformations are offered in

Table 5.3 Relation of TOMAL-2 Standard Scores and Percentile Ranks

Subtest Scores[a]	Index Scores[b]	Percentile
20	150	99.9+
19	145	99.87
18	140	99.62
17	135	99
16	130	98
15	125	95
14	120	91
13	115	84
12	110	75
11	105	63
10	100	50
9	95	37
8	90	25
7	85	16
6	80	9
5	75	5
4	70	2
3	65	1
2	60	0.38
1	55	0.13

[a]$M = 10, SD = 3$

[b]$M = 100, SD = 15$

≡ Rapid Reference 5.4

Score Metrics Offered in the TOMAL-2 Examiner's Manual

In addition to traditional subtest scaled scores with a mean of 10 and standard deviation of 3 and index scores with a mean of 100 and standard deviation of 15, as well as percentile ranks for all scores, the TOMAL-2 examiner's manual offers the following supplementary score conversions:

Normal Curve Equivalents (NCEs): Mean = 100 SD = 21.06

T-scores: Mean = 50 SD = 10

z-scores: Mean = 0 SD = 1

Stanines: Mean = 5 SD = 2

the TOMAL-2 examiner's manual as a convenience to those who may have a need for other metrics. These are available in Appendix E, Table E.1 on page 158 of the examiner's manual and include transformations for Normal Curve Equivalents, T-scores, z-scores, and stanines (also see Rapid Reference 5.4 for a summary).

Age-equivalent scores are provided for ages 5 years 0 months through 14 years 9 months. However, age equivalents have very limited uses and examiners must be careful in their use and interpretation. We do not recommend them for routine usage.

DON'T FORGET

The standard battery for the TOMAL-2 consists of eight (four verbal, four nonverbal) subtests, yielding a Verbal, Nonverbal, Composite Memory, and a Verbal Delayed Recall Index.

Standard Battery

The standard battery for the TOMAL-2 consists of eight (four verbal, four nonverbal) subtests, yielding a Verbal, Nonverbal, Composite Memory, and a Verbal Delayed Recall Index (see Table 5.4 for the composition of each scale). The subtests on each primary scale (Verbal and Nonverbal) provide a breadth of assessment of memory in each domain, sampling free and associative recall, meaningful and abstract memory functions, sequential recall, and the learning process, among other factors of memory. This battery of eight core sub-

Table 5.4 TOMAL-2 Supplementary Indexes and Their Subtest Composition

Index	Subtests
Sequential Recall[a]	Visual Sequential Memory Digits Forward Letters Forward Manual Imitation
Free Recall[b]	Facial Memory Abstract Visual Memory Memory for Location
Associative Recall[b]	Memory for Stories Paired Recall
Attention/Concentration[a]	Digits Forward Digits Backward Letters Forward Letters Backward Manual Imitation
Learning[a]	Word Selective Reminding Visual Selective Reminding Object Recall Paired Recall

[a]Requires at least one supplementary subtest. Learning or acquisition curves can be plotted against standardized learning curves from the standardization sample.

[b]May be derived entirely from core subtests.

tests will answer most questions concerning memory function; however, additional supplementary subtests and memory indexes are available, as previously noted.

Supplementary Subtests and Indexes

The four verbal and two nonverbal supplementary subtests (see Table 5.4) are used to augment the core battery when an even more detailed view of memory is desired, and they may be especially useful to neuropsychologists and to researchers. The administration of these six subtests typically requires less than 25 minutes for an experienced examiner, although very adept examinees may require more time. The use of these subtests allows the derivation of additional indexes, including the Sequential Recall Index, Free Recall Index, the Attention/Concentration Index, the Associative Recall Index, and the Learning Index. Composition of each supplementary index is illustrated in Table 5.4. Use of the supplementary indexes is facilitated by Section V on the TOMAL-2 Profile Summary Form.

LEARNING AND LEARNING CURVES

As previously noted, a Learning Index may be derived from those subtests that require repetitive presentation of common stimuli across trials. These four subtests (Word Selective Reminding, Object Recall, Paired Recall, and Visual Selective Reminding) allow for the assessment of immediate recall for the first trial and the generation of a learning curve across subsequent trials of

> **DON'T FORGET**
> ....
> Learning or acquisition curves can be plotted against standardized learning curves from the standardization sample for four subtests: Word Selective Reminding, Object Recall, Paired Recall, and Visual Selective Reminding.

the same stimulus. The Learning Index provides a psychometric method of evaluating learning as assessed on these subtests. Section VI on the TOMAL-2 Profile Summary Form also facilitates the plotting of learning curves for a visual display. The TOMAL-2 scoring software will automatically calculate and plot these learning curves and will plot a comparison learning curve for the same age group from the responses of the standardization sample.

DESCRIPTION OF SUBTESTS

The following text describes each of the eight core subtests, four verbal and four nonverbal, as well as the six supplementary subtests.

Verbal Subtests

Memory for Stories (MFS)

MFS is a verbal subtest requiring recall of a short story heard from the examiner's reading. The subtest provides a measure of meaningful recall, in which many examinees will form semantic associations as part of their recall strategy (however, some examinees may recall phrases or words correctly, unaided by the semantic aspects of the story, and still receive a good score) and is also related to sequential recall in some instances.

Word Selective Reminding (WSR)

WSR is a verbal free-recall task on which the examinee learns a word list and repeats it, only to be reminded of words left out in each case. It tests learning and immediate recall functions in verbal memory. Trials continue until mastery is achieved or until six trials have been attempted. Sequence of recall is unimportant. Depth of processing may be reflected in forgetting or retention of words previously recalled that are not "reminded," and are later forgotten or continuously recalled.

Object Recall (OR)

For OR, the examiner presents a series of pictures, pointing at each one while saying the name of the picture aloud. The pictures are removed and the examinee is to recall them. The examiner repeats this process until mastery is achieved or until five trials have been attempted. Verbal and nonverbal stimuli are thus paired, and recall is entirely verbal, creating a situation found to interfere with recall for many children with learning disabilities but to be neutral or facilitative for nondisabled children (e.g., Swanson & Saez, 2003).

Paired Recall (PR)

PR is a verbal paired-associate learning task on which the examinee is required to recall a list of word pairs when the first word of each pair is provided by the examiner. A classic task of experimental psychology, easy and hard pairs (easy pairs of words are those with common associations like *hot-cold* that almost no one fails to recall, while hard pairs have no logical reason for being paired) are included. The easy pairs serve as a measure of cooperation and effort for all but the most egregiously impaired, since most of the variance in performance across examinees is seen in the hard pairs.

Nonverbal Subtests

Facial Memory (FM)

FM is a nonverbal subtest requiring recognition and identification of faces from a set of distractors—black-and-white photos of faces of individuals of various ages, male and female, and of various ethnic backgrounds. The faces are carefully cropped to reduce extraneous clues and force the examinee to use the facial configuration as the primary element of recall. The subtest assesses nonverbal meaningful memory in a highly practical fashion and is one that has been extensively researched over the years. Recalling faces is quite different than recalling inanimate objects and abstract stimuli. Sequencing of responses is unimportant.

Abstract Visual Memory (AVM)

AVM assesses immediate recall for meaningless figures when order is unimportant. The examinee is presented with a standard stimulus with a brief (5 second) viewing opportunity and is then required to recognize the standard from any of six distractors (six distractors were used to reduce the impact of guessing). Attempts at verbal cueing by examinees tends to retard or interfere with performance on AVM as well, as it emphasizes visual memory. None of the standard stimuli or the distractors appears more than once during the subtest as well, also denigrating verbal encoding as a strategy.

Visual Sequential Memory (VSM)

VSM requires recall of the sequence of a series of meaningless geometric designs for which verbal cues are very difficult to derive or apply. The ordered designs are presented, followed by presentation of a standard order of the stimuli, and the examinee shows the order in which they originally appeared.

Memory for Location (MFL)

MFL assesses spatial memory to a large extent. The examinee is presented with a set of large dots distributed on a page and is then asked to recall the locations of the dots in any order.

Supplementary Subtests

Digits Forward (DF)

A standard verbal number recall task, DF measures low-level rote recall of a sequence of numbers. For all digits and letter recall tasks on the TOMAL-2, a unique scoring system is followed that is explained in detail in Chapter 2 of the TOMAL-2 Examiner's Manual.

Visual Selective Reminding (VSR)

VSR is a nonverbal analogue to WSR whereby examinees point to specified dots on a card, following a demonstration by the examiner, and are reminded only of items recalled incorrectly. As with WSR, trials continue until mastery is achieved or until five trials have been attempted.

Letters Forward (LF)

This task is a language-related analog to common digit span tasks using letters as the stimuli in place of numbers.

Manual Imitation (MI)

MI is a psychomotor, visually based assessment of sequential memory. The examinee is required to reproduce a set of ordered hand movements in the same sequence as presented by the examiner. A favorite task of Luria, it involves visual attention as well as visual memory and sequencing via motor pathways.

Digits Backward (DB)

This is the same basic task as Digits Forward, except the examinee recalls the numbers in reverse order.

Letters Backward (LB)

This task is a language-related analog to the Digits Backward task, using letters as the stimuli instead of numbers.

Verbal Delayed Recall

There are two delayed recall tasks: MFS and WSR. These tasks assess learning and the decay of memory and have been found to differentiate strongly among children, adolescents, and adults with specific neurological diseases and lesions in specific brain sites. They are also related to attentional mechanisms and the relative intactness of a variety of cognitive processes. The Verbal Delayed Recall Index may also serve as a measure of *forgetting* and may be of particular interest when contrasted with the Composite Memory Index and the Learning Index. Immediate versus delayed recall also has implications in assessing level of effort and in differential diagnosis of depression and functional versus organically based memory disturbances, especially in TBI, PTSD, and dementia cases.

TOMAL-2 PSYCHOMETRIC PROPERTIES

The TOMAL-2 examiner's manual contains extensive information regarding the psychometric characteristics of the TOMAL-2. Extensive information is provided on the development, standardization, and scaling of all of the TOMAL-2 scores, as well as information on test score reliability and data as well as theory to support the recommended interpretations of TOMAL-2 scores.

Standardization Sample

The TOMAL-2 was standardized on 1,921 individuals drawn in a population-proportionate stratified random sampling of the United States (including 28 different states) and drawn to mimic the 2002 U.S. Bureau of the Census statistics on the basis of geographic region, race, family income, educational attainment (parent educational level was used for the under-age-18 sample), and exceptionality status. Nearly equal numbers of males and females were tested. The resulting sample was a close match to the target 2002 census data. These responses were used to derive the various standard scores for the TOMAL-2 by the method of continuous norming, using the Roid (1989) method of scaling.

Reliability of TOMAL-2 Scores

Test score reliability was assessed on the TOMAL-2 using Cronbach's alpha to assess internal consistency and Pearson correlations to evaluate interscorer reliability and test-retest stability of TOMAL-2 performance. Table 5.5 (from Chapter 5 of the TOMAL-2 examiner's manual, reproduced here by permission of the copyright holder, Pro-Ed Inc.)

Table 5.5 Reliability Estimates[a] of Subtests and Indexes by Age

Subtest or Index	Age																			M[b]
	5	6	7	8	9	10	11	12	13	14	15	16	17	18	19	20–29	30–39	40–49	50–59	
Core Subtests																				
Memory for Stories	.90	.87	.89	.84	.84	.84	.84	.88	.87	.90	.90	.89	.86	.90	.93	.86	.89	.92	.87	.88
Facial Memory	.46	.66	.53	.67	.68	.71	.60	.72	.68	.47	.69	.76	.79	.79	.79	.51	.63	.75	.69	.67
Word Selective Reminding	.92	.92	.88	.88	.89	.83	.85	.89	.86	.91	.92	.89	.82	.80	.86	.91	.90	.92	.84	.88
Abstract Visual memory	.78	.93	.96	.95	.95	.96	.96	.95	.95	.96	.96	.96	.96	.96	.97	.94	.96	.96	.94	.95
Object Recall	.85	.88	.90	.83	.82	.83	.84	.89	.82	.82	.89	.82	.82	.84	.87	.84	.90	.91	.88	.86
Visual Sequential Memory	.79	.90	.84	.78	.89	.89	.86	.92	.91	.90	.92	.88	.86	.92	.90	.80	.91	.88	.81	.88
Paired Recall	.86	.87	.84	.85	.86	.87	.87	.88	.87	.85	.89	.86	.85	.72	.86	.88	.94	.92	.88	.87
Memory for Location	.77	.91	.92	.91	.90	.92	.90	.91	.91	.90	.91	.93	.89	.92	.93	.89	.92	.93	.89	.91
Supplementary Subtests																				
Digits Forward	.95	.96	.97	.96	.97	.96	.97	.97	.97	.97	.97	.97	.97	.97	.96	.96	.97	.96	.96	.96
Visual Selective Reminding	.92	.90	.87	.89	.86	.90	.88	.88	.89	.91	.90	.85	.82	.87	.82	.90	.89	.90	.88	.88
Letters Forward	.93	.95	.95	.95	.97	.95	.96	.98	.98	.97	.98	.97	.97	.97	.97	.97	.96	.97	.96	.97
Manual Imitation	.93	.95	.95	.95	.95	.96	.95	.96	.96	.97	.97	.96	.96	.97	.97	.93	.95	.96	.93	.96
Digits Backward	.87	.92	.92	.93	.96	.96	.96	.97	.97	.97	.97	.97	.97	.97	.97	.97	.97	.97	.96	.96
Letters Backward	.88	.87	.92	.93	.94	.94	.95	.97	.97	.97	.97	.98	.97	.98	.98	.97	.97	.97	.95	.96
Delayed Recall Subtests																				
Memory for Stories-Delayed	.88	.89	.91	.80	.84	.84	.89	.90	.87	.88	.91	.94	.94	.88	.94	.87	.91	.92	.84	.89
Word Selective Reminding-Delayed	.86	.90	.83	.87	.93	.93	.93	.91	.94	.94	.96	.93	.96	.93	.96	.67	.86	.87	.81	.91
Core Indexes																				
Composite Memory Index	.93	.96	.95	.95	.95	.95	.95	.96	.96	.95	.96	.96	.95	.96	.97	.95	.96	.97	.95	.96
Verbal memory Index	.94	.95	.94	.93	.93	.93	.93	.95	.93	.94	.95	.94	.92	.91	.94	.94	.96	.96	.94	.94
Nonverbal Memory Index	.85	.93	.91	.91	.93	.93	.91	.94	.93	.90	.94	.94	.94	.95	.95	.89	.93	.94	.91	.93
Supplementary Indexes																				
Attention/Concentration Index	.96	.97	.98	.98	.98	.98	.98	.99	.99	.98	.99	.99	.99	.99	.99	.98	.99	.99	.98	.98
Sequential Recall Index	.95	.97	.97	.96	.97	.97	.97	.98	.98	.98	.98	.99	.97	.98	.98	.96	.98	.97	.96	.97
Free Recall Index	.80	.90	.88	.90	.90	.91	.89	.91	.91	.86	.91	.93	.90	.93	.94	.86	.90	.93	.90	.90
Associative Recall Index	.91	.91	.90	.89	.89	.90	.90	.91	.91	.91	.93	.91	.90	.86	.93	.91	.94	.94	.90	.90
Learning Index	.94	.94	.93	.93	.93	.93	.93	.94	.93	.93	.95	.93	.91	.90	.92	.94	.95	.95	.93	.93
Verbal Delayed Recall Index	.90	.92	.90	.87	.91	.91	.93	.93	.93	.93	.95	.95	.96	.93	.96	.82	.91	.92	.86	.92

[a]Coefficient Alpha

[b]Median value across age

From C. R. Reynolds and J. K. Voress (2007), TOMAL-2 Examiner's Manual, copyright Pro–Ed Inc., with permission.

demonstrates very high Alpha coefficients for the TOMAL-2 subtest and index scores. A review of Table 5.5 reveals subtest score reliabilities routinely in the high .80s, with many in the .90s. Index score reliability coefficients are typically in the mid to high .90s. For the test-retest studies across several age ranges, the Pearson correlations are primarily in the .70s and .80s. Based on independent scoring by two examiners, interscorer reliability coefficients of agreement were found to be .94 or higher for all TOMAL-2 scores.

The overall reliability of the various scaled scores and composite indexes yielded by the TOMAL-2 are thus quite good. Relative to Anastasi and Urbina's (1997) three (interrelated) sources of test error (content, as represented by internal consistency reliability estimates such as Alpha; time, represented as test-retest correlations; and scorer, represented by agreement between independent scorers), the coefficients determined demonstrate very acceptable levels of score reliability. The internal consistency reliability of the TOMAL-2 scores is consistently high across demographic classifications as well. The magnitude of these reliability coefficients strongly suggests that the TOMAL-2 scores generally possess relatively small, acceptable amounts of error and that test users can have confidence in the consistency of TOMAL-2 results when obtained after carefully following the standardized administration and scoring procedures detailed in the examiner's manual.

Validity of Test Score Interpretation on the TOMAL-2

In conjunction with reliability, the psychometric concept of validity represents the primary technical aspect of psychological testing and evaluation. Often we refer to *test validity* or hear professionals who use tests pose the question, "Is this a valid test?" Validity is thus often misinterpreted as referring to a test. Tests per se are neither valid nor invalid. As Messick so eloquently stated, "[Validity] is an integrated judgment of the degree to which empirical evidence and theoretical rationales support the *adequacy* and *appropriateness* of *inferences* and *actions* based on test scores" (1989, p. 13 [emphasis added]). According to the *Standards for Educational and Psychological Testing* (AERA, APA, & NCME, 1999), *validity*, in the context of psychological testing, refers to "the degree to which evidence and theory support the interpretations of test scores entailed by proposed users of tests" (p. 9). Reynolds (1998) defines validity similarly, arguing that validity refers to the appropriateness and accuracy of the interpretation of performance on a test. On objective measures of aptitude or cognitive skills such as memory, test performance is usually quantified and expressed as a test score. Hence, it is not tests that undergo validations but our interpretations of test performances that are the appropriate subjects of validity research. Validation of the meaning of test scores is also a process that involves an ongoing, ever-changing effort to accumulate evidence for a sound scientific basis for proposed test score interpretations, and it is not then static but a constantly moving target. Validity, like reliability, will always be a relative concept, as the validity (i.e., evidence to support an interpretation of performance on a test) required to support an interpretation of test performance will vary according to the purpose for which test scores are being used, the types of individuals or populations being examined, and the specific interpretations being made.

The 1999 *Standards* provides one suggested scheme for organizing sources of evidence to evaluate proposed interpretations of test scores, although clearly recognizing that other organizational systems may be appropriate. The *Standards* propose five categories of evidence that clearly vary in their importance, according to how

DON'T FORGET

Validity refers to test score interpretations, not to the tests themselves.

test scores are used. Rapid Reference 5.5 provides a readily accessible summary of these five categories. It is also important to understand that the categories proposed in the *Standards* are not at all independent but overlap considerably and in many ways can be viewed as transactional.

As noted in the *Standards,* these areas of validity evidence are not discrete but overlap significantly. This is especially true of the TOMAL-2, wherein the evidence related to the first three areas noted previously (evidence based on test content, the response processes, and

---

≡ *Rapid Reference 5.5*

Structure of the **TOMAL-2** Validity Evidence

The TOMAL-2 Examiner's Manual presents evidence from multiple perspectives—being theory based, logic based, and empirically based—related to the interpretation of performance on the TOMAL-2. The empirically and logically based evidence presented therein is organized into five areas as suggested in the 1999 *Standards.* These areas are:

1. *Evidence based on test content* (i.e., themes, wording, and format of the items; guidelines for administration and scoring; and the scoring elements);

2. *Evidence based on response processes* (i.e., the fit between the latent constructs of the test and the detailed nature of performance by the examinee and conduct of the examiner);

3. *Evidence based on internal structure* (i.e., the degree to which the relationships among the component parts of the test conform to the hypothesized constructs);

4. *Evidence based on relations to other (external) variables* (i.e., the relationships between test scores and variables external to the test, including developmental variables and scores on other tests of similar and dissimilar constructs); and,

5. *Evidence based on consequences of testing* (i.e., the intended and unintended outcomes of the use or application of a test).

the internal structure of the test) are inextricably intertwined. Theory as well as empirical evidence in support of test score interpretations is considered to be important in the standards. The *Standards* also note that evidence may be logical and not just empirical, especially with regard to evidence based on content and response processes. Logical evidence is thus summarized where appropriate. The TOMAL-2 is offered as a measure of memory skills, both general and specific, and the examiner's manual presents a variety of evidence, as described previously, to support its interpretation as such.

Of particular interest to practitioners are the correlations of TOMAL-2 scores to other instruments. The TOMAL-2 examiner's manual reports correlations between the TOMAL-2 and several measures of intelligence, multiple reading and language measures, as well as correlations with the WRAML2. These results are summarized only very briefly here.

Achievement and Language

Correlational analyses were calculated between the various Core and Supplementary Index scores on the TOMAL-2 and three measures of achievement and language development. In these studies, the TOMAL-2 CMI and the VMI correlate highest with reading, with rs of .54 and .50, respectively, with one reading measure. The NMI correlates much lower at .35. Among the supplementary indexes, the *r*'s trend lower, with ACI, SRI, and the LI correlating in the mid to low .40s. In the other study, the VMI correlated with reading at .60 and the CMI at .50. While the correlation of the VMI with reading increased, the correlation between the NMI and reading as assessed in the second study declined to only .22. In reviewing these two studies and the pattern of correlations observed, it seems that the more complex the reading task, the higher overall the correlations with memory.

In a correlational study with the *Comprehensive Expressive and Receptive*

Vocabulary Test–Second Edition (CREVT-2), a very interesting pattern emerged. The TOMAL-2 core indexes correlated at relatively low levels with the CREVT-2 scores; although as one would expect, the VMI has the higher correlations relative to NMI and CMI. The supplementary indexes, however, have surprisingly higher correlations. The highest correlations observed in this study were between the Verbal Delayed Recall Index and the three CREVT-2 scores, with r's ranging from .55 to .60. This is a very positive indication regarding the utility of the VDRI, as vocabulary is indeed a long-term and very robust form of memory, being resistant to decline on all but the most severe forms of brain injury and CNS disease. Intuitively, one would expect the VDRI to be a good predictor of vocabulary, but it is also the least reliable of all the supplementary indexes. Delayed recall in general is also one of the most sensitive tasks to organically based disruptions of memory functions. Of the remaining supplementary indexes, the highest correlations are seen with ACI, SRI, and ARI with the CREVT-2 scores.

Correlations with Measures of Intelligence

Studies were completed correlating the TOMAL-2 with two individually administered measures of intelligence. In general, the TOMAL-2 indexes correlate in the .50s and .60s with intelligence test scores with some notable, higher, correlations evident. The FRI and the VDRI consistently correlate higher with IQs, with values running in the .70s with Verbal IQs.

As with the original TOMAL, the TOMAL-2 was found to be related to intelligence but at a level consistently below the level of correlation typical between measures of intelligence for the majority of its indexes. These results are quite similar to patterns seen with the other major memory battery currently available, e.g., the WRAML2 (Sheslow & Adams, 2003). The TOMAL-2 then is not simply another attempt at measuring distinct aptitudes that result in an intelligence test. The TOMAL-2 has only about a 16 to 50% overlap with intelligence tests, which tend to overlap from 50 to 64% among themselves. Thus, the TOMAL-2 (and the WRAML2) clearly adds unique information to the assessment.

WRAML2 and TOMAL-2

In a correlational study of these two scales, the WRAML-2 and the TOMAL-2 means were within 3 points of each other on all scales. The correlations between the TOMAL-2 CMI, VMI, and NMI and the WRAML-2 General Memory were .79, .79, and .60, respectively, indicating a strong relationship between the two scales at the adult level, even more so than with children and adolescents. These values also exceed the correlations of the two instruments with measures of intelligence, once again indicating these assessments are not simply redundant with measures of intelligence, but are assessing different constructs.

Readministration of the TOMAL-2

As we noted in our discussion of retesting on the WRAML2, often examiners wonder how soon a readministration of a test can be completed following the initial testing. Although a 6- to 12-month estimate is often heard to be suggested for many tests, such an interval has no empirical basis that we can discover. Instead, it would be sounder to look at the data reported for test-retest results in order to make this determination for any test. The TOMAL-2 reports a test-retest median interval of 14 days, a briefer interval than reported for the WRAML2. Test-retest data are provided for subtests and indexes. However, even over this brief interval, and with normal samples, changes in scores occur at relatively low levels on most subtests, with no practice effects evident on some subtests at either the child or the adult level. However, practice effects on the order of .3 to .5 standard deviations were not uncommon, especially on the core and supplementary indexes, with larger increases at the adult ages. Sequential memory tasks tended to show the smallest effects, and more purely verbal measures showed the largest effects. It is anticipated that such effects will fade relatively soon, but no longer-term data are available at this time. However, in the case of recent retesting, examiners can use the data in the TOMAL-2 examiner's manual (p. 86, Table 5.4) to estimate corrections for retest effects in the short term.

SUMMARY

The assessment of children and adolescents is a particularly complex task, requiring knowledge of child development, individual differences, psychometrics, and clinical acumen and experience not only with the tools of assessment but also with children and youth. Memory is a complex phenomenon that, as we have discussed earlier in this book, can be broken into numerous components, not all of which can be assessed with the TOMAL-2, nor with competing scales of memory.

The TOMAL-2 is a well-standardized, psychometrically sound instrument for evaluating memory function for ages 5 years, 0 months, 0 days, through 59 years, 11 months, 30 days. It yields four core Memory Indexes: Verbal, Nonverbal, Composite, and Verbal Delayed Recall. Supplementary Indexes are available to assess Learning, Attention/Concentration, Associative Recall, Free Recall, and Sequential Memory.

These eight core subtests and two Verbal Delayed Recall tasks of the TOMAL-2 should answer most but not all questions regarding memory function in children and adolescents. The six remaining supplementary subtests should address further questions. By reviewing overall memory function and by carefully analyzing task-by-task performance, an appropriate approach for tests with the very high reliability of subtest scores and high level of subtest specificity as possessed by the TOMAL-2 (see Reynolds & Kamphaus, 2003, for an explanation), one may acquire a clear picture of memory functions, which should have both diagnostic and treatment implications.

⟐ TEST YOURSELF ⟐

1. **Which of the following indexes is not part of the TOMAL-2?**
   (a) Composite Memory Index
   (b) Nonverbal Memory Index
   (c) Verbal Memory Index
   (d) Verbal Delayed Recall Index
   (e) Recognition Memory Index

2. **The age range for the TOMAL-2 is**
   (a) 5 to 17 years.
   (b) 6 to 21 years.
   (c) 16 to 79 years.
   (d) 21 to 90 years.
   (e) 5 to 59 years.

3. **Separate forward and backward recall subtests are provided on the TOMAL-2 because**
   (a) these recall processes primarily tap differing neurological substrates.
   (b) factor-analytic data separate these factors.
   (c) TBI patients often score differently on forward versus backward recall.
   (d) injury location in TBI patients affects scores on forward and backward recall differently.
   (e) all of the above

(continued)

4. Administration of the TOMAL-2 Core Battery takes approximately

(a) 20 minutes.

(b) 30 minutes.

(c) 40 minutes.

(d) 50 minutes.

(e) At least 1 hour or more.

5. The TOMAL-2 contains all the following except

(a) rote learning measures.

(b) procedural memory measures.

(c) visual memory measures.

(d) sequential memory measures.

(e) new learning (over trials) measures.

6. The internal consistency reliability estimates for the TOMAL-2 subtests scores

(a) hover around .50.

(b) are mostly in the high .80s and .90s.

(c) are not reported.

(d) are below that of most individually administered intelligence tests' subtest score reliability coefficients.

(e) cannot be accurately determined for most of the subtests.

7. TOMAL-2 standard scores are

(a) age-corrected deviation scaled scores.

(b) linear transformations of specific raw scores.

(c) Rasch-derived distribution-free scores.

(d) normalized using the negative hypergeometric function described by Lord and Novick.

(e) an excellent example of Pearson type-3 distributions.

8. **Learning or acquisition curves can be plotted against standardized leaning curves from the standardization sample for four subtests of the TOMAL-2. Which are they (select all that apply)?**

   (a) Word Selective Reminding

   (b) Object Recall

   (c) Paired recall

   (d) Visual Selective Reminding

   (e) Memory for stories

9. **Which of the following common stratification variables was not used in selecting the TOMAL-2 standardization sample?**

   (a) race

   (b) a measure of socioeconomic status

   (c) geographic region of residence

   (d) urban versus rural residence

   (e) gender

10. **Interscorer reliability estimates for TOMAL-2 scores, from correlating scores of independent scorers, were**

   (a) .50–.60.

   (b) .60–.70.

   (c) .80–.90.

   (d) above .90.

   (e) not reported.

Answers: 1e; 2e; 3e; 4b; 5b; 6b; 7a; 8a, b, c, and d; 9d; 10d

Six

ADMINISTRATION AND SCORING OF THE TOMAL-2

The TOMAL-2 examiner's manual should be consulted for step-by-step administration procedures for all TOMAL-2 procedures. What follows is intended to supplement that important information. As we did with the WRAML2, we will use the standardized sequence of subtest administration to guide the order of this chapter's administration and scoring commentary, and we will attempt to present parallel information where this approach works well. A part of the information provided includes estimates of subtest administration times, assuming a skilled examiner, but it should be noted that administration times will vary depending on the examinee's age, memory ability, and idiosyncratic test-taking characteristics (e.g., expect younger adults with good memory skills to take longer than children on subtests for which a discontinue rule applies). In addition, older adults often are more reflective and slower moving, so they may take longest. Some perfectionist, anxious, or compulsive clients will need encouragement to move along. In our own clinical work, we have found that some impaired examinees, particularly adults, recognize they are having difficulties and will begin to linger or become more labored and deliberate in their approach on many if not most items. These clients need to be encouraged to keep moving along once it is clear they cannot recall the necessary material. However, the majority of clients will perform within the administration time intervals provided in Rapid Reference 6.1. As we recommended with the WRAML2, these time approxima-

≡ *Rapid Reference 6.1*

Estimated Administration Times for the TOMAL-2 Subtests

Core Battery: 28 to 37 minutes
Memory for Stories: 3 to 4 minutes
Facial Memory: 4 to 5 minutes
Word Selective Reminding: 3 to 4 minutes
Abstract Visual Memory: 4 to 5 minutes
Object Recall: 3 to 4 minutes
Visual Sequential Memory: 3 to 4 minutes
Paired Recall: 2 to 3 minutes
Memory for Location: 6 to 8 minutes
Supplementary Subtests: 13 to 19 minutes
Digits Forward: 2 to 3 minutes
Visual Selective Reminding: 3 to 4 minutes
Letters Forward: 2 to 3 minutes
Manual Imitation: 2 to 3 minutes
Digits Backward: 2 to 3 minutes
Letters Backward: 2 to 3 minutes
Delayed Recall Subtests: 4 to 5 minutes
Memory for Stories—Delayed: 2 to 3 minutes
Word Selective Reminding—Delayed: 2 minutes

tions may be especially beneficial in estimating appropriate elapsed time intervals to use before administering Delay Recall subtests when undertaking a partial administration of the TOMAL-2.

Tests of problem solving, such as IQ and related aptitude measures, and comprehensive memory batteries such as the WRAML2 and the TOMAL-2 are experienced as mentally taxing and can be exhausting for many examinees. It is thus best not to administer such tests at the end of a long or detailed testing or interview session. It is preferable to administer such tests earlier in the evaluation process rather than later.

There are four subtests with a timed presentation (Facial Memory, Abstract Visual Memory, Visual Sequential Memory, Memory for Location), wherein a standard is exposed to the examinee for memorization in a specified time. For these subtests, having a stopwatch or some other means of precisely determining 5 or 10 seconds of elapsed time is necessary. A wall clock or watch with a second hand can be made to work satisfactorily. However, keeping track of how long a client takes to complete a task is unnecessary for the entire TOMAL-2; there are no "bonus points" or other scoring adjustments based on time. Object Recall is the only subtest with a time-limited response. Examinees are allowed 90 seconds for recall. As a practical matter, this subtest remains a power test, since virtually all examinees recall all objects they could recall, even with unlimited time within this 90-second time constraint.

Following is commentary organized by TOMAL-2 subtest; for each, there are three subsections: an estimated time range likely needed for administration, subtest-specific observations

---

CAUTION

Always be careful to observe the age-designated starting points on each subtest.

CAUTION

It is usually best to administer detailed memory batteries like the TOMAL-2 and the WRAML2 early in the testing process since they can be mentally fatiguing for many examinees, especially those with central nervous system compromise.

DON'T FORGET

There are four TOMAL-2 subtests with a timed presentation of the standard stimulus: Facial Memory, Abstract Visual Memory, Visual Sequential Memory, and Memory for Location.

worth noting, and a listing of the most commonly made errors for that subtest. Regarding the subsection entitled "Interesting Observations," most examiners are aware of the many generic happenings that are important to observe whenever conducting any assessment, such as consistency of response, cooperation, quality of speech and language, frustration tolerance, persistence when encouraged, distractibility, body language, and so on. These important domains of observation are not mentioned in the commentary that follows because it is assumed that examiners will already be vigilant observers of the spontaneous behaviors, reactions, and mannerisms important in any evaluation. Instead, what "Interesting Observations" lists are those that are specific to the subtest, or in some cases, unique to the TOMAL-2 overall.

Similarly, within the concluding subsection entitled "Common Examiner Administration Errors," general administrative mistakes that examiners may make are not included (e.g., not following standardized procedures, using a noisy or poorly lit room). As with our discussion of the WRAML2, basic examiner test-administration skills are assumed. It is always crucial that standardized test-administration procedures are followed, or the reliability and the validity test results are questionable (Lee, Reynolds, & Willson, 2004). Changes in standardized procedures result in unintended variations in performance that are often counterintuitive and difficult to predict (Lee, Reynolds, & Willson, 2004). Rapid Reference 3.1, from our discussion of test administration for the WRAML2, applies here as well and is useful to consider when administering almost any standardized test. Instead, "Common Examiner Administration Errors" highlights either those errors that have been noted during teaching the TOMAL-2 to graduate students or those errors commonly discovered during professional workshop presentations. The number associated with each subtest that follows corresponds to the order of subtest administration and the subtest numbering found on the Examiner Form.

Each subtest ends with a checklist that can be used by those learning or teaching the TOMAL-2 to check accuracy of test administration. Ideally, after video recording her/his subtest administration with a practice client, the checklist can be used to help establish the examiner's level of accuracy achieved.

SUBTEST DURATION, UNIQUE OBSERVATIONS, AND ERRORS TO AVOID

The core subtests are presented first, followed by the supplementary subtests and the delayed-recall subtests. The TOMAL-2 Examiner Record Booklet contains all of the necessary instructions for the administration of each of the TOMAL-2 subtests, as a convenience to the examiner. It is not necessary to have the TOMAL-2 manual open to administer the test correctly, as all of the necessary instructions are on the record booklet. Nevertheless, examiners should have already read and familiarized themselves with the more extended discussions in the manual regarding administration and scoring of the TOMAL-2.

DON'T FORGET

The TOMAL-2 examiner record booklet contains the verbatim instructions and rules for administration of each TOMAL-2 subtest, but this is not a substitute for a careful reading of the examiner's manual.

1. Memory for Stories (Core subtest)

Approximate administration time: 3 to 4 minutes.

Interesting Observations

There is adequate space on the examiner record form to record the examinee's responses, and the content recalled by the examinee should be written on the record form in the space provided. This information is especially important to capture for possible use in subsequent diagnostic exploration. Be alert for the following:

- Retelling the content but in a disorganized manner, or other displays of organizational (i.e., frontal lobe) deficits. It is typical for examinees to recall the story in the order it was read, even when material is left out. Earning credit does not depend on retelling story content in the correct sequence, but a disjointed recall style is unusual and may have clinical significance. Those new to the subtest may find it helpful to record the client response and score it later.
- Any recency and primacy effects. It is unusual for a client to tell only the beginning (or end) of the story (i.e., demonstrating only a primacy or a recency effect). It is even rarer to have only the middle content reported. Be sure to encourage the client to tell more of the story in order to help determine if you are observing an oversight, impulsiveness, or a real recall deficit (this kind of encouragement is consistent with the administration guidelines found in the manual).
- Confabulations (that is, renditions of parts of or the entire story that contain distortions or inventions). These should be recorded verbatim when possible. Omitting small *chunks* throughout a story is a more typical recall pattern, and this is especially characteristic for details found in the middle of a story. Distorting or embellishing the gist of the story is atypical, whereas omitting or distorting a detail is more common.
- Incorrect renditions of any portion of a story. Like confabulations, these smaller errors can be helpful in understanding the nature of the memory deficit. Affective attributions to characters in the story are sometimes interesting. Blending portions of the content of the first story with that of the second story is atypical and suggestive of a significant information-processing deficit.
- Behaviors triggered by differential difficulty levels between the stories. The second story is usually experienced as harder than the first. Therefore, note if the examinee seems to give up prematurely with the increased work demand. If so, does

examiner encouragement reengage the examinee? Sometimes the little bit of extra difficulty causes a fragile memory system to become overloaded, resulting in very poor performance with the second story.

Common Examiner Administration Errors

- Not first establishing rapport with a shy or anxious child or adult. This is especially important with this TOMAL-2 subtest, since it is the first one administered. So if the examinee is not responding easily to informal chit-chat, delay starting memory testing and invest more time helping to get the client at ease, or administer an alternate procedure, tapping the examinee's likely strengths.

- Stories are read too quickly, too slowly, or robotically. The TOMAL-2 stories should be read in a conversational manner with appropriate affect, inflection, and intonation (when learning the test, record your administration of the subtest, and then check its accuracy).

- Not encouraging the anxious or reluctant client sufficiently. Reluctant examinees should be encouraged as directed in the manual by using the given prompts as appropriate (i.e., "Tell me more," and "What else can you recall from the story?").

- Client's responses are not correctly recorded because of client speed of response or examiner's unfamiliarity with the story content. Developing beforehand some kind of shorthand recording system is helpful. Taping the client's responses (and subsequently recording and scoring them) is an acceptable practice for beginning examiners, although be cautious using this approach with more paranoid or anxious clients. Experience indicates taping is seldom necessary once you have administered and scored the test only a handful of times, as most examiners develop a rapid coding or shorthand system. Most examiners can write the story as retold verbatim without difficulty after only a few administrations. It is also permissible to develop a personalized system of abbreviations in writing the retold story as a form of personal shorthand if it enables you to take down the story verbatim.

- Reading a second story when even the examinee earns one or more points on the first story.
- Reading a story not appropriate for the examinee's age. Rapid Reference 6.2 provides a checklist to use to avoid common administration errors for the Memory for Stories subtest.

Rapid Reference 6.2

Memory for Stories Subtest

	Yes	No
1. Instructions read verbatim.		
2. All instructions included.		
3. Instructions read clearly.		
4. Two age-appropriate stories are read.		
5. Stories read with appropriate pace, inflection, and clarity.		
6. Story recall requested after each story.		
7. Examinee prompted using verbatim manual prompts as needed.		
8. Items scored correctly for each story (guides in manual consulted).		
9. Total Raw Score is accurate.		
10. Correct Standard Score obtained.		
11. Verbatim, accurate synonyms, and ethnically appropriate name and nickname substitutions given credit.		

2. Facial Memory (Core subtest)

Approximate administration time: 4 to 5 minutes.

Interesting Observations
Be alert for the following:

- Portions of the stimulus cards that seem to be ignored in the examinee's response. This is especially true for those "ignoring" most of the right or left side (or top or bottom) of the cards, since this may be suggestive of a field cut (resulting from injury to the retina or optic nerve) or visual neglect. This should be noted on all subtests in which visual stimuli are presented and will not be mentioned for all of the subtests on the TOMAL-2 that involve picture book presentations.
- Motor difficulties in placing the chips over the examinee's choices of faces. To the extent that this causes significant slowing of the examinee's ability to respond, it may confound accurate assessment of memory due to short-term memory decay over a longer time period than experienced by the average examinee without such significant motor problems.
- Pattern of eye movements, to examine whether the client is looking at all parts of the card on items with multiple faces (all items after Item 1).
- Squinting or moving his/her face noticeably close to the stimulus card or off to one side, which may indicate visual acuity problems. For this and all other visual memory tasks on the TOMAL-2, be sure to always ask if the client wears glasses at the outset of the evaluation and uses them if he/she needs them for reading or other close-up work .
- Affective responses to any particular faces or set of faces. The faces in the TOMAL-2 represent a wide range of ethnic groups and both genders, as well as some individuals with dis-

abilities or impairments—some obvious, others not—and also children and adults.

Common Examiner Administration Errors

- Not strictly adhering to the timed stimulus card exposure. Extra or shortened time can radically alter an examinee's performance.
- Not providing the chips immediately or giving the examinee the wrong number of chips.
- Failing to encourage the examinee to use of all of the chips provided when identifying the faces seen on the stimulus card.
- Turning multiple pages when moving to the next item, thus exposing some faces prematurely. Rapid Reference 6.3 provides a checklist to use to avoid common administration errors for the Facial Memory subtest.

> ## DON'T FORGET
>
> When administering Facial Memory, the timing of the stimulus presentation changes across items: Allow 5 seconds for Items 1–4; 10 seconds for Item 5; 15 seconds for Item 6; and 20 seconds for Item 7.

≡ Rapid Reference 6.3

Facial Memory Subtest

	Yes	No
1. Picture book displayed flat on the table.		
2. Timing of stimulus exposure is correct on each item.		
3. All instructions included and read verbatim and clearly.		

(continued)

	Yes	No
4. Examiner points to picture book with verbal instructions.		
5. Correct number of chips are given for each item.		
6. Item is scored correctly before going to next item.		
7. Examinee is encouraged to use all chips provided, if necessary.		
8. All items are administered.		
9. Total Raw Score computed accurately.		
10. Standard Score accurately obtained.		

3. Word Selective Reminding (Core subtest)

Approximate administration time: 3 to 4 minutes.

Interesting Observations
Be alert for the following:

- Strategies such as grouping by conceptual or semantic category for recall or other strategies indicating sophisticated approaches to remembering (e.g., recalling all animals first, then food-related items).
- Are primacy and recency effects seen in order of recall? Although not necessary for scoring the correctness of a response (since order of recall on WSR is irrelevant) the examiner may wish to record the order in which the examinee recalls words by numbering the words in the order they are recalled (rather

than just checking the item off). As with Memory for Stories, noting order of recall can allow the examiner to explore various performance aspects better and develop a stronger or more in-depth understanding of the examinee's memory skills and needs for rehabilitation (e.g., are primacy and recency effects apparent?).

- If an examinee recalls a word on one trial, is that word recalled on subsequent trials without a reminder? This is the most common pattern with most nonclinical clients. However, selective reminding as a task is useful in evaluating depth of processing in memory, and it is important clinically to note items that are recalled correctly on one trial and dropped out of the recall on a later trial and when this occurs (e.g., on the very next trial or later).

- Are intrusion errors retained? Do different intrusion errors occur on different trials?

- Are semantic associations apparent by the third and/or fourth trials? For example, with older children and adults, it is common to hear *plate* and *spoon* or *apple* and *bread* or *pencil* and *eraser* reported together by Trial 3 or 4. It is sometimes valuable, at the conclusion of all parts of this subtest, to ask the client "How did you remember all of the words?"

- Does the client ask or use his/her fingers to determine the total number of words administered? Gaining such knowledge is a reasonable strategy and suggests productive (and independent) problem-solving ability. This may be more common in a capable person with a relatively weak short-term verbal memory.

- On occasion, after the first trial following the reading of the omitted words by the examiner, when asked to say the list again, an examinee would repeat only the words originally omitted, and of which they were just reminded. When this occurs, be sure to note it and repeat the instructions, prompting the examinee to say all the words.

Common Examiner Administration Errors

• Reading the words too slowly or too quickly (when learning the test, record your administration of the subtest and then check its accuracy).

≡ Rapid Reference 6.4

Word Selective Reminding Subtest

	Yes	No
1. All instructions included and read verbatim.		
2. Words pronounced clearly.		
3. Words read in a conversational tone and rate.		
4. Correct word list is used, as determined by client age.		
5. Intrusions recorded but not corrected.		
6. Testing discontinued after successful recall of all words on a single trial.		
7. All six trials are administered if all words are not recalled in any one trial.		
8. Credit given for all items remaining after the discontinue criterion is met.		
9. Total Raw Score obtained accurately.		
10. Accurate Standard Score obtained.		

- Not enunciating words clearly or speaking too quickly and running words together.
- Incomplete recording of the client's performance because of the client's fast word recall. This is sometimes a problem for examiners new to the test. Initially, one may use a tape recorder and score the subtest later; however, the words are given on the examiner record booklet in alphabetical order for each trial. It is only necessary to record whether the word is recalled by placing a check or other easily made mark next to the word. Numbering them is recommended for a variety of clinical reasons, most already noted, but this typically becomes very easy after only a few practice sessions once examiners are familiar with the form and the words—they are listed in the same order for every trial.
- Telling the examinee how many words make up the list, how many trials are to be administered, or that "we just have one more trial to go."
- Failing to stop and give credit for all remaining trials after all of the words are successfully recalled on one trial. Rapid Reference 6.4 provides a checklist to use to avoid common administration errors for the Word Selective Reminding subtest.

> ## DON'T FORGET
> ....
> On Word Selective Reminding use the 8-word list for ages 5–8 years and the 12-word list at all other ages.

4. Abstract Visual Memory (Core subtest)

Approximate administration time: 4 to 5 minutes.

Interesting Observations
Be alert for the following:

- Attempts to use verbal encoding strategies for recall of these visually presented items. This is an ineffective strategy that actually makes the task more difficult for most examinees due to the nature of the drawings.
- Such severe motor difficulties that pointing responses are extremely slow, which may affect remembering on this subtest. Milder motor problems should have no adverse impact.
- The examinee focuses on a small detail in the standard drawings as a means of recalling the entire drawing. This too is an ineffective strategy and also reveals anxious and obsessive tendencies along with a lack of flexibility in processing that can be helpful in deriving more astute and successful strategies for recall.
- Squinting or moving his/her face noticeably close to the standard stimulus and recall alternatives, which may indicate a client's visual acuity problems. This may be a problem on all or some of the visually presented tasks for which details of the pictures are important. Is the examinee wearing his/her glasses?

Common Examiner Administration Errors

- The standard stimulus is not displayed for exactly 5 seconds.
- Failure to demonstrate the correct response if the first item administered is failed.
- More than one page is turned at a time, inadvertently exposing drawings to be recalled later in the subtest.
- Failing to prompt hesitant examinees.
- Failure to discontinue testing after an examinee fails two of three consecutive items.
- "Testing the limits" before the entire test battery is completed by allowing extra time on items after the ceiling item or other accommodative procedures. Rapid Reference 6.5 provides a

≡ Rapid Reference 6.5

Abstract Visual Memory Subtest

	Yes	No
1. Picture book presented in correct position.		
2. All instructions included, read verbatim and clearly.		
3. Standards for recall exposed for exactly 5 seconds and then removed.		
4. Correct response demonstrated if first item administered is failed.		
5. Discontinue or end rule applied correctly.		
6. Hesitant examinees are encouraged to point.		
7. Testing is started on correct item as determined by examinee's age.		

checklist to use to avoid common administration errors for the Abstract Visual Memory subtest.

5. Object Recall (Core subtest)

Approximate administration time: 3 to 4 minutes.

Interesting Observations
Be alert for the following:

- Semantic or other groupings of objects to occur as a strategy. Compare this with strategies observed on other subtests on the

TOMAL-2 in which a common set of items is administered over multiple trials.

- It is useful, as on other subtests, to record the order of recall (although this is not necessary for scoring) to assess primacy and recency effects.
- Determine whether objects recalled correctly on an earlier trial drop out or are not recalled on a later trial.
- Make a record of intrusion errors in the blank space on the record booklet below the scoring columns for the subtest. Intrusions were relatively rare in the normal standardization sample but occur more often with frontal impairment and may reach the point of confabulation if numerous.
- Lapses in attention. On tasks on the learning index, such as Object Recall, in which the same stimuli are repeated, poor attentional processes may become evident.
- Sometimes examinees will substitute a word or object label that is highly similar to the picture (e.g., an examinee might say "fly" instead of "bee" or "ribbon" instead of "bow"), indicating recall of the visual image, but the wrong label, demonstrating difficulty with the multisensory input.

Common Examiner Administration Errors

- Reading the items too quickly and/or failing to point to the pictures as you read the items. The items are designed to be named at a rate of one per second by the examiner. Reading faster or slower will alter recall for any task with a timed presentation (e.g., see Lee, Reynolds, & Willson, 2003).
- Reading the items in the order listed on the examiner record booklet instead of the order presented in the picture book. The items are randomized across each presentation in the picture book but are listed, for ease of scoring, in alphabetical order on the record booklet. Name the items and point to the pictures

simultaneously by looking at the picture booklet and score responses looking at the record booklet.

- Hesitating or forgetting to turn from the picture page to the blank page on any trial before asking the examinee to recall the objects seen. After each picture page with the randomized objects pictured, a blank page is inserted into the picture book for display during the recall trial.
- Allowing extra time beyond the 90-second limit for recall of the pictured objects.
- Failure to discontinue or to give credit for all remaining items once all picture names are recalled correctly on a single trial.
- Penalizing a client for immature articulation or other examinees for articulation problems. Give credit if the name is pronounced well enough to be recognizable as the object presented. Rapid Reference 6.6 provides a checklist to use to avoid common administration errors for the Object Recall subtest.

≡ Rapid Reference 6.6

Object Recall Subtest

	Yes	No
1. Directions read verbatim and clearly.		
2. Examiner points to pictures as he/she also names them aloud.		
3. Pictures are named at rate of one per second.		
4. Picture page is turned to blank page and oral recall requested immediately after naming of all pictures by the examiner.		

(continued)

	Yes	No
5. Pictures are named in the order shown in the picture book on each trial, not from the record form order.		
6. Examinee is allowed 90 seconds to recall as many picture names as possible on each trial.		
7. Testing terminated and credit for all remaining items given if examinee recalls all picture names on any one trial.		
8. Accurate Total Raw Score computed.		
9. Accurate Standard Score obtained.		

6. Visual Sequential Memory (Core subtest)

Approximate administration time: 3 to 4 minutes.

Interesting Observations
Be alert for the following:

- Since most examinees tell the stories from Memory for Stories in sequence, even though this is not required, contrasting the score on Visual Sequential Memory with the Memory for Stories score potentially provides a comparison of sequential memory where meaningful associations are present (Memory for Stories) with abstract sequences where no apparent associations occur.
- Such severe motor difficulties that pointing responses are extremely slow may affect remembering on this subtest. Milder motor problems should have no adverse impact.

- Attempts to use verbal encoding strategies for recall of these visually presented items. This is an ineffective strategy that actually makes the task more difficult for most examinees, due to the nature of the drawings.
- Examinees who fail to scan the entire page may have some form of visual field defect or neglect.
- Examinees who scan from right to left instead of left to right may experience difficulty with early print conventions in languages such as English or display other areas of confusion. Some follow-up with design-copying tasks might be done when such observations are made.

Common Examiner Administration Errors
- The standard stimulus is not displayed for exactly 5 seconds.
- Items are scored as pass/fail (i.e., 0,1) instead of giving credit for each design recalled in the correct sequence within each item.
- Not demonstrating the correct response when the examinee earns a raw score of zero on the first item administered.
- Starting at the wrong age-designated starting point.
- Turning multiple pages, exposing standard or response pages to be used with later items.
- Placing the picture book at an uncomfortable distance from the examinee.
- Giving points for items below the start point for the examinee's age level.
- Failing to encourage hesitant examinees to try. At first glance this subtest can appear more difficult or intimidating to examinees than is actually the case. Rapid Reference 6.7 provides a checklist to use to avoid common administration errors for the Visual Sequential Memory subtest.

≡ Rapid Reference 6.7

Visual Sequential Memory Subtest

	Yes	No
1. Standard pictures are presented for exactly 5 seconds.		
2. Instructions read verbatim and clearly.		
3. Correct starting item selected, based on age.		
4. Correct response demonstrated if a raw score of zero on the first item.		
5. Items are scored based on number of designs recalled in correct sequence.		
6. Picture book placed at a comfortable distance for the examinee to give a pointing response.		
7. Discontinue rule is followed correctly.		
8. Hesitant examinee is encouraged appropriately.		
9. Total Raw Score correctly summed.		
10. Standard Score accurately obtained.		

7. Paired Recall (Core subtest)

Approximate administration time: 2 to 3 minutes.

Interesting Observations
Be alert for the following:

- Compare raw scores on the easy pairs and hard pairs as a means of considering effort. Very few examinees miss more than one of the easy pairs, as most of the variance in scores on this subtest is in the hard pair recall.

- Confusion or mixing of the stimulus pairs (i.e., attaching the wrong word to the stimulus word).
- Record any intrusions for consideration to determine if there is a pattern of intrusions across multiple subtests. Intrusions are relatively unusual on this subtest.
- Impulsive responding during the presentation of the word lists after the first trial. Some examinees will begin to answer when they are supposed to be listening to the second presentation trial and may have difficulty inhibiting responses even once cautioned to wait.

Common Examiner Administration Errors

- Administering the wrong word list. Be sure to use the six-paired recall list for ages 5 through 8 years and the eight-paired recall list for all other ages.
- Reading the word list too fast or too slowly. Read the words at the rate of one per second. Alterations in presentation speed affect recall.
- Not pausing two seconds between word pairs. Some examiners read all of the word pairs at a continuous rate, which makes it more difficult for the examinee to make the correct associations.
- Rereading the word pairs from the prior ordered list. The word pairs, although they are the same for all trials, are randomized for presentation order across trials. Occasionally an examiner will look down at the record booklet and read from the wrong list. Rapid Reference 6.8 provides a checklist to use to avoid common administration errors for the Paired Recall subtest.

≡ Rapid Reference 6.8

Paired Recall Subtest

	Yes	No
1. Instructions read verbatim and clearly.		
2. Correct responses given if either sample item is failed.		
3. Correct list of word pairs is used for examinee's age.		
4. Correct randomized list is read for each trial.		
5. Total Raw Score correctly summed.		
6. Standard Sore accurately obtained.		

8. Memory for Location (Core subtest)

Approximate administration time: 6 to 8 minutes.

Interesting Observations

Be alert for the following:

- As on all visually presented subtests in which stimuli are scattered about the page or there is not a single focal point, watch how the examinee scans the page to check for evidence of visual neglect or poor strategies for scanning.
- Observe for evidence of acuity problems.
- Motor difficulties in placing the chips in the examinee's choices of squares. To the extent that this causes significant slowing of the examinee's ability to respond, it may confound accurate assessment of memory due to short-term memory de-

cay over a longer time period than experienced by the average examinee without such significant motor problems.

- Observe that the examinee places the chips to determine whether he/she uses a sequential or a simultaneous strategy. If the examinee places the chips one after the other in a sequence, most likely a linear approach to processing the stimuli to memory has been invoked on what is largely a spatial task. Typically, examinees who score well on this subtest invoke simultaneous processing strategies in which they memorize the pattern, as opposed to sequence of filled squares. When placing chips, these examinees will invoke visualization strategies to recreate the visual pattern. After the entire battery of TOMAL-2 subtests has been administered, it is sometimes fruitful to ask highly successful or notably unsuccessful examinees how they attempted to perform this task. It is useful in understanding memory problems to know whether examinees have knowledge or skills in the development and deployment of effective strategies for remembering. Several examinees in the standardization sample were noted to count the number of dots and then count out chips, thus sacrificing time better spent observing the stimulus.

Common Examiner Administration Errors
- The standard stimulus is not displayed for exactly 5 seconds.
- Not providing the examinee with 10 chips before beginning the subtest instructions.
- Not demonstrating the correct response when the examinee earns a raw score of zero on the first item administered.
- Starting at the wrong age-designated starting point.
- Turning multiple pages, exposing standard or response pages to be used with later items.

- Placing the picture book at an uncomfortable distance from the examinee.
- Giving points for items below the start point for the examinee's age level.
- Continuing past the discontinue rule (three of five consecutive items failed). Rapid Reference 6.9 provides a checklist to use to avoid common administration errors for the Memory for Location subtest.

⟰ Rapid Reference 6.9

Memory for Location Subtest

	Yes	No
1. Instructions read verbatim and clearly.		
2. Chips are given to examinee before reading instructions.		
3. Correct age-designated starting point is used.		
4. Picture book is placed at a comfortable distance for examinee to place chips.		
5. Correct response is demonstrated if first administered item failed.		
6. Standard pages are displayed for 5 seconds.		
7. Discontinue rule observed (three of five consecutive items failed).		
8. Total Raw Score computed accurately.		
9. Standard Score accurately obtained.		

9. Digits Forward (Supplementary subtest)

Approximate administration time: 2 to 3 minutes.

These observational notes and examiner cautions apply equally well to Letters Forward (subtest 11), Digits Backward (subtest 13), and Letters Backward (subtest 14). These are all also supplementary subtests and have a common administration time of 2 to 3 minutes. The checklist in Rapid Reference 6.10 will also be applicable to all four of these subtests.

Interesting Observations

Be alert for the following:

- As we pointed out in the discussion of the WRAML2, there are differences in accurately recalling letters versus numbers. Numbers are easier, and this is borne out by examining the raw score to scaled score transformations of Digits Forward versus Letters Forward on the TOMAL-2. While the string length (number of elements recalled) may vary between these two tasks and other auditory rote recall tasks, the scaled scores should nevertheless be similar to other tasks of immediate rote verbal memory. When they are not, first look to behavioral observations related to attention as well as to effort before making interpretations related to differences in processing, encoding, or recalling the particular stimulus. Digits, letters, and other symbols do have different levels of correlation with other tasks and salient distinctions in their surface characteristics, but be sure to rule out easily observed behavioral dimensions before making such interpretations.
- Note whether primacy and recency effects are present on items with less than perfect recall and compare this to other subtests.
- On any rote auditory recall task, it is important to be a careful

observer of attention. Many times, attention will be the most salient determinant of an individual's ability to recall auditory strings. If any external distractors occur, such as a siren outside or other noises that distract the examinee significantly, note this carefully and consider whether the subtest should be invalidated altogether.

- Note any strategies such as chunking or rehearsal that may be attempted by the examinee. As on other memory tasks, always be looking for obvious strategies an examinee may employ. On such brief rote recall tasks as Digits Forward and similar tasks, many strategies will actually interfere with recall.

- On backward recall tasks, be certain the examinee does not become confused after the first or a later item and begin to recall the stimuli in forward order. If this occurs, repeat the instructions as needed regarding backward recall.

- Some examinees will say each number/letter immediately after the examiner.

Common Examiner Administration Errors

- Numbers are read too fast or too slowly (versus one per second). Alterations in speed clearly have an effect on the length of the string an examinee can recall.

- The examiner's voice does not fall with the presentation of the last digit on each item (in order to signal the end of the series).

- Elements are not enunciated well or loudly enough by the examiner.

- Failure to record the examinee's response on the record booklet. This is useful for later checking of scoring but also to examine evidence of intrusions, primacy and recency effects, and any other obvious patterns to recall that may not be evident from only listening. This subtest is also difficult to score accurately without recording the examinee's response.

- Repeating an item if requested by the examinee. Rapid Reference 6.10 provides a checklist to use to avoid common administration errors for the Digits Forward, Letters Forward, Digits Backward, and Letters Backward subtests.

≡ *Rapid Reference 6.10*

Digits Forward, Letters Forward, Digits Backward, Letters Backward Subtests

	Yes	No
1. Instructions read verbatim and clearly.		
2. Numbers/letters read one per second.		
3. Examiner's voice drops slightly with last digit/letter of each item.		
4. Items 1 through 4 administered to all examinees.		
5. Examinee's response is recorded on record booklet.		
6. Discontinue rule observed—after Item 4, if less than three points on each of two consecutive items.		
7. Total Raw Score computed accurately.		
8. Standard Score accurately obtained.		

10. Visual Selective Reminding (Supplementary subtest)

Approximate administration time: 3 to 4 minutes.

Interesting Observations
Be alert for the following:

- Although order of recall is irrelevant to scoring, examiners should note if an examinee points to the dot in each square in a different sequence than presented by the examiner. This type of responding was relatively rare in the normal standardization sample.

- As on several other subtests noted previously, after the entire battery of TOMAL-2 subtests has been administered, it is sometimes fruitful to ask highly successful or notably unsuccessful examinees how they attempted to perform this task. For understanding memory problems, it is useful to know whether examinees have knowledge or skills in the development and deployment of effective strategies for remembering.

- Motor difficulties in pointing correctly to the examinee's choice of dots. To the extent that this causes significant slowing of the examinee's ability to respond, it may confound accurate assessment of memory due to short-term memory decay over a longer time period than experienced by the average examinee without such significant motor problems.

- If an examinee recalls a dot correctly on one trial, is that dot recalled on subsequent trials without being a reminder? This is the most common pattern with most nonclinical clients. However, selective reminding as a task is useful in evaluating depth of processing in memory, and it is important clinically to note when items recalled correctly on one trial are dropped out of the recall on a later trial and when this occurs (e.g., on the very next trial or later).

- On rare occasions, an examinee will not attend accurately to the instructions to "Now point to all the dots again," and this should be noted (and the examinee reminded).
- It is common for the examinee to point to more than one dot per square on the grid, especially after the first trial. The examiner should ignore any incorrect dots touched for scoring purposes but still note the occurrence of such intrusions for clinical purposes should a pattern of intrusion errors emerge throughout the assessment.

Common Examiner Administration Errors

- Choosing the wrong side of the standard card relative to the examinee's age.
- Positioning the client and the examiner in an awkward position. Although there is no steadfast rule on the positioning of the examiner and the examinee, they must each have an unobscured view of the other's pointing cues and responses.
- Be sure the card is oriented as directed in the manual. It is easy to place it upside down on occasion and this will result in the examiner pointing to the wrong dots when cueing the examinee.
- Failure to give credit to all remaining trials once an examinee gets all of the items correct on a single trial. Rapid Reference 6.11 provides a checklist to use to avoid common administration errors for the Visual Selective Reminding subtest.

≣ Rapid Reference 6.11

Visual Selective Reminding Subtest

	Yes	No
1. Standard card presented at a comfortable distance for examinee to point accurately.		
2. Examiner positions client correctly and is in a clear position to observe responses.		
3. Age-appropriate selective reminding card is used (six-block card for ages 5 to 8 years, and eight-block card thereafter).		
4. Card is oriented as directed on the record booklet.		
5. Instructions read verbatim and clearly.		
6. Examiner points at designated items correctly.		
7. Examinee's responses are recorded for each item.		
8. Examiner points only to items missed on all trials after Trial 1.		
9. Examiner ignores intrusions.		
10. Discontinue rule followed accurately and credit given for all remaining trials after examinee earns a perfect score on any one trial.		
11. Total Raw Score accurately computed.		
12. Standard Score accurately obtained.		

II. Letters Forward (Supplementary subtest)

Approximate administration time: 2 to 3 minutes.
See subtest 9, Digits Forward.

12. Manual Imitation (Supplementary subtest)

Approximate administration time: 2 to 3 minutes.

Interesting Observations
Be alert for the following:

- Any significant motor problems the examinee may have that slow responding on this subtest as well as particular difficulty in forming the hand movements. Inordinate levels of motor slowing may interfere with recall on this task.
- As on any visually presented task, visual impairments may interfere with performance on Manual Imitation.
- Watch for counting aloud, labeling of the hand movements, or other attempts at verbal encoding of the sequence. Unlike tasks that are highly abstract visually or that include faces, Manual Imitation lends itself to the development of verbal strategies in those adept at verbal processing, and this can enhance performance.
- Observe and note any primacy or recency effects in the examinee's recall. This can be determined after testing if you have recorded the examinee's responses on the record booklet in the manner instructed.
- Manual Imitation is another very good task for which it is fruitful, after the entire battery of TOMAL-2 subtests has been administered, to ask highly successful or notably unsuccessful examinees how they attempted to perform this task. For understanding memory problems it is useful to know

whether examinees have knowledge or skills in the development and deployment of effective strategies for remembering.

- Perseverative responses are sometimes encountered on this task, which was a favorite of the Russian neuropsychologist, Luria, and they are generally taken to denote frontal lobe or related executive system difficulties.

Common Examiner Administration Errors

- Failure to administer items 1 through 6 to all examinees, no matter how poorly they may perform.
- Failure to ensure the examinee can make a recognizable approximation of the hand movements to be imitated prior to beginning the testing.
- When teaching the hand movements, offering a verbal label to each hand position, as necessary. This will greatly facilitate the performance of many examinees but restrict the performance of a few.
- Presenting the hand movements at a rate that is too slow or too rapid. As with digit and letter recall tasks, items should be presented at the rate of one per second.
- Failure to record the sequence of recall and write it on the record booklet as instructed.
- Scoring the items as pass/fail as opposed to scoring according to the number of hand movements reproduced in the correct position in the sequence. Rapid Reference 6.12 provides a checklist to use to avoid common administration errors for the Manual Imitation subtest.

≡ *Rapid Reference 6.12*

Manual Imitation Subtest

	Yes	No
1. Instructions read verbatim and clearly.		
2. Examinee determined to be able to make recognizable approximations of the examiner's hand movements.		
3. Examiner teaches the hand movements, without labeling them, if necessary.		
4. Hand movements are presented at a constant, standard rate of one per second.		
5. Response sequence is recorded as directed on record booklet.		
6. Items 1 through 6 administered to all examinees.		
7. Discontinue rule followed correctly.		
8. Total Raw Score computed accurately.		
9. Standard Score correctly obtained and recorded.		

13. Digits Backward (Supplementary subtest)

Approximate administration time: 2 to 3 minutes.
   See subtest 9, Digits Forward.

14. Letters Backward (Supplementary subtest)

Approximate administration time: 2 to 3 minutes.
   See subtest 9, Digits Forward.

15. Memory for Stories—Delayed (Delayed recall subtest)

Approximate administration time: 2 to 3 minutes.

Interesting Observations
Be alert for the following:

- Retelling the content but in a disorganized manner or other displays of organizational (i.e., frontal lobe) deficits. It is typical for examinees to recall the story in the order it was read, even when material is left out. Earning credit does not depend on retelling story content in the correct sequence, but a disjointed recall style is unusual and may have clinical significance. Those new to the subtest may find it helpful to record the client response and score it later.

- Any confusion evidenced by blending the two stories. Blending portions of the content of the first story with that of the second story is atypical and suggestive of a significant information processing deficit, but it does tend to occur more often on the delayed recall of the stories than on the initial recall.

- Confabulations (that is, renditions of parts of or the entire story that contain distortions or inventions). These should be recorded verbatim when possible. Omitting small *chunks* throughout a story is a more typical recall pattern, and this is especially characteristic for details found in the middle of a story. Distorting or embellishing the gist of the story is atypical, whereas omitting or distorting a detail is more common.

- Incorrect renditions of any portion of a story. Like confabulations, these smaller errors can be helpful in understanding the nature of the memory deficit. Affective attributions to characters in the story are sometimes interesting behaviors triggered by differential difficulty levels between the stories. The second story is usually experienced as harder than the first. Therefore, note if the examinee seems to give up prematurely with the increased work demand. If so, does examiner encouragement reengage the examinee? Sometimes the little bit of extra difficulty causes a fragile memory system to become overloaded, resulting in very poor performance with the second story. This remains true on the delayed recall, as it did with the initial recall administration.

- Once the client starts making errors, is most of the meaning of the story preserved (despite the errors), or do important aspects of the meaning get distorted or lost? While a paraphrased recall may earn zero points, such an item failure is much better than remembering only the first and last few words, and is a reflection of more effort at recall than a simple "I can't" or "I don't remember any of it." The interpretation of the score should reflect these features in addition to the total score earned.
- Note if errors are predominantly semantic or verbatim, as described earlier. Compare the type of errors made to those noted in the immediate recall administration of the subtest.

Common Examiner Administration Errors
- Failure to prompt the examinee with the name of the story.
- Prompting with the name of a different story not previously administered.
- Failure to record the examinee's responses verbatim in the space provided. Rapid Reference 6.13 provides a checklist to use to avoid common administration errors for the Memory for Stories—Delayed subtest.

≡ *Rapid Reference 6.13*

Memory for Stories—Delayed Subtest

	Yes	No
1. Correct story titles chosen and read.		
2. Instructions read verbatim and clearly.		
3. Requests recall of second story even if examinee earns a raw score of zero on the first story.		
4. Records examinee's response verbatim on the record booklet.		
5. Encourages hesitant examinee as needed.		
6. Items scored correctly for each story (guides in manual consulted).		
7. Total Raw Scores computed correctly.		
8. Accurate Scaled Score obtained.		

16. Word Selective Reminding—Delayed (Delayed recall)

Approximate administration time: 2 minutes.

Interesting Observations
Be alert for the following:

- Compare responses to see whether any strategies evident on initial recall persist, such as grouping by conceptual or semantic category for recall or other strategies, indicating sophisticated approaches to remembering (e.g., recalling all animals first, then food-related items).

- Are intrusion errors retained?
- It is sometimes valuable, at the conclusion of all parts of this subtest, to ask the client "How did you remember all of the words?"
- Does the examinee use his/her fingers to determine the total number of words recalled, or remember how many words were initially presented?

Common Examiner Administration Errors

- Incomplete recording of the client's performance because of the client's fast word recall. This is sometimes a problem for examiners new to the test. Initially, one may use a tape recorder and score the subtest later; however, the words are given on the examiner record booklet in alphabetical order for the delayed recall trial. It is only necessary to record whether the word is recalled by placing a check or other easily made mark next to the word. Numbering them is recommended for a variety of clinical reasons, most already noted, but this typically becomes very easy after only a few practice sessions once examiners are familiar with the form and the words, since they are listed in the same order for every trial.
- Telling the examinee how many words they have yet to recall.
- If using the cued recall condition, cueing for all of the words instead of just those that were not recalled during the free recall. Rapid Reference 6.14 provides a checklist to use to avoid common administration errors for the Word Selective Reminding—Delayed subtest.

≡ Rapid Reference 6.14

Word Selective Reminding—Delayed Subtest

	Yes	No
1. Reads instructions verbatim and clearly; all instructions included.		
2. Clarifies the task if the examinee has questions.		
3. Using cued recall only for items not recalled correctly during the free recall.		
4. Total Raw Score correctly calculated.		
5. Accurate Scaled Score obtained.		

🔍 TEST YOURSELF 🔍

1. **The TOMAL-2 Examiner Record Booklet presents instructions for administration of which of the TOMAL-2 subtests?**

   (a) the core battery only

   (b) the supplementary subtests only

   (c) the delayed recall subtests only

   (d) none of the subtests

   (e) all of the subtests

2. **Recording the speed at which a task is completed is an examiner's responsibility for which subtest?**

   (a) Abstract Visual Memory

   (b) Facial Memory

   (c) Visual Selective Reminding

   (d) Paired Recall

   (e) none of the above

3. **The only TOMAL-2 subtest with a time-limited response is _____.**

   (a) Abstract Visual Memory

   (b) Facial Memory

   (c) Visual Selective Reminding

   (d) Paired Recall

   (e) Object Recall

4. **The subtest thought to be most difficult for many examiners to learn to administer properly is _____.**

   (a) Abstract Visual Memory

   (b) Facial Memory

   (c) Visual Selective Reminding

   (d) Paired Recall

   (e) Word Selective Reminding

5. **Which memory phenomenon is not associated with recall on the Memory for Stories subtest?**

   (a) primacy effect

   (b) recency effect

   (c) commission errors

   (d) forgetting verbatim but remembering gist features

   (e) recognition memory

Answers: 1e; 2e; 3e; 4c; 5e

Seven

INTERPRETATION OF THE TOMAL-2

I n Chapter 4, an approach to interpreting WRAML2 scores was presented that is useful in many ways with the TOMAL-2, but that more closely reflects the preferences for interpretation of the WRAML2 author and that is more specific to the WRAML2. In this chapter an approach to interpreting the TOMAL-2 is presented that is similar in some ways to the approach to WRAML2 interpretation, but that also differs in that it more strongly reflects the preferences for interpretation of the TOMAL-2 authors and is more specific to the TOMAL-2. Where it is reasonable and useful to do so, a parallel organization is used for the organization of the two interpretive chapters. Where the coauthors of this book present different or conflicting views of interpretive models (you will find them overall to be more similar than different) in these two chapters (4 and 7 of this volume), we trust that readers will view these as nuances of legitimate professional disagreements as to the "best" approach to apply and choose the best of the two approaches presented (where they do differ) that matches their own knowledge and skills in test score interpretation. As did the WRAML2 interpretive chapter, this chapter on TOMAL-2 interpretation begins with a general overview of interpretation of test scores as related to the TOMAL-2. The complete TOMAL-2 renders a large number of scores, divided into those that are highly specific (the subtest scores); scores representing clusters of subtests that reflect some common, clinically useful constructs (the core and supplementary indexes); and one core index reflecting the most global level of performance, the Composite Memory Index. In general, all of these scores, if obtained under valid, standardized conditions, should be interpreted. The question, of course, is what is the best, most valid interpretation of any particular score, and it is important to recall that it is the interpretation of test scores to which the construct of validity applies, not to tests or test scores themselves (e.g., see AERA et al., 1999; Reynolds, Livingston, & Willson, 2009).

The primary approach given in the following is an integration of Kaufman's (1979; Reynolds & Kaufman, 1985) psychometric approach to interpretation of test scores and actuarial approaches. The emphasis of the interpretation is on the levels of scores (i.e., specificity) that best account for the examinee's performance. Unlike intelligence test interpretation, which should focus on IQs and index level scores almost exclusively, avoiding subtest level interpretations (e.g., see Kamphaus, 2000; McDermott, Fantuzzo, & Glutting, 1990; Reynolds & Kamphaus, 2003; Watkins, 2000, 2003; and Watkins, Glutting, & Lei, 2007) on memory batteries such as the WRAML2 and TOMAL-2 are more often recommended as being appropriate. There are several reasons for this distinction. Unlike intelligence tests, memory batteries tend to have smaller average intercorrelations among subtests (which is the essential determinant of the strength of any g-factor present), subtests with relatively higher internal consistency reliability coefficients, and greater levels of subtest specificity, thereby representing more reliable and distinguishable differences in various memory constructs than are typically represented on subtests of an intelligence battery. There are many different manipulations of stimuli and methods of presentation of tasks in the memory domain, and small changes in stimuli or presentation or modes of recall can create substantial changes in performance, reflecting different memory systems within the brain. As one example, for which there is strong evidence from functional behavioral neuroimaging, recalling or recognizing faces versus recalling or recognizing inanimate objects (both of which are visual memory to a large extent) invoke enhanced cerebral activation in clearly distinguishable regions of the cortex (e.g., Grelotti et al., 2005; Schultz, 2005; Shultz et al., 2000, 2003). Forward and backward recall represent another such example with strong psychometric as well as clinical differentiation, as forward recall tasks can be very well preserved in cases with only localized right-hemisphere damage, while backward recall is substantially impaired; and backward recall can be preserved in cases with localized left-hemisphere damage but forward recall is impaired (e.g., see Ramsay & Reynolds, 1995, and Reynolds, 1997, for reviews and analyses of forward and backward recall). In factor analyses, forward and backward recall load most highly on distinct factors as well. Seldom do the subtests of an intelligence test reflect such a level of distinctive activation in the brain. Comparison of composite scores permits the examiner to form clinical hypotheses about the nature of a memory problem; to recommend various treatment programs, including cognitive rehabilitation strategies and educational programming and placement; to diagnose specific memory conditions; and to make prognoses for successful remedial or special interventions. In cases where there has been some injury to the brain, the TOMAL-2 will be an excellent assessment battery to evaluate recovery of function. Statistical comparison of the TOMAL-2 subtests to their respective composite mean scaled score should also be undertaken, as described in the following.

Also included in this chapter is a brief section on a neuropsychological model of interpretation of performance on the TOMAL-2.

CAUTION

The subtest level of interpretation of any test, TOMAL-2 included, is the most tenuous level of score interpretation.

LEVELS OF ANALYSIS

The TOMAL-2 may be interpreted using different levels of analysis, which may receive different degrees of emphasis in different cases; commonly included are (a) a combined index level (i.e., the Composite Memory Index, CMI), (b) a separate index level (e.g., Verbal and Nonverbal Memory Indexes, VMI and NMI, and one or more of the supplementary indexes, including the Verbal Delayed Recall Index, Attention/Concentration Index, and Sequential Recall Index, among others), and (c) the individual subtest level (including the eight core subtests, two delayed-recall subtests, and the remaining six supplementary subtests). In most cases, some combination of these scores will be emphasized.

Test interpretation based on multiple test findings is always the preferred basis of interpretation because, generally, more scores (i.e., more samples) provide stronger psychometric properties for the resultant estimate(s). Consequently, using the Composite Memory Index provides the strongest psychometric basis for formulating a TOMAL-2 interpretation, since the CMI is made up of two index (VMI and NMI) and eight subtest scores, which themselves are each made up of numerous memory items. Using a combined score is always preferred unless the component scores contributing to that summary score are found to be highly variable, first deviating at a statistically significant level from the average subtest score, and then showing a level of infrequency in the normal or nonreferred population.

The first step in clinical interpretation of the TOMAL-2 is to complete the Profile Summary Form. This form is for the examiner's use in deriving all of the necessary standard scores for the TOMAL-2 subtests and indexes and provides a means of profiling and summarizing the examinee's performance as reflected in these scores. It allows for easy comparisons of various scores, and its use greatly facilitates the interpretive process.

THE PROFILE SUMMARY FORM

Space is provided on the Profile Summary Form pages for (a) specifying pertinent information about both the examiner and the examinee; (b) recording TOMAL-2 subtest results in terms of raw scores, percentiles, standard scores, and age equivalents (if desired); (c) computing indexes for the composites; (d) recording pertinent information about the examinee's history and presenting problems; (e) other test results that are available; (f) completing a learning curve analysis; (g) profiling the examinee's TOMAL-2 subtest performance; (h) comparing composite scale differences; and (i) the examiner's interpretations and recommendations. Detailed instructions as well as an example of a completed Profile Summary Form are provided in Chapter 3 (see especially Figure 3.2) of the TOMAL-2 Examiner's Manual and so are not duplicated here. If using the TOMAL-2 software, much of this information will be contained on the printout provided by the scoring program, including the learning curve analysis, and need not be duplicated on the Profile Summary Form. However, many examiners find it helpful to at least plot the TOMAL-2 scores on the Profile Summary Form anyway if they plan to make direct comparisons of TOMAL-2 scores to other assessments, such as intelligence test scores. Those who interpret the TOMAL-2 should be strongly conversant with the Profile Summary Form provided as a standard component of the TOMAL-2 test kit.

Although the study of intraindividual differences may be done with subtest scaled scores, the use of composite indexes provides a more general indication of certain types of memory processes and provides a superior basis for evaluating subtest level performance as well. Composite scores are preferable, in large part, because their results are more reliable than individual subtests. Similarly, from a neuropsychological perspective, more clinical relevance is often obtained from composite scores because of the contrasts that can be made between verbal and nonverbal and delayed recall. More will be said about this topic in the next section.

There are four core composite indexes on the TOMAL-2: Composite Memory Index (CMI), Verbal Memory Index (VMI), Nonverbal Memory Index (NMI), and Verbal Delayed Recall Index (VDRI). Supplementary indexes are provided for the advanced user. The structure of these scales and indexes was reviewed in Chapter 4 of this book. Each index score is based on the sum of the subtest scaled scores

DON'T FORGET

The TOMAL-2 supplementary indexes provide logical regroupings of the TOMAL-2 subtests, based on expert reviews of the subtests' content. Often these regroupings will explain any discrepancies or high levels of variability in subtest-level performance and should be consulted before moving to the subtest level of interpretation. Index or composite score interpretations are always preferred over individual subtest-level performance whenever appropriate.

that comprise the index. The composite index is a standard score computed on various combinations of subtests. It is useful because it allows the examiner to estimate an examinee's ability on categorically related memory tasks or *constructs* incorporated into the TOMAL-2. That is, an examinee's ability relative to different aspects of memory function can be assessed in addition to specific subtest performance in relation to the composite or other indexes. The use and interpretation of the composite indexes are first addressed, since they are the first layer of interpretation of an examinee's performance on the TOMAL-2, followed by a discussion of the more detailed information that may be available at the level of the individual subtest.

THE COMPOSITE MEMORY INDEX (CMI)

The CMI is the most global of memory indicators on the TOMAL-2, as well as the most reliable and the most robust indicator of overall or general memory skills. This index is composed of all the core subtests of the verbal and nonverbal indexes. It is a global index of memory function. Obviously, the score can be enhanced by exceptional performance on one or both of its composite indexes (VMI and NMI) or markedly impaired by a deficient performance on either one or both of the verbal and nonverbal composite measures. When the CMI is diminished it is a sign of dysfunctional memory, but we do not know immediately if this is due to a generalized memory deficit or some specific problem(s). When the score is diminished because of deficient verbal and nonverbal memory performance, it may be a sign of generalized memory dysfunction. From a neuropsychological standpoint, such a finding has implications for either diffuse cerebral dysfunction or bilateral temporal lobe damage (especially in the hippocampal region) or dysfunction as well as difficulties with attention and concentration. When presenting the CMI, despite its high level of reliability, it is important to give some indication in a report as to its relative level of precision. Most often this is accomplished by reporting the obtained score on the CMI accompanied by a confidence interval of the examiner's choosing (most often the 85% or 95% confidence interval in clinical settings), and values for attaching these confidence intervals are given in the TOMAL-2 Examiner's Manual.

When the VMI and the NMI are similar in magnitude, the CMI should be the value from the TOMAL-2 chosen by the examiner for emphasis in explaining the examinee's level of memory skills. The CMI should be accompanied by its percentile rank in most instances as an aid to interpretation and a qualitative description of the overall level of memory performance, such as provided in Table 7.1.

When the VMI and NMI differ at a level of magnitude that is unusual in the population, the CMI should be deemphasized and the focus of interpretation should move more toward the other core and supplementary indexes. Roid's (1989) continuous norming procedure was used to develop the standard scores for the TOMAL-2. This

Table 7.1 Suggested Qualitative Descriptors for TOMAL-2 Indexes

Index Intervals	Description	Percentage Included in Each Interval
> 130	Very Superior	2.34
121–130	Superior	6.87
111–120	Above Average	16.12
90–110	Average	49.51
80–89	Below Average	16.12
70–79	Impaired	6.87
< 70	Significantly Impaired	2.34

method uses polynomial regression to fit the progression of means, standard deviations, skewness, and kurtosis across age groups. These fitted values were estimated at 6-month intervals for ages 5–0 through 8–11; 1-year intervals for ages 9–0 through 19–11; and 10-year intervals for ages 20–0 through 59–11. Given the fitted values of skewness and kurtosis from the regression, the shape of the distribution of the scores was determined and standard scores then derived. The use of these methods in the derivation of the TOMAL-2 standard scores, and the fact that all TOMAL-2 scores are derived from a common sample, permits direct comparisons of the various standard scores provided by the TOMAL-2, including the various indexes as well as the individual subtests. These types of comparisons are useful in telling us which scores to emphasize in the interpretation of test performance as well as in providing the examiner with an intraindividual measure of the examinee's memory abilities.

After reviewing the CMI, this process begins with contrasting the VMI and the NMI scores to determine whether they differ at a statistically significant level (i.e., is any observed difference in these two indexes considered reliable or is it most likely due to chance or other random influences on the two scores?). The absolute value of the difference, VMI – NMI, is used in this assessment. Once the two index scores have been subtracted, the difference score can be compared to the values in Table 7.2 to determine whether the difference is reliable or not and at what level of confidence it may be determined that the two indexes differ. As seen in Table 7.2, a difference between the VMI and NMI of 11 standard score points represents a statistically significant difference between performance on these indexes at $p \leq .05$. While this indicates a real difference in performance in these two global areas of memory function, such differences are relatively common in the general population, and in most cases will not reflect a disability. Examiners should nevertheless interpret this difference as indicative of a real difference in how the examinee is likely to function in each general area of memory function. And while a statistically significant difference that is common in the population at large is not usually reflective of a disability, it may have implications for learning and instruction as well as vocational

Table 7.2 Differences Required for Statistical Significance when Comparing TOMAL-2 Core Composites

Indexes Compared	Size of Difference Required for Significance	
	.05	.01
VMI – NMI	11	14
VMI – VDRI	11	14
NMI – VDRI	12	15
CMI – VDRI	10	14

Note: VMI = Verbal Memory Index; NMI = Nonverbal Memory Index; VDRI = Verbal Delayed Recall Index; CMI = Composite Memory Index.

DON'T FORGET

When reviewing difference scores, it is important to consider the statistical significance or reliability of the difference score, but one must also consider the frequency with which such differences occur. The statistical significance testing of the difference tells you about its relative reliability and how often it occurs due to chance factors alone. Reliable differences in performance on various composite scores on many tests are relatively common. The cumulative frequency distribution of difference scores should be consulted to determine how often any particular difference score occurs in the total population of test takers as estimated from the standardization sample. The reliability of a difference score as determined by statistical significance testing (e.g., determining that a difference score is statistically significantly different from zero at $p \leq .05$), and its actual rate of occurrence in the population are often confused.

choice and success. Next we examine the relative frequency of occurrence of a difference score of this size in the normal population.

Table 7.3 provides the cumulative distribution of difference scores for the key comparisons of TOMAL-2 core indexes. In evaluating this table we see that about 40% of the population has real differences in memory skills as reflected in their test performance. At what point does the difference become more interesting clinically, possibly denoting a disability, and reflecting a point where the emphasis of the interpretation of performance should shift strongly to the indexes beyond the CMI? There is no uniform or gold standard for answering this question. Reynolds and Kamphaus (2003) reviewed this issue, as have others, and have suggested that frequency of occurrence in the normal population provides a basis for such decision making about test score interpretation, and that whenever a difference is seen to occur in less than 10% of the population, the difference score should be accorded greater importance, and overall composites such as the CMI should not be taken as representative of the examinee's memory skills. In such in-

Table 7.3 Cumulative Percentages of Difference Scores for Core Indexes on the TOMAL-2

Amount of Discrepancy	VMI – NMI	VMI – VDRI	NMI – VDRI	CMI – VDRI
> 39	.1	.1	.8	.4
39	.3	.3	1.3	.6
38	.4	.5	1.4	.7
37	.4	.5	1.9	.7
36	.5	.6	2.3	1.0
35	.7	1.2	2.8	1.1
34	1.3	1.2	3.1	1.2
33	1.6	1.4	3.6	1.4
32	2.0	1.6	3.9	1.6
31	2.8	1.6	4.4	2.4
30	3.1	2.2	4.6	2.6
29	3.8	2.4	5.1	3.2
28	4.8	2.6	5.6	3.8
27	5.4	3.0	7.0	4.3
26	6.4	3.6	9.0	4.6
25	7.5	4.0	11.1	5.6
24	9.1	4.8	12.2	6.2
23	10.4	5.9	13.6	6.9
22	12.1	6.7	14.6	7.5
21	13.7	7.8	16.4	8.7
20	16.0	8.0	17.7	9.7
19	17.7	9.2	20.4	11.5

Table 7.3 Continued

Amount of Discrepancy	VMI – NMI	VMI – VDRI	NMI – VDRI	CMI–VDRI
18	19.6	10.7	22.8	13.2
17	22.0	13.8	24.6	13.8
16	24.1	15.2	28.2	15.2
15	27.6	16.4	31.5	17.7
14	30.5	20.1	33.9	20.1
13	35.0	23.9	37.0	23.9
12	38.5	27.4	40.9	27.3
11	42.4	29.9	44.2	29.9
10	47.4	34.4	46.9	35.3
9	50.2	38.7	50.8	39.4
8	54.3	43.1	55.3	45.6
7	59.0	49.6	58.8	51.3
6	63.4	54.5	64.8	57.9
5	68.7	61.4	71.8	64.5
4	74.3	68.6	76.8	70.0
3	80.2	75.3	81.3	74.9
2	86.6	82.9	87.2	84.8
1	92.4	90.2	93.5	90.1
0	100.0	100.0	100.0	100.0

Note: VMI = Verbal Memory Index; NMI = Nonverbal Memory Index; VDRI = Verbal Delayed Recall Index; CMI = Composite Memory Index.

stances, examinees' memory skills will vary widely depending upon the tasks before them, and a more detailed review and explanation of memory skill is required. When reviewing the cumulative frequency of difference scores for the TOMAL-2 core indexes in Table 7.3, it is seen that a difference of about 23 points between VMI and NMI is necessary to reach the 10% criterion. Of course, this value is arbitrary in many regards, being only a recommendation, and examiners may have a rationale for using other cutoff points to designate unusualness of a difference score. Table 7.4 presents the cumulative frequency distributions for comparing each of the TOMAL-2 supplementary indexes to the CMI in order to determine whether any of these indexes show an unusual amount of variation from the examinee's overall level of memory performance. We recommend applying the same 10% rule to assessing the relative rarity of any observed differences between a supplementary index and the CMI.

INDEX VERSUS SUBTEST LEVELS OF ANALYSIS

Similarly, each of the TOMAL-2 indexes should be used for interpretation, provided that the subtests contributing to an index score are reasonably similar. However, once again, if the subtests contributing to an index score differ significantly from their overall mean, then the index taken alone may be a misleading summary statistic. Table 7.5 provides values necessary to evaluate whether any of the subtests comprising the VMI and the NMI differ at a statistically significant level from the mean subtest scaled score on each of these indexes. Due to the relatively high reliability of the TOMAL-2 subtests, differences between the individual subtest score and the mean subtest scaled score of only two to three points will be significant in most instances, although it is best to use the tabled values rather than a single, quick rule of thumb.

Each of the core composites, VMI and NMI, are composed of four subtests, and it is not unusual for one of the four to be disparate from the

Table 7.4 Cumulative Percentages of Difference Scores for CMI and Supplementary Indexes

Amount of Discrepancy	CMI – ACI	CMI – SRI	CMI – FRI	CMI – ARI	CMI – LI
36	1.0				
35	1.2	0.3			
34	1.5	0.6			
33	2.2	1.0			
32	2.9	1.3			
31	3.1	1.4	0.3	0.1	
30	3.5	1.6	0.3	0.2	
29	4.3	1.9	0.4	0.3	0.1
28	5.3	2.7	0.5	0.4	0.3
27	6.1	3.4	0.6	0.8	0.6
26	7.0	4.1	0.6	1.4	0.7
25	7.8	5.2	0.8	1.6	0.8
24	9.6	5.9	0.8	2.0	0.8
23	10.8	7.8	1.0	2.3	2.0

(continued)

Table 7.4 Continued

Amount of Discrepancy	CMI – ACI	CMI – SRI	CMI – FRI	CMI – ARI	CMI – LI
22	12.1	9.2	1.4	3.2	2.3
21	13.9	10.8	1.9	4.1	2.7
20	15.6	12.9	2.6	5.1	3.5
19	17.3	15.2	3.7	5.9	4.4
18	20.9	17.3	4.8	7.5	5.0
17	23.5	19.7	5.7	9.3	6.3
16	26.6	22.0	7.5	10.8	8.8
15	29.4	26.3	10.1	12.6	10.9
14	33.2	29.7	11.9	15.9	13.1
13	36.7	33.5	14.9	19.6	16.6
12	40.3	38.4	18.4	23.8	20.2
11	43.3	42.5	23.6	27.8	23.8

10	47.8	47.4	27.3	31.9	29.5
9	51.3	52.3	33.7	37.0	33.0
8	56.6	57.3	39.6	43.9	39.1
7	61.7	61.7	45.4	50.3	45.8
6	67.0	66.7	51.6	57.7	52.9
5	72.3	72.5	60.8	66.6	60.0
4	78.0	79.2	67.9	73.0	69.2
3	83.4	86.4	78.5	81.2	78.0
2	89.6	91.5	86.7	89.1	86.8
1	96.8	97.3	95.4	96.2	96.2
0	100.0	100.0	100.0	100.0	100.0

Note: ACI = Attention/Concentration Index; SRI = Sequential Recall Index; FRI = Free Recall Index; ARI = Associative Recall Index; LI = Learning Index.

Table 7.5 Differences Required for Significance when Each TOMAL-2 Subtest Is Compared to the Mean Score for Any Child

Subtest	4 Verbal Memory Subtests		4 Nonverbal Memory Subtests		8 Composite Memory Subtests	
	.05	.01	.05	.01	.05	.01
Memory for Stories	2	3	—	—	3	3
Word Selective Reminding	2	3	—	—	3	3
Object Recall	2	3	—	—	3	3
Paired Recall	2	3	—	—	3	3
Facial Memory	—	—	3	4	4	5
Abstract Visual memory	—	—	2	2	2	2
Visual Sequential Memory	—	—	2	3	3	
Memory for Location	—	—	2	3	2	3

Note: Values calculated after Davis (1959) and corrected for the number of comparisons using the Bonferroni inequality.

overall mean. When none of the subtest scores differs from the overall mean subtest score on the composite index, the index tells pretty much the whole story of performance on that scale. The examiner can be confident in noting a high level of consistency in performance on all tasks making up the index under discussion. When one of the subtests deviates from the mean of all subtests on an index, the index composite score should remain the primary focal point of interpretation, but the examiner should explain and interpret the deviaht subtest scaled score. In so doing, the examiner should remain cautious and conservative about the interpretation of such a single deviant score. If two (which would be half) or more of the scores deviate at a statistically significant level (see Table 7.5) from the overall mean subtest scaled score on the index to which they are assigned, then the examiner should be most cautious in interpreting the index score and give more weight to the pattern of subtest scores seen within the index.

With these general guidelines in mind, we will turn to the topic of the meaning of performance on various aspects of the TOMAL-2, beginning with a review of the index scores, which is provided in Rapid Reference 7.1.

≡ Rapid Reference 7.1

TOMAL-2 Subtests Sorted by Core and Supplementary Index

Composite Memory Index

Verbal Memory Index	*Nonverbal Memory Index*
Memory for Stories	Facial memory
Word Selective Reminding	Abstract Visual Memory
Object Recall	Visual Sequential Memory
Paired Recall	Memory for Location

Verbal Delayed Recall Index

Memory for Stories—Delayed   Word Selective Reminding—Delayed

Attention/Concentration Index

Digits Forward	Letters Backward
Letters Forward	Manual Imitation
Digits Backward	

Sequential Recall Index

Visual Sequential Memory	Letters Forward
Digits Forward	Manual Imitation

Free Recall Index

Facial Memory	Memory for Location
Abstract Visual Memory	

Associative Recall Index

Memory for Stories   Paired Recall

Learning Index

Word Selective Reminding	Paired Recall
Object Recall	Visual Selective Reminding

INDEX SCORE INTERPRETATION

Following the guidelines discussed in the preceding sections of this chapter, featuring the CMI makes sense when the VMI and NMI are generally in agreement or any observed difference is not of an unusual nature. Therefore, a low CMI (with similarly low VMI and NMI) would suggest that an examinee has general impairment in laying down new memories, regardless of content or sensory modality. This overall difficulty with immediate memory (and long-term) processes would be expected for an examinee with a severe congenital condition, such as overall developmental delay or other significant neurodevelopmental disorder, or it could result from a major generalized acute insult such as a sustained anoxic episode associated with drowning, massive generalized head injury, or a variety of central nervous system diseases.

Verbal Memory Index (VMI)

As the title implies, the VMI represents a measure of verbal memory. Because verbal memory tends to be a function mediated more by dominant, typically left-hemispheric functions, selective reduction in the VMI in contrast to normal Nonverbal Memory Index values has implications for left or dominant cerebral dysfunction. Individuals with prominent verbal or language-related learning disabilities perform poorly on VMI subtests—especially on those for which sequencing of recall is important—and therefore have diminished or deficient VMIs. Verbal memory is particularly important in formal learning environments, especially for school-aged children, and it is a strong correlate of academic achievement in school-aged children. However, it also has significant implications for predicting performance in vocational training programs for adults when, as is often the case, such programs rely heavily on written manuals, lecture, or related verbal strategies. Severe problems with verbal memory will interfere with most aspects of life, including such seemingly simple activities as following the plot in a story or carrying on all but the simplest of conversations.

Nonverbal Memory Index (NMI)

The NMI taps nonverbal aspects of memory. Research indications are that, unlike verbal memory, nonverbal memory processes are mediated more by the right (or nondominant) hemisphere. Accordingly, a selective deficit in NMI may have implications for right-hemisphere dysfunction. Learning-disabled individuals with primary deficits in perceptual-motor, spatial, and related nonverbal functions will likely have greater NMI than VMI deficits. The category of individuals that have become known as experiencing nonverbal learning disabilities (noting the existence of this as a discrete diagnosis remains controversial) will often experience difficulties on the NMI more so than on the VMI. Poor NMI performance will have implications for vocational functioning as well in jobs for which intact spatial skills and visualization are important.

Verbal Delayed Recall Index (VDRI)

The VDRI assesses the crucial aspect of delayed recall. In numerous research studies, the delayed recall system is the area most significantly affected by brain injury. There are no particular focal points to discuss from an anatomical standpoint, but where delayed recall is impaired, the VMI would apply. Impairments in delayed recall relative to immediate recall are also more likely to denote the presence of organic phenomena as opposed to functional and chronic developmental problems. Delayed recall is often more impaired than immediate and short-term memory in cases of TBI and especially in the various dementias. Delayed recall is more likely to fall below the CMI when organically based memory problems are evident, while the two indexes are more likely to be comparable or VDRI even higher than the CMI when a functional memory impairment is present.

As noted previously, one key to TOMAL-2 interpretation rests on the comparison of various scores, assuming that, in general, cognitive functions are somewhat uniformly distributed within a certain range. Just as we recommended comparing the VMI and NMI scores as the basis for some interpretations, the VDRI should likewise be compared to the other core indexes. Values for these comparisons are in Tables 7.2 through 7.4. In TBI cases delayed recall is often the most sensitive index to impaired memory function. As such, if an examinee performs in the average range on the Verbal, Nonverbal, and Composite Indexes, but the Verbal Delayed Recall Index is *more than 13 points* below the other indexes, this would be significant at the $p < .05$ level. This would be an indication of disturbed retention of information in this examinee, the seriousness of which will depend in part on the magnitude or frequency of occurrence of the given discrepancy as seen in the cumulative frequency distribution tables mentioned previously.

It is difficult also for individuals to know how much recall is appropriate on delayed recall tasks when they are attempting to mislead an examiner. When a very low CMI is apparent and the VDRI is at a higher level and the examinee has reason to benefit from the diagnosis of significant memory deficiencies, malingering or less than optimal effort or cooperation with the evaluation might be suspected as well. This will require confirmation from collateral sources, however, and a determination of malingering or lack of effort is seldom justified on the basis of a single indicator.

Supplementary Indexes on the TOMAL-2

The TOMAL-2 provides a variety of supplemental indexes that were derived purely based on expert analysis of the content of the subtests. Additionally, unlike the core indexes of Verbal and Nonverbal Memory, the supplementary indexes have overlap among the subtests assigned to some of the indexes. On VMI and NMI, the four core subtests belonging to each index belong only to that index, and they are not shared across VMI and NMI. The supplementary indexes do share subtests, the greatest overlap occurring between the Attention/Concentration Index and the Sequential Recall Index. These supplementary indexes are offered to assist in understanding overall patterns of memory skills that may surface in a detailed subtest analysis but that are more clearly evident when combined into indexes, for reasons explained throughout this chapter. Essentially, the supplementary indexes on the TOMAL-2 provide for logical, content groupings of the 14 subtests that assist the examiner in locating alternative interpretations of performance that are helpful, especially when the VMI and NMI may differ or when several subtests show significant deviations from the core indexes to which they contribute.

The major exception to this caveat regarding subtest level interpretation is when one desires to compare forward and backward recall, which can have localizing advantages in cases of TBI and also assist in revealing strategies for recall. The TOMAL-2 has separate digits forward and backward scale scores as well as separate letters forward and backward recall, so that examiners may compare performance on several forward and backward recall tasks using common stimuli. These subtests are highly reliable due to the method of scoring provided for these tasks on the TOMAL-2 and differences of three or more scaled score points between Digits Forward and Digits Backward or between Letters Forward and Letters Backward represent a significant difference in performance that should be considered for interpretation.

Subtest Level Interpretations

It is particularly important when interpreting performance at the level of the individual subtest to pay careful attention to the behavioral observations and nuances of performance by examinees, noted in Chapter 6. Often such observations will confirm standard interpretations of subtest-scaled scores, but more importantly they may disconfirm what might otherwise be the most common interpretation of a score. For example, a low-scoring examinee who attempts to encode the squares on Memory for Location via numbering the squares mentally and recalling the locations of the dots using their self-styled numerical grid may not, in fact, have a deficit in spatial memory. The culprit may be poor planning and execution of strategies for remembering. Observations made by the examiner, performance on other subtests that may assess a common or overlapping skill, and follow-up questioning of the examinee ("How did you go about trying to remember . . . ?") after all tests have been administered will be more important for the finer distinctions the examiner attempts to make in the interpretation of TOMAL-2 performance. The subtest level is the finest level of distinction that should be attempted as well. Attempts to interpret performance on the basis of any individual item on a subtest are not recommended, nor are they supported in the literature. Table 7.6 provides qualitative descriptors of performance levels on the subtest scaled scores for all TOMAL-2 subtests, all of which are scaled to a mean of 10 and a standard deviation of 3.

Table 7.6 Qualitative Descriptors for TOMAL-2 Subtest Scaled Scores

Scaled Score Intervals	Description	Percentage Included in Each Interval
17–20	Very Superior	2.34
15–16	Superior	6.87
13–14	Above Average	16.12
8–12	Average	49.51
6–7	Below Average	16.12
4–5	Impaired	6.87
1–3	Significantly Impaired	2.34

Memory for Stories Subtest

This subtest assesses the examinee's auditory processing (often sequential) and consolidation of verbal information presented in paragraph form. The structure of this test places heavy demands on attention, the ability to process sequentially relevant verbal information, and consolidation of that information for meaningful retrieval. Extensive research using this format indicates that the neural structures required to perform this task tend to be more left- or dominant-hemisphere mediated and temporal lobe in origin (Bigler, 1988). Accordingly, a clinically significant deficit in the Memory for Stories (MFS) subtest may have implications for impaired left-hemisphere functioning. Typically, when left-hemisphere dysfunction is present, other verbal memory tests will be impaired as well. Of the individual subtests on the TOMAL-2, MFS has the highest correlation with school learning, as one might expect, given the heavily verbal nature of schooling and the heavy use of didactic instruction.

Word Selective Reminding Subtest

This task requires retrieval of words from short- and long-term storage. Because the child hears only the words that she or he has not recalled from the previous trial, the words recalled that were not from the prompt are being retrieved from longer storage processes. This test specifically addresses this type of retrieval process, which has been demonstrated to be affected by neurological dysfunction (Buschke & Fuld, 1974; Fletcher, 1985). As with the Memory for Stories subtest, performance on verbal selective reminding tasks tends to be more affected by left-hemisphere dysfunction, particularly the temporal lobe. However, an advantage that the Word Selective Reminding subtest has in comparison to the Memory for Stories subtest is that it is given over trials, and a learning curve can be established. There are two aspects of interpreting a learning curve. First, the slope of the line is critical. In normal learning of the words on the Word Selective Reminding subtest, there is a positive slope that is quite steep. (Figure 7.1 includes sample learning curves as output by the TOMAL-2 software scoring system.) A slope that deviates from this may be considered abnormal. Second, the actual performance level on each trial can be compared with age-matched normal controls. For example, a child may have what appears to be a normal slope, but the individual trial performance on one, several, or all trials is in the impaired range. Learning curves are easily plotted and reviewed on the Profile Summary Form or via the scoring software for TOMAL-2. Selective reminding tasks also allow one to examine forgetting and depth of processing. Words recalled on a first trial are not reminded, and when they are forgotten or not recalled on a later trial, problems may be evident with transferring information from short-term into long-term store. In such cases, the VDRI will be important to examine carefully.

Occasionally, examinees will give words that are not on the list at all. Such words are termed *intrusions*. These can be recorded directly on the record form, if desired. While no normative interpretation is offered, due to the infrequency of intrusions, certain words (e.g., *fork*) may be revealing as an indicator of use of a particular memory strategy. Also, in certain cases of differential diagnosis (e.g., Alzheimer's Disease versus Korsakoff's Disease), multiple intrusions are of great clinical interest.

Object Recall Subtest

Although all TOMAL-2 subtests require multiple processing/retrieving modalities, the Object Recall subtest places specific demands on visual recognition with verbal recall. This crossing of visual processing with linguistic matching involves numerous association pathways of both hemispheres. However, because the final response is verbal and the task itself is predominantly linguistic, functions such as Object Recall are thought principally to be left-hemisphere mediated. Because this task crosses several modalities, Object Recall can be disrupted by neural impairment at a variety of levels. For this subtest, clinical inter-

TOMAL-2
Cecil R. Reynolds and Judith Voress
Copyright 2008 by PRO-ED, Inc.

	Year	Month	Day
Examinee Paul Miller **Date of Evaluation**	2008	2	24
Examiner Charles Szasz **Birth Date**	1999	10	21
Age	**8** years	**4** months	

Core Subtests

Raw Score

Memory for Stories: 10

Facial Memory: 19

Word Selective Reminding:
Profile Trial Scores
2 + 7 + 8 + 8 + 8 + 8 = 41

Abstract Visual Memory: 5

Object Recall:
Profile Trial Scores
3 + 5 + 6 + 6 + 4 = 24

Visual Sequential Memory: 3

Paired Recall:
Profile Trial Scores
4 + 4 + 6 + 6 = 20

Memory for Location: 4

Supplemental Subtests

Raw Score

Digits Forward: 16

Visual Selective Reminding:
Profile Trial Scores
2 + 4 + 5 + 6 + 6 = 23

Letters Forward: 21

Manual Imitation: 17

Digits Backward: 9

Letters Backward: 7

Memory for Stories Delayed: 5

Word Selective Reminding Delayed: 5

Page 1

Figure 7.1 Example of a TOMAL-2 Scoring Software Printout

TOMAL-2
Cecil R. Reynolds and Judith Voress
Copyright 2008 by PRO-ED, Inc.

Examinee: Paul Miller   **Examiner:** Charles Szasz

Core Subtests / Verbal Subtests	Raw Score	Scaled Score	Percentile Rank	Description	Age Equivalent	Subtest Significance
Memory for Stories	10	6	9	Below Average	below 5-0	ns
Word Selective Reminding:	41	10	50	Average	8-9	.05/.01
Object Recall:	24	3	1	Very Deficient	below 5-0	.05/.01
Paired Recall:	20	12	75	Average	9-3	.05/.01
Nonverbal Subtests						
Facial Memory:	19	7	16	Below Average	5-6	ns
Abstract Visual Memory:	5	8	25	Average	6-3	ns
Visual Sequential Memory:	3	1	below 1	Very Deficient	below 5-0	.05/.01
Memory for Location:	4	5	5	Deficient	below 5-0	.05
Supplemental Subtests / *Verbal Subtests*						
Digits Forward:	16	5	5	Deficient	below 5-0	
Letters Forward:	21	8	25	Average	6-6	
Digits Backward:	9	8	25	Average	6-6	
Letters Backward:	7	7	16	Below Average	5-6	
Nonverbal Subtests						
Manual Imitation:	17	8	25	Average	6-3	
Visual Selective Reminding:	23	9	37	Average	6-9	
Verbal Delayed Recall Subtests						
Memory for Stories:	5	5	5	Deficient	below 5-0	
Word Selective Reminding:	5	10	50	Average	8-3	

Page 2

Figure 7.1 Continued

pretation will rely heavily on the comparison with other subtests. For example, the two subtests discussed previously—Memory for Stories and Word Selective Reminding—represent more *pure* auditory verbal processing and retention tasks and tend to be affected more by left-hemisphere damage, particularly to the temporal lobes. Accordingly, if

TOMAL-2 Summary

Cecil R. Reynolds and Judith Voress
Copyright 2008 by PRO-ED, Inc.

Examinee: Paul Miller   **Examiner:** Charles Szasz

Index Scores	SS Total	Index Score	85% CI	Percentile Rank	Description	Cumulative Intersubtest Scatter
Verbal Memory Index (VMI)	31	85	80-90	16	Below Average	3.7%
Nonverbal Memory Index (NMI)	21	66	60-72	1	Very Deficient	14.4%
Composite Memory Index (CMI)	52	72	67-77	3	Deficient	4.3%

Supplemental Index Scores

Verbal Delay Recall Index (VDRI)	15	83	77-89	13	Below Average	
Attention/Concentration Index (ACI)	36	81	78-84	10	Below Average	
Sequential Recall Index (SRI)	22	69	65-72	2	Very Deficient	
Free Recall Index (FRI)	20	77	70-84	6	Deficient	
Associative Recall Index (ARI)	18	94	88-100	35	Average	
Learning Index (LI)	34	89	83-95	23	Below Average	

Core Comparisons

	Difference	Significance Level	Discrepancy Frequency
VMI vs. NMI	19	.01	19.6%
VMI vs. VDRI	2	ns	90.2%
NMI vs. VDRI	17	.01	28.2%
CMI vs. VDRI	11	.05	35.3%

Supplementary Comparisons

	Difference	Significance Level	Discrepancy Frequency
CMI vs. ACI	9	.01	51.3%
CMI vs. SRI	3	ns	86.4%
CMI vs. FRI	5	ns	60.8%
CMI vs. ARI	22	.01	3.2%
CMI vs. LI	17	.01	6.3%

Page 3

Figure 7.1 Continued

an examinee has a generalized verbal memory deficit, it would be expected that Memory for Stories, Word Selective Reminding, and Object Recall would all be impaired. In contrast, if a child has a deficiency in visual memory, Object Recall may be affected, with Memory for Stories and Word Selective Reminding being unaffected. It may be that this

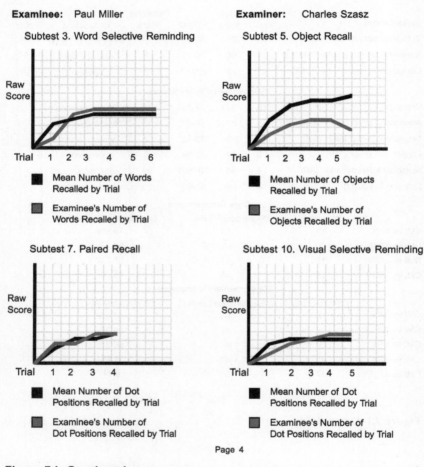

TOMAL-2 Learning Curve Analysis
Cecil R. Reynolds and Judith Voress
Copyright 2008 by PRO-ED, Inc.

Examinee: Paul Miller   **Examiner:** Charles Szasz

Subtest 3. Word Selective Reminding

- Mean Number of Words Recalled by Trial
- Examinee's Number of Words Recalled by Trial

Subtest 5. Object Recall

- Mean Number of Objects Recalled by Trial
- Examinee's Number of Objects Recalled by Trial

Subtest 7. Paired Recall

- Mean Number of Dot Positions Recalled by Trial
- Examinee's Number of Dot Positions Recalled by Trial

Subtest 10. Visual Selective Reminding

- Mean Number of Dot Positions Recalled by Trial
- Examinee's Number of Dot Positions Recalled by Trial

Page 4

Figure 7.1 Continued

subtest will permit a unique analysis between verbal and nonverbal memory disorders in some examinees because of its cross-modality basis. Such tasks are often especially impaired in children with learning disabilities, as the pairing of stimuli tends to interfere with rather than facilitate learning (common mythology being that pairing modalities during learning facilitates recall for such individuals—in fact, it divides attention and most often *impairs* recall when the stimuli are presented simultaneously as opposed to sequentially).

Paired Recall Subtest

The Paired Recall subtest is a verbal associative learning task wherein the examinee has to learn to pair words with one another. This type of learning task assesses well the degree of connection between the hippocampal regions and the neocortex, where learning and association are stored. The version on the TOMAL-2 uses easy pairs (word pairs with a clear, logical association) and hard pairs (words with no logical association). Most of the variance in performance is attributable to the hard pairs. Examinees who do poorly on the easy pairs (recalling less than half) either have such severe memory impairments that even short conversations become nearly impossible, or they are simply not putting forth sufficient effort. Paired Recall contributes to the VMI and the LI.

Digits / Letters Forward / Backward Subtests

Digit and letter recall tasks have cognitive demands that are increased by having the examinee repeat the numbers or letters in reverse direction. Backward recall also requires a manipulation that is not present in forward recall. Although digit/letter span abilities are affected by a wide variety of neurological deficits, numerous studies failed to demonstrate one particular brain region more critical than another in controlling this function, provided that the individual is not aphasic, except for the forward/backward distinction (see the following). These tasks also place heavy demands on attention/concentration skills and freedom from distractibility. One clinical caveat that is often used is that if these digit/letter tasks are intact, then the examinee is assumed to have "normal" attention/concentration. Therefore, if other TOMAL-2 subtests are distinctly below Digit/Letter subtests span performance, then it can be assumed that the deficits are attributable to impaired memory performance and not just a deficit in attentional processes. However, these tasks are also quite brief and do not give information on sustained levels of concentration (e.g., see Riccio et al., 2001, for discussion).

Forward recall and backward recall have different associations with regard to anatomical locale. Individuals with impairments in forward recall are more likely to have left-hemisphere deficits while problems with backward recall are more likely to insinuate right-hemisphere deficiencies (e.g., see Ramsay & Reynolds, 1995, and Reynolds, 1997, for a detailed explanation of the interpretation of forward versus backward recall performance). Forward and backward recall should thus be interpreted separately, and these tasks continue to be divided on the TOMAL-2 as they were on the TOMAL. This distinction seems related to the requirement of manipulation on backward recall and the process of choice for such a manipulation by most examinees. Visualization is a common strategy, for example, that is employed for backward recall as opposed to rehearsal for forward recall. Backward recall is also considerably more demanding mentally and has about twice the correlation with general ability levels as does forward recall (e.g., see Jensen, 1980). Concentration problems and mental fatigue may be more evident on backward recall as well. These scores are nevertheless combined along with Manual Imitation in the Attention/Concentration Index on the TOMAL-2 to aid in viewing attentional disturbances—for purposes of evaluating different aspects of memory skill, or if the examiner is interested in localization effects, forward recall and backward recall should be viewed separately.

Facial Memory Subtest

Neuropsychological studies demonstrate the role of occipital-temporal-parietal regions, particularly of the right hemisphere, in visual discrimination and retention of faces (Benton, Hamsher, Varnay, & Spreen, 1983; Kolb & Whishaw, 2003; Lezak, 1983). The TOMAL-2 Facial Memory subtest examines the individual's ability to process and retain facial memory. Accordingly, this task taps many important aspects of complex visual memory. Isolated deficits on this task, in comparison to normal visual-spatial processing, would implicate right temporal lobe dysfunction. Research also demonstrates that faces are recognized and recalled on the basis of the face as a whole, and not on the basis of an analysis of its component parts. For this reason and to enhance the right-hemisphere orientation of this task (by further defeating the use of verbal cueing as an aid to recall of the faces) on the TOMAL-2, the faces used for the recall portion sometimes have a different facial expression or a slightly different orientation.

Abstract Visual Memory Subtest

This subtest permits the assessment of the child's ability to process and retain obtuse geometric patterns as they increase in complexity. Naturally, this task taps visual processing, attention to detail, and the ability to match a retained abstract figure with its counterpart in an array of similar figures. As with the Visual Selective Reminding subtest, this task requires little, if any, verbal mediation. As such it is a measure of visual-spatial memory, with such functions based more in right-hemisphere processing. Attempts at verbal mediation, given the abstract nature of the figures and the short exposure time, appear to impair the performance of most examinees.

> **CAUTION**
>
> Only use standardized or scaled scores for making comparisons of index scores or between specific subtests and overall levels of performance. Raw scores should never be used in such contrasts.

Visual Sequential Memory Subtest

As discussed previously, retention tasks that place demands on sequential processing typically require the highest order of cognitive processing and integration. As a counterpart to the verbal subtests that require sequential processing (e.g., Letters Forward), the Visual Sequential Memory subtest was developed to assess sequential visual processing and retention. The figures are abstract forms, and the task places little, if any, demand on linguistic skills. Accordingly, just like the other nonverbal memory subtests of the TOMAL-2, Visual Sequential Memory assesses a nonlanguage visual memory construct. Because of its similarity to the Abstract Visual Memory subtest, a comparison between the two can assist in evaluating whether a particular visual memory problem is more general in nature (in which case both subtests would be impaired) or more specific to sequential processing (in which case only the Visual Sequential Memory subtest would be impaired). As indicated previously, this test can be directly compared to verbal sequential memory tasks as well. Research on such sequential visual processing tasks has not demonstrated a specific anatomic basis for disorders in nonverbal sequential processing, but a deficit in such tasks may be a more sensitive indicator of neurological dysfunction than some nonsequential processing tasks.

Visual Selective Reminding Subtest

This test is the visual analog of the verbal Word Selective Reminding subtest (Fletcher, 1985). Because language is not a major factor in processing and retaining these patterns, this task is thought of as a rather *pure* measure of visual memory. If the Visual Selective Reminding is significantly below the Word Selective Reminding, then implications for possible right-hemisphere dysfunction would be expected. Likewise, because these two tasks are so closely matched, a quick comparison between visual and verbal memory can be made by examining scaled score comparisons between the two.

Memory for Location Subtest

As part of the TOMAL-2, Memory for Location was deemed essential to assess spatial memory, in addition to the traditional visual memory tasks. Because the stimulus objects in this test are merely large black dots in a fixed pattern, the key characteristic to their pattern recall is the spatial placement. Research on spatial memory typically implicates a greater role of the right hemisphere, particularly the temporal-parietal regions (Kolb & Whishaw, 2003) in control of such aspects of spatial memory.

Manual Imitation Subtest

Manual Imitation is another sequential processing task with a simple motor component. Purposely, motor skill was avoided in the TOMAL-2 because of the significant confound between motor development and visual-motor functioning, as assessed by a variety of so-called "visual" recall tasks (e.g., *Benton Visual Retention Test;* Benton, 1974). To avoid such confounds the TOMAL-2 does not include any visual-copying tasks. However, the motor-output component to memory is an important one. Hence, Manual Imitation appears to be an excellent compromise in which a nonverbal task with a simple motor response can be examined. As indicated by previous discussions of the other subtests, most do not place significant demands on frontal-lobe integrity. Thus, the Manual Imitation subtest permits an examination of sequential processing and visual imitation with a motor response.

Delayed Recall Subtests

The TOMAL-2 has two delayed recall subtests that are both verbal, Memory for Stories—Delayed and Word Selective Reminding—Delayed, and that form the VDRI. When these two scores differ by more than three scaled score points, it may be useful to interpret the two subtests independently of the VDRI. While the two scores will most often correspond, when they do differ the primary distinction has to do with the contextual clues and associations available in Memory for Stories versus

> # DON'T FORGET
>
> Coordination of test results across observations, history, and scores from other types of tests produces the best, most cohesive, and productive report of the examination of the individual.

Word Selective Reminding. Differences in performance then may reflect the examinee's abilities in forcing associations or inabilities to relate isolated words and to develop strategies for unstructured recall, such as in WSR, as opposed to recall of meaningful material that is logically associated and structured for the examinee, as in MFS. If one observes carefully the pattern of recall of words and whether associated clusters are recalled (see Chapter 6) on WSR-Delayed as well as the level of coherence of the stories on MFS-Delayed, such strategies and the underlying reasons for the differences should become apparent.

Cautions on Subtest Score Interpretation

As noted earlier, subtest interpretation is fraught with considerable risk of clinical error given the lower reliability of those scores. The literature and personal experience clearly show that psychologists are very prone to use subtest comparisons in order to form diagnostic impressions. While interpreting disparate subtest results should be cautiously undertaken, their interpretation can have value, especially if such findings are supported by other test results and/or history. Therefore, subtest diagnostic guidelines and interpretive suggestions are presented here, but as mentioned several times already, they must be used cautiously and only within the context of other corroborative quantitative findings and qualitative (i.e., ecologically meaningful) support.

Learning Curves

Four of the TOMAL-2 subtests involve the repeated presentation of a common set of stimuli: Word Selective Reminding, Object Recall,

Paired Recall, and Visual Selective Reminding. Since a common set of stimuli are to be learned across multiple trials, one can examine the learning or acquisition curve for the information. In general, as material is repeated, an examinee will retain more information. The TOMAL-2 Profile Summary Form provides graphs for these four subtests that allow the examiner to plot the raw scores on each trial of each of these four subtests and to also plot on the same graph the mean (rounded to the nearest whole number) raw score of individuals of the same age from the standardization sample. The TOMAL-2 scoring software also plots these curves automatically (see Fig. 7.1). By reviewing the commonality of the curve on each subtest for the examinee with that of an age-matched cohort, a visual display of the examinee's learning rate relative to that of age mates is obtained. This view offers a greater understanding of the acquisition of material under conditions of repeated presentation than does a simple summary score, and it reveals patterns associated with learning. For example, an examinee who has substantial attention problems is less likely to improve across trials than an examinee with even less well-developed memory skills, but who can and does pay attention well on each trial. An examinee who has special problems with consolidation in the memory process may show an absence of improvement relative to age mates or even a decline across trials that may not be evident from a simple summary score. Examiners are thus encouraged to review the examinee's learning curve against the age-standardized learning curve in most every instance. An illustration of an additional application of learning curves is given in the brief case discussion at the end of this chapter.

Ceiling and Floor Effects in Interpretation

Whenever test examiners prepare to interpret a test result using norms, they should be aware of how well those norms cover the full range of ability. It is common for cognitive tests to have less rigorous norms "coverage" at the ability and age extremes. In part, this is related to lower reliability often found at ability extremes (very few persons are included that represent those extremes) and lower reliability at age extremes (i.e., very young children and very old adults tend to demonstrate more variability than other age groups). The easiest way for an examiner to check on adequacy of norm coverage is to simply look at the norms tables provided, and then look for dashes or blanks. If one does that using the TOMAL-2 Manual, one will notice, for young 5-year-olds, several blanks rather than numbers associated with some subtest scaled score listings, usually those at or below scaled scores of four. Scores down to a subtest-scaled score of four represent two full standard deviations below the mean subtest scaled score and are not problematic, except for those who are severely impaired. For example, one can spot that Abstract Visual Memory and the two delayed verbal recall subtests have but minimal measurement precision when the youngest age groups do poorly on this subtest. That is, a 5-year-old cannot score below a scaled score of five or six on these subtests. Therefore, an examiner can conclude that a child with a raw score of zero or one who is performing at least two standard deviations below average (a scaled score of four), but is unable to determine whether the child may be scoring three, four, or more standard deviations below the mean. Clinically, such precision in defining deficits may not have much importance (that is, does it matter if it represents a severe or very severe deficit?). However, if this is the case over several subtests, then the examiner needs to recognize that, for a given age, poor performance may yield a score that may be an overestimate of a child's true ability because of a weak psychometric floor (i.e., less precision). The same can happen in

DON'T FORGET

Floor effects occurring when testing individuals at young ages may cause scaled scores and indexes to overestimate some types of memory skills.

detecting strengths if so-called ceiling scores do not have adequate range on one or more subtests.

On the TOMAL-2, inspection of the norms suggests that there are some floor limitations in interpreting individual subtest scaled scores for 5-year-olds who earn raw scores of zero or 1 on Abstract Visual Memory or the two delayed recall subtests. The use of composite scores typically helps examiners overcome this problem, and this is evident on the TOMAL-2 as well, with the exception of the Verbal Delayed Recall Index at age 5 years, where the entire index has a floor effect when examinees in this age group (5 years) earn raw scores of zero. For the most part, this floor effect is problematic for 5 to 7 years of age but only for AVM and the Verbal Delayed Recall Index and only when these young children earn raw scores of zero. In this instance, and at these age levels, examiners should interpret these low scores as reflecting performance that is impaired but note that "due to floor effects present on [AVM and/or the VDRI subtests], Johnny's memory skills may be even more impaired than represented by even these low levels of performance." The use of index scores is notably helpful in this regard, however, as a 5-year-old who earns all raw scores of zero or 1 on the eight TOMAL-2 core subtests (a scaled score total of 24), earns a Composite Memory Index of only 45, a score nearly four standard deviations below the mean. But that child may, in fact, be performing even below this very low level of estimated memory skill in specific areas represented by AVM and on delayed recall. The instrument, like many others, is simply unable to measure very specific extreme deficits at this age. For

> **CAUTION**
>
> At ages 5 to 7 years, the Verbal Delayed Recall Index has a floor effect and raw scores of zero on one or both of the subtests making up this index may cause the level of skill typically reflected in the obtained index score to be an overestimate of the child's true delayed recall skills.

DON'T FORGET

Ceiling effects when testing individuals in early adulthood when memory skills are strongest may result in the underestimation of memory skills in some particularly adept adults.

most clinicians, documenting the significant deficit(s) present and knowing that overall memory skill is impaired at such an extreme remains valuable, even if pin-pointing the degree of extreme deficits in highly specific areas is not possible.

However, *ceiling* effects do not seem to exist when using the TOMAL-2, with the exception of AVM and the WSRD (which have but limited ceiling effects, with maximum scaled scores of 13 at some age levels); and the use of the composite scores to which these subtests contribute readily rectifies any issue of ceiling effects. The top performance range for memory (which tends to be in the early to mid-twenties) has adequate raw score range at the upper levels of all subtests. Therefore, it is possible for scaled scores of 13 to 19 to be earned, and consequently, relative levels of *memory giftedness* can legitimately be determined easily with reasonable psychometric precision for all of the many TOMAL-2 indexes and nearly all of the TOMAL-2 subtests.

Item Bias: Gender and Minority Groups

The TOMAL-2 Manual presents considerable data that should provide confidence to examiners that there is evidence for no item bias between genders as well as across minority groups. Detailed statistical analyses of potential item bias were conducted for the TOMAL and the TOMAL-2, and items showing bias with regard to gender or ethnicity were eliminated during the test-development process. The TOMAL-2 Manual also reports various item-bias statistics for the final items selected for the various subtests, principally in the form of correlations between the difference in item difficulties for pairs of adjacent items across gender and ethnicity, with virtually all of these values exceeding .90 (with a single value out of 42 such comparisons reaching as low as .89). Correlations between age and raw scores for each of the TOMAL-2 subtests were also observed to be constant across gender and ethnicity, demonstrating a common pattern of change in TOMAL-2 raw scores across group as a function of age. Prior research with the TOMAL (e.g., see Lowe, Mayfield, & Reynolds, 2003; Reynolds & Bigler, 1997) indicated a common factor solution of the intercorrelation matrix of the subtests was appropriate across gender and ethnicity. TOMAL-2 items as well as total subtest scores show an absence of bias in research conducted thus far.

CLINICAL SYNDROMES AND THE INTERPRETATION OF THE TOMAL-2

There are no syndrome-specific memory profiles for comprehensive batteries of memory tasks, although there are some patterns of interest that have been noted in the literature. Based on what is known about various clinical syndromes and their impact on memory function, some general guidelines can be noted. What follows is based on the TOMAL-2 authors' use of the TOMAL and the TOMAL-2 to date; clinical inference based on research using other memory assessment techniques; as well as the known neurodevelopmental underpinnings of some disorders. The TOMAL-2 is just over a year old as of this writing, and there has not yet been sufficient time for independent research to be published regarding the use of the TOMAL-2 with these exceptional populations.

Learning Disability

It is beyond the scope of this manual to address the myriad clinical aspects involved in assessing and identifying learning disabilities. For such a comprehensive discussion, the reader is referred to Fletcher-Janzen and Reynolds (2008), Kaufman and Kaufman (2001), Myers and Hammill (1990), and Swanson, Harris, and Graham (2003). Nonetheless, some general statements can be made. Many children with learning disabilities have some form of deficient memory function (Ceci, 1984; De Renzi & Lucchelli, 1990; Fletcher, 1985; Lorsbach & Gray, 1985). Although a great oversimplification, one way to divide learning disabilities is by whether they affect verbal or nonverbal abilities or a combination of the two (Rourke, Fisk, & Strang, 1986). For example, a reading disability in a child with no deficits in visual processing and fully intact visual-motor abilities is typically considered to be a verbal learning disorder. Such children often have a component of impaired verbal retention. Preliminary evidence with the TOMAL-2 suggests that children with reading disorders will have a pattern of lower verbal memory than nonverbal. This line of thinking is consistent with the postulates of Boder (Boder & Jarrico, 1982) in terms of her conceptualization of reading disorders into dyseidetic and dysphonetic groups, depending on whether the impairment was more visually or verbally mediated, respectively.

Rourke et al. (1986) discussed at length the neuropsychological factors in various learning disorders, including disabilities of nonverbal learning. In such disorders, these children display a deficit pattern quite opposite to that noted previously. These children typically display primary deficits in visual-spatial processing and recall of information. Accordingly, on the TOMAL-2 one might expect to see a deficit pattern wherein the nonverbal subtests were more selectively impaired than verbal.

Children with learning disabilities generally also tend to have greater difficulties with sequential memory than any other aspect or type of memory. This likely reflects a tendency for individuals with disturbances in the ability to process and acquire information using sequential processing approaches to be diagnosed with a learning disability.

Traumatic Brain Injury (TBI)

TBI ranks as one of the top three medical problems inducing disability in children (Goldstein & Levin, 1990). Accordingly, this is a common problem encountered not only by clinicians but also by professionals in the public schools who are required to serve children with TBI. The two most frequent, chronic problems following TBI at all ages are attentional deficits and memory deficits. The interpretation of memory problems on the TOMAL-2 in children is complicated by their potentially greater ability for neural plasticity (which creates a problem for lesion-location theories of brain injury in children) and variations in developmental progress. With these limitations in mind, there are some general rules that can be given that will apply more readily to adults assessed with the TOMAL-2 (with greater caution in their application to child and adolescent cases). Although it is a great oversimplification to dichotomize the brain into a left hemisphere that is dominant for language-mediated tasks and a right hemisphere dominant for visual-spatial function, this dichotomy does have some clinical utility. For example, damage to the left hemisphere tends to disrupt verbal memory more than visual, with the opposite pattern obtained when the right hemisphere is involved. As discussed earlier in this volume, the temporal lobes are very vulnerable to injury in TBI and, accordingly, the most frequent cognitive sequelae of TBI are deficits in memory followed by attentional problems. Thus, any child with a history of TBI should be evaluated carefully for significant deficits in memory. A Verbal Memory Index that is significantly below a Nonverbal Memory Index may have particular relevance in implicating left-hemisphere dysfunction, particularly left temporal lobe. When the Nonverbal Memory Index is significantly below a Verbal Memory Index, right hemisphere with right temporal lobe dysfunction may be indicated. Also, it is anticipated that some TOMAL-2 subtests may be very specific to certain brain regions. A distinctly deviant subtest performance on a particular TOMAL-2 subtest in a TBI child may be reflective of focal damage. Among adults, TBI produces similar symptoms and can produce memory deficits that interfere with work and aspects of daily living. The TOMAL-2 can quantify and assess the levels of such problems in more memory domains than any other scale at the time of this writing.

Attention-Deficit/Hyperactivity Disorder (ADHD)

The core symptom of ADHD is an impairment in attention/concentration (Nussbaum & Bigler, 1990). Because attention and concentration are such elemental aspects of efficient memory, any deficit in attentional mechanisms will affect memory performance. Typically, the pattern of deficit in these children and adults is on tasks that are more pure measures of attention span, such as Digits and Letters Forward/Backward. These tasks are not as engaging as the other tasks on the TOMAL-2 that have either visual stimuli or more interesting examiner–examinee interaction (e.g., Memory for Stories). Thus, in ADHD individuals one expects to see some reduction in overall memory performance, but the most significant reduction should be on the tasks that require the greatest amount of sustained attention.

Affective Disorders

Children and adults with affective disturbance may have altered memory performance. Typically, memory deficits secondary to affective disturbance are subtle and often related to deficits in attention and alteration in level of motivation. In a person being assessed with the TOMAL-2 wherein depression is suspected or there is a history of depression, some lowering of memory performance is to be expected. It should also be noted that many individuals with TBI have significant changes in emotional status, and these factors, not just the brain injury, may alter memory performance. In cases of depression as a functional impairment of memory, Verbal Delayed Recall tasks are less likely to be impaired relative to overall memory performance than in cases of organic impairments to the brain.

The Dementias and Neurological/Neurodevelopmental Disorders Other than TBI

Neurological impairment, regardless of its etiology and location, often impairs memory function (Bigler, 1988). The same lateralization implications of significantly discrepant TOMAL-2 findings discussed in the TBI section apply here. Also, neurological impairment often affects delayed recall function disproportionately. Thus, in all cases where an individual with known or suspect neurological dysfunction is being evaluated with the TOMAL-2, careful attention should be directed to examining the Verbal Delayed Recall Index with all other indexes.

Chronic neurodevelopmental disorders that express in childhood persist into adulthood (e.g., Mental Retardation, Prader-Willi Syndrome, Angelmann Syndrome) and commonly cause memory problems, but they also have highly variable expressivity. Individual evaluation of memory function in such patients often reveals strengths that can lead to improved rehabilitation planning.

The various dementing disorders (of which Alzheimer's is the best known but of which there are hundreds) can strike adults at any age (e.g., Binswanger's Disease, Huntington's Disease), although after age 40 is the most common time. Memory deficits are hallmarks of the dementias; however, the pattern of memory disturbances evident in each of the dementias is different. TOMAL-2 findings may have an important diagnostic role in some cases but consistently will reveal the pattern of deficits present. The latter can often lead the astute clinician and rehabilitation specialist to means of developing appropriate memory and other cognitive prostheses to delay the loss of independent living and reduce the burden on caretakers.

AN APPLICATION OF THE TOMAL-2 WITH A CHILD REFERRAL

Memory batteries, in general, are most useful in the context of additional data, as we have noted repeatedly throughout this book. What follows here is an example of the application of the TOMAL-2 in the assessment of an 8-year-old boy referred by his teacher due to a variety of learning problems that developed in conjunction with fine motor problems subsequent to treatment for lead exposure. Academic progress in first grade had been unremarkable. As part of a comprehensive evaluation, he was administered the TOMAL-2 along with a variety of other measures. The TOMAL-2 software provides a rapid conversion of raw to scaled scores and summaries of TOMAL-2 performance, an analysis of the spread of scores, and a look at the four learning curves that can be derived from the TOMAL-2. The TOMAL-2 printout for this case is presented in Figure 7.1.

To assess overall levels of intellectual function, Paul was administered the KABC-II and the RIAS. On these measures he earned scores within the average range. On the KABC-II he earned a Fluid Reasoning score of 96 and a Crystallized Score of 106. These were comparable to his RIAS scores, for which he obtained a Verbal Intelligence Index of 108 and a Nonverbal Intelligence Index of 99. His Koppitz-2 Developmental Bender-Gestalt Test Visual Motor Index was only 71, however, indicating significant problems with visual-motor integration skills. Achievement testing indicated low average levels of performance across the board, with standard scores ranging from 80 to 91 on the KTEA-II, except in math, for which he earned a lower score of 73. Prior to the last year, no academic problems had been evident.

A review of his TOMAL-2 scores as seen in Figure 7.1 reveals quite a few difficulties not evident on intellectual assessment. Paul has difficulties in most areas of memory, some far more pronounced than others, with the exception of his skills in associative recall. This strength indicates he may have some compensatory strategies and it is consistent with his relatively intact intellectual skills. However, his academic problems are likely due to his difficulties with short-term recall, especially in the area of nonverbal recall and aspects of sequential memory, for which he is unable to invoke his intact intellectual skills to form associations that can aid his level of recall. Once he makes associations, he is able to retain material well, as evidenced by his Verbal Delayed Recall Index score, which is comparable to his Verbal Memory Index, although both are still below average. When information is repeated, he performs relatively better as well, although the lowered learning curve on Object Recall demonstrates the type of interference that can occur due to divided attention in individuals with attention and concentration difficulties, when one pairs verbal and visual stimuli as opposed to allowing the individual to focus on a single aspect of the stimulus to be recalled. Relative to his Composite Memory Index of 72, his Associative Recall Index of 94 represents a relative strength that will be useful in developing remedial plans, especially in light of intact reasoning skills as reflected in his intelligence test scores.

Overall, Paul is seen to have substantial memory problems but he can definitely be aided by the introduction and use of strategies that help him to form associations and learn rules related to generating conceptual understanding as opposed to rote recall. A follow-up assessment with the School Motivation and Learning Strategies Inventory revealed a highly motivated student but one who did not have skills in the development and application of learning and study strategies on his own. As part of the intervention process, it was recommended that Paul be taught and that his teachers model associative learning strategies (i.e., when he is to learn something new, it should be made as explicit as possible how the new material relates to material Paul already knows and understands). Additionally, rote learning should be deemphasized in favor of developing concepts for understanding and the development of heuristics. Instead of memorizing math facts, which still occurs at Paul's grade level, for instance, rules for deriving math facts and their relationships to numerical systems can be emphasized more profitably. Given the recency of Paul's treatment for lead exposure, it is also hopeful that he will experience additional recovery of some of his memory skills. Lead at low to moderate levels of exposure, such as in this case, has no signature injury, but deficits in memory, attention, and fine-motor problems such as are associated with peripheral neuropathy are common. The pattern of results seen here are consistent with much of the literature on low to moderate levels of lead exposure and are more easily revealed through assessment of memory and learning than through assessment of intellectual function, as illustrated in Paul's case. In general, memory measures tend to be more sensitive to central nervous system dysfunction than general measures of ability or reasoning skills. Difficulties with memory and attention are the most common complaints to surface secondary to central nervous system insult at all ages. The TOMAL-2 examiner's manual (Reynolds & Voress, 2007) offers an additional and more detailed case presentation as well.

🐟 TEST YOURSELF 🐟

....

1. **With which age group should TOMAL-2 examiners show greatest caution when interpreting very low scores?**

    (a) Any person from a minority group

    (b) 5-year-olds

    (c) 10- to 12-year-olds

    (d) 20- to 25-year-olds

    (e) Low scores for all age groups should be interpreted with the same degree of caution

2. **TOMAL-2 performance for children with a learning disability diagnosis tends to show**

   (a) a lower Attention/Concentration Index than Nonverbal Memory Index.

   (b) overall, low average to borderline memory ability (i.e., CMI = 70–85).

   (c) lower scores overall than children with a diagnosis of ADHD.

   (d) weaknesses in most memory domains.

   (e) lowest levels of performance on sequential recall tasks.

3. **The TOMAL-2 subtest that is best for assessing level of effort is often _____?**

   (a) Memory for Stories

   (b) Word Selective Reminding

   (c) Visual Selective Reminding

   (d) Paired Recall

   (e) Facial Memory

4. **Generally speaking, which TOMAL-2 score would have the greatest psychometric soundness?**

   (a) CMI

   (b) Verbal Memory Index

   (c) Nonverbal Memory Index

   (d) Attention/Concentration Index

   (e) Verbal Delayed Recall Index

5. **The best approach to interpreting the TOMAL-2 is to**

   (a) begin with the individual items and work up.

   (b) begin with the subtest scores and work up to the indexes.

   (c) begin with the CMI and work down toward more detailed explanations.

   (d) start with the supplementary indexes.

   (e) review the learning curves to see if there is evidence of malingering.

(continued)

6. **When comparing indexes, be sure**
   (a) to use raw scores only.
   (b) to use standard scores only.
   (c) to use age-equivalents.
   (d) to use percentile ranks.
   (e) it is okay to use any of these score metrics.

7. **The supplementary indexes with the greatest amount of subtest overlap are**
   (a) Associative Recall and Sequential Recall.
   (b) Associative Recall and Learning.
   (c) Free Recall and Sequential Recall.
   (d) Sequential Recall and Attention/Concentration.
   (e) Free recall and Learning.

8. **Depth of processing is usually assessed via which form of memory task?**
   (a) Selective reminding
   (b) Sequential recall
   (c) Declarative memory tasks
   (d) Semantic memory tasks
   (e) Procedural memory tasks

9. **A statistically significant difference ($p \leq .05$) of 11 points between the VMI and the NMI occurs in approximately what percentage of cases in the population at large?**
   (a) 1%
   (b) 5%
   (c) 15%
   (d) 33%
   (e) 43%

10. **The TOMAL-2 Supplementary Indexes were derived via**
    _____.

    (a)   structural equation modeling

    (b)   factor analysis using principal components

    (c)   factor analysis using maximum likelihood solutions

    (d)   confirmatory factor analysis

    (e)   expert content analysis

Answers: 1:b; 2:e; 3:d; 4:a; 5:c; 6:b; 7:d; 8:a; 9:e; 10:e

References

Alvord, S., Adams, W., Shaver, G., Rosengren, K., Garner, B., & Barker, R. (November, 2001). *Relationship between relevant WRAML and NEPSY subtest performance and reading readiness.* National Academy of Neuropsychology Annual Meeting, San Francisco.

American Educational Research Association (AERA), American Psychological Association (APA), & National Council on Measurement in Education (NCME). (1999). *Standards for educational and psychological testing.* Washington, DC: American Psychological Association.

Anastasi, A., & Urbina, S. (1997). *Psychological testing* (7th ed.). Upper Saddle River, NJ: Prentice Hall.

Baddeley, A. (1992). Working memory. *Science, 255,* 556–559.

Bender, L. (1938). A visual motor gestalt test and its clinical use. *American Orthopsychiatric Association research monograph* (Vol. 3). New York: American Orthopsychiatric Association.

Benton, A. L. (1946). *Benton visual retention test.* New York: Psychological Corp.

Benton, A. L. (1974). *The revised visual retention test* (4th ed.). San Antonio, TX: Psychological Corp.

Benton, A. L., Hamsher, K. deS., Varnay, N. R., & Spreen, O. (1983). *Facial recognition test.* New York: Oxford University Press.

Bigler, E. D. (Ed.). (1990). *Traumatic brain injury: Mechanisms of damage, assessment, intervention, and outcome.* Austin, TX: PRO-ED.

Blumenfeld. H. (2002). *Neuroanatomy through clinical cases.* Sunderland, MA: Sinauer Associates.

Boder, E., & Jarrico, S. (1982). *Boder reading-spelling pattern test: A diagnostic screening test for developmental dyslexia.* San Antonio, TX: Psychological Corp.

Brown, A. L. (1975). The development of memory: Knowing, knowing about knowing, and knowing how to know. In H. W. Reese (Ed.), *Advances in child development and behavior* (pp.103–152). New York: Academic Press.

Buschke, H., & Fuld, P. A. (1974). Evaluating storage, retention, and retrieval in disordered memory and learning. *Neurology, 11,* 1019–1025.

Butcher, J. N., Dahlstrom, W. G., Graham, J. R., Tellegen, A., & Kaemmer, B. (1989). *Minnesota Multiphasic Personality Inventory–2 (MMPI-2): Manual for administration and scoring.* Minneapolis: University of Minnesota.

Butcher, J. N., Williams, C. L., Graham, J. R., Archer, R., Tellegen, A., Ben-

Porath, Y. S., & Kaemmer, B. (1992). *MMPI-A manual for administration, scoring and interpretation*. Minneapolis: University of Minnesota Press.

Ceci, S. J. (1984). A developmental study of learning disabilities and memory. *Journal of Experimental Child Psychology, 38,* 352–371.

Corkin, S. (2002). What's new with the amnestic patient, HM? *Nature Reviews, Neuroscience, 3,* 153–160.

De Renzi, E., & Lucchelli, F. (1990). Developmental dysmnesia in a poor reader. *Brain, 113,* 1337–1345.

Ebbinghaus, H. (1885). *Uber das Gedachtnis.* Leipzig: Duncker.

Fletcher, J. M. (1985). Memory for verbal and nonverbal stimuli in learning disability subgroups: Analysis of selective reminding. *Journal of Experimental Child Psychology 40,* 244–259.

Fletcher-Janzen, E., & Reynolds, C. R. (Eds.). (2008). *Neuropsychological perspectives on the diagnosis and treatment of learning disabilities in the era of RTI.* NY: Wiley.

Fuster, J. M. (1995). *Memory in the cerebral cortex: An empirical approach to neural networks in the human and nonhuman primates.* Cambridge, MA: MIT Press.

Goldstein, F., & Levin, H. S. (1990). Epidemiology of traumatic brain injury: Incidence, clinical characteristics, and risk factors. In E. D. Bigler (Ed.), *Traumatic brain injury* (pp. 51–68). Austin, TX: PRO-ED.

Goldstein, S., & Reynolds, C. R. (Eds.). (2005). *Handbook of neurodevelopmental and genetic disorders in adults.* New York: Guilford.

Gordon, R. A. (1984). Digits backward and the Mercer-Kamin law: An empirical response to Mercer's treatment of internal validity of IQ tests. In C. R. Reynolds & R. T. Brown (Eds.), *Perspectives on bias in mental testing* (pp. 357–506). New York: Plenum.

Grelotti, D. J., Klin, A. J., Gauthier, I., Skudlarski, P., Cohen, D. J., Gore, J. C., Volkmar, F., & Schultz, R. T. (2005). fMRI activation of the fusiform gyrus and amygdala to cartoon characters but not to faces in a boy with autism. *Neuropsychologia, 43*(3), 373–385.

Haberlandt, K. (1999). *Human memory: Exploration and application.* Needham Heights, MA: Allyn & Bacon.

Hannay, H. J., Howieson, D. B., Loring, D. W., Fischer, J. S., and Lezak, M. D. (2004). Neuropathology for neuropsychologists. In M. D. Lezak, D. B. Howieson, and D. W. Loring (Eds.), *Neuropsychological assessment* (4th ed.). New York: Oxford University Press.

Jensen, A. R. (1980). *Bias in mental testing.* NY: The Free Press.

Kamphaus, R. W. (2000). *Clinical assessment of child and adolescent intelligence* (2nd ed.). Needham Heights, MA: Allyn & Bacon.

Kaplan, E. (1996, March). *Discussant.* Symposium presented at the annual meeting of the National Association of School Psychologists, Atlanta.

Kaufman, A. S. (1979). *Intelligent testing with the WISC-R.* New York: Wiley.

Kaufman, A. S., & Kaufman, N. L. (Eds.). (2001). *Specific learning disabilities and difficulties in children and adolescents.* New York: Cambridge University Press.

Kolb, B., & Whishaw, I. Q. (2003). *Fundamentals of human neuropsychology* (5th ed.). New York: Worth.

Lashley, K. D. (1950). In search of the engram. *Symposium of the Society for Experimental Biology, 4,* 454–482.

Levin, H. S., Eisenberg, H. M., & Benton, A. L. (1989). *Mild head injury.* New York: Oxford University Press.

Lezak, M. D. (1983). *Neuropsychological assessment.* New York: Oxford University Press.

Lorsbach, T. C., & Gray, J. W. (1985). The development of encoding processes in learning disabled children. *Journal of Learning Disabilities, 18,* 222–227.

Lowe, P. A., Mayfield, J. W., & Reynolds, C. R. (2003). Gender differences in memory test performance among children and adolescents. *Archives of Clinical Neuropsychology, (18),* 865–878.

Lowther, J. L., & Mayfield, J. W. (2004). Memory functioning in children with traumatic brain injuries: A TOMAL validity study. *Archives of Clinical Neuropsychology, 19,* 105–118.

Luria, A. R. (1966). *Higher cortical functions in man* (B. Haigh, Trans.). New York: Basic Books.

Luria, A. R. (2006). *The mind of a mnemonist.* Cambridge, MA: Harvard University Press.

McCarthy, D. (1972). *McCarthy scales of children's abilities.* San Antonio, TX: Psychological Corp.

McDermott, P., Fantuzzo, J., & Glutting, J. (1990). Just say no to subtest analysis: A critique of Wechsler theory and practice. *Journal of Psychoeducational Assessment, 8,* 290–302.

Messick, S. A. (1989). Validity. In R. Linn (Ed.), *Educational measurement* (3rd ed., pp.13–103). Washington, DC: American Council on Education.

Miller, G. A. (1956). The magical number seven, plus or minus two: Some limits on our capacity for processing information. *Psychological Review, 63,* 81–97.

Miller, M., Bigler, E., & Adams, W. (2003). Comprehensive assessment of child and adolescent memory: The Wide Range Assessment of Memory and Learning, the Test of Memory and Learning, and the California Verbal Learning Test-Children's Version. In C. R. Reynolds & R. W. Kamphaus (Eds.), *The handbook of psychological and educational assessment of children, Vol. I, intelligence, aptitude, and achievement—second edition.,* pp. 275–304). New York: Guilford.

Miyake, A., & Shah, P. (1999). Toward unified theories of working memory:

Emerging consensus, unresolved theoretical issues, and future research directions. In A. Miyake, & P. Shah (Eds.), *Models of Working Memory* (pp. 442–481). Cambridge, UK: Cambridge University Press.

Myers, P. I., & Hammill, D. D. (1990). *Learning disabilities: Basic concepts, assessment practices, and instructional strategies.* Austin, TX: PRO-ED.

Nussbaum, N. L., & Bigler, E. D. (1990). *Identification and treatment of attention deficit disorder.* Austin, TX: PRO-ED.

Osterrieth, P. A. (1944). Le test de copie d'une figure complexe. *Archives de Psychologie, 30,* 206–356.

Prigatano, G. P. (1978). Wechsler memory scale: A selective review of the literature. *Journal of Clinical Psychology, 34,* 816–832.

Ramsay, M. C., & Reynolds, C. R. (1995). Separate digit tests: A brief history, a literature review, and a reexamination of the factor structure of the Test of Memory and Learning (TOMAL). *Neuropsychology Review, 5*(3), 151–171.

Reitan, R. M., & Wolfson, D. (1985). *The Halstead-Reitan neuropsychological test battery: Theory and clinical interpretation.* Tucson, AZ: Neuropsychology Press.

Rey, A. (1941). L'examen psychologique dans les cas d'encephalopathie traumatique. *Archives de Psychologie, 28,* 286-340.

Rey, A. (1958). *L'Examen Clinique en psychologie.* Paris: Presses Universitaires de France.

Reynolds, C. R. (1985). Critical measurement issues in learning disabilities. *The Journal of Special Education, 18,* 451–476.

Reynolds, C. R. (1986). Measurement and assessment of exceptional children. In R. T. Brown & C. R. Reynolds (Eds.), *Psychological perspectives on childhood exceptionality: A handbook* (pp. 91–135). New York: Wiley Interscience.

Reynolds, C. R. (1987) Intelligent testing. In C. R. Reynolds & L. Mann (Eds.), *Encyclopedia of special education* (pp. 855-857), New York: Wiley Interscience.

Reynolds, C. R. (1997). Forward and backward memory span should not be combined for clinical analysis. *Archives of Clinical Neuropsychology, 12*(1), 29–40.

Reynolds, C. R. (1998). Fundamentals of measurement and assessment in psychology. In A. Bellak & M. Hersen (Series Eds.) & C. R. Reynolds (Vol. Ed.), *Comprehensive clinical psychology: Vol. 4. Assessment* (pp. 33–56). Oxford, England: Elsevier Science.

Reynolds, C. R., & Bigler, E. D. (1994b). *Test of Memory and Learning.* Austin, TX: PRO-ED.

Reynolds, C. R., & Bigler, E. D. (1994a). *Manual for the Test of Memory and Learning.* Austin, TX: PRO-ED.

Reynolds, C. R., & Bigler, E. D. (2001). *Clinical assessment scales for the elderly.* Odessa, FL: Psychological Assessment Resources.

Reynolds, C. R., & Fletcher-Janzen, E. (Eds.). (1997). *Handbook of clinical child neuropsychology, (second edition)*. New York: Plenum.

Reynolds, C. R., & Kaufman, A. S. (1985). Assessing intelligence with the Wechsler Scales. In B. Wolman (Ed.), *Handbook of intelligence*, 601–662. New York: Wiley-Interscience.

Reynolds, C. R., & Kamphaus, R. W. (2003). *Reynolds intellectual assessment scales*. Lutz, FL: PAR, Inc.

Reynolds, C. R., & Kamphaus, R. W. (2004). *Behavior assessment system for children, second edition*. Bloomington, MN: Pearson Assessments.

Reynolds, C. R, & Richmond, B. O. (2008). *Revised children's manifest anxiety scale, second edition*. Los Angeles: Western Psychological Services.

Reynolds, C. R., Richmond, B., & Lowe, P. (2003a). *Adult manifest anxiety scale*. Los Angeles: Western Psychological Services.

Reynolds, C. R., Richmond, B., & Lowe, P. (2003b). *Elderly anxiety scale*. Los Angeles: Western Psychological Services.

Reynolds, C. R., & Voress, J. K. (2007). *Test of Memory and Learning–second edition* (TOMAL-2). Austin, TX: PRO-ED.

Reynolds, C. R., & Voress, J. K. (in press). *Elderly memory schedule*. Austin, TX: PRO-ED.

Riccio, C., & Reynolds, C. R. (1998). Neuropsychological assessment of children. In M. Hersen & A. Bellack (Series Eds.) & C. R. Reynolds (Vol. Ed.), *Comprehensive clinical psychology: Vol. 4, Assessment* (pp. 267–301). New York: Elsevier.

Riccio, C., Reynolds, C. R., & Lowe, P. A. (2001). *Clinical applications of continuous performance tests: Measuring attention and impulsive responding in children and adults*. New York: Wiley.

Riccio, C., & Wolfe, M.E. (2003). Neuropsychological perspectives on the assessment of children. In C. R. Reynolds & R. W. Kamphaus (Eds.), *The handbook of psychological and educational assessment of children, Vol. I, Intelligence, aptitude, and achievement, second edition* (pp. 275–304). New York: Guilford.

Roid, G. H. (1989). *Programs to fit skewed distributions and generate percentile norms for skewed or kurtotic distributions: Continuous norming with the first four moments* (Tech. Rep. No. 89-02). Salem, OR: Assessment Research.

Rourke, B. P., Fisk, I. L., & Strang, J. D. (1986). *Neuropsychological assessment of children: A treatment oriented approach*. New York: Guilford.

Schultz, R. T. (2005). Developmental deficits in social perception in autism: The role of the amygdala and fusiform face area. *International Journal of Developmental Neuroscience, 23,* 125–141.

Schultz, R. T., Gauthier, I., Klin A., Fulbright, R., Anderson, A., Volkmar, F., Skudlarski, P., Lacadie et al. (2000). Abnormal ventral temporal cortical activity during face discrimination among individuals with autism and Asperger syndrome. *Archives of General Psychiatry, 57,* 331–340.

Schultz, R. T., Grelotti, D. J., Klin, A., Kleinman, J., Van der Gaag, C., Marois, R., & Skudlarski, P. (2003). The role of the fusiform face area in social cognition: Implications for the pathobiology of autism. *Philosophical Transactions of the Royal Society, Series B, 358,* 415–427.

Shaver, G., & Adams, W. (2005). Distinguishing simulated malingerers from head injured patients and controls on the Wide Range Assessment of Memory and Learning, second edition. *Dissertation Abstracts International, Section B: The Sciences and Engineering. 65(12B), 6674.*

Sheslow, D. V., & Adams, W. V. (1990). *Wide range assessment of memory and learning.* Wilmington, DE: Wide Range, Inc.

Sheslow, D. V., & Adams, W. V. (2003). *Wide range assessment of memory and learning—second edition.* Wilmington, DE: Wide Range.

Snyderman, M., & Rothman, S. (1987). Survey of expert opinion on intelligence and aptitude testing. *American Psychologist, 42,* 137-144.

Squire, L. R., & Schacter, D. L. (Eds.). (2002). *Neuropsychology of memory.* New York: Oxford University Press.

Swanson, H. L., Harris, K. R., & Graham, S. (Eds.). (2003). *Handbook of learning disabilities.* New York: Guilford.

Swanson, H. L, & Saez, L. (2003). Memory difficulties in children and adults with learning disabilities. In H. L. Swanson, K. R. Harris, & S. Graham (Eds.), *Handbook of learning disabilities* (pp. 182–198). New York: Guilford.

Tombaugh, T. (1996). *Test of memory malingering.* N. Tonawanda, NY: Multi-Health Systems, Inc.

Watkins, M. W. (2000). Cognitive profile analysis: A shared professional myth. *School Psychology Quarterly, 15,* 465–479.

Watkins, M. W. (2003). IQ subtest analysis: Clinical acumen or clinical illusion. *Scientific Review of Mental Health Practice, 2,* 118–141.

Watkins, M. W., Glutting, J., & Lei, P. (2007). Validity of full-scale IQ when there is significant variability among WISC-III and WISC-IV factor scores. *Applied Neuropsychology, 14*(1), 13–20.

Wechsler, D. (1945). *Wechsler memory scale.* New York: Psychological Corporation.

Weniger, R., and Adams, W. (November, 2006). *Differences in performance on the WRAML2 for children with ADHD and reading disorder.* National Academy of Neuropsychology annual meeting, Tampa, FL.

Zillmer, E. A., Spiers, M. V., & Culbertson, W. (2008). *Principles of neuropsychology, second edition.* Belmont, CA: Wadsworth.

Annotated Bibliography

American Educational Research Association, American Psychological Association, & the National Council on Measurement in Education. (1999). *Standards for educational and psychological testing.* Washington, DC: Author.

This sixth version of the Standards *represents by far the most massive and thorough revision of the* Standards *ever prepared. It is featured here for three reasons: (a) these* Standards *apply to memory tests; (b) they contain a comprehensive reconceptualization of the notion of validity that is not widely understood even this many years after its publication; and (c) we have cited this document periodically throughout this book and strongly suggest reading it in its entirety if you are involved in testing and assessment at any level. Additionally, the* Standards *have been reviewed and adopted by most major membership organizations in the field of psychology and also have been adopted by a number of state licensing boards as part of their rules of practice. The* Standards *also serves as a useful text to understanding how tests should be developed, the documentation that should be provided by test developers and publishers, and discussions of the rights and responsibilities of test users. In addition to excellent chapters on psychometrics (e.g., reliability, validity, scaling), the* Standards *also address the difficult issues of fairness in testing, testing of the linguistically and culturally diverse examinee, and testing individuals with disabilities. In addition to presenting standards of practice in each of these areas, the* Standards *provides an excellent discussion of the concepts underlying each of these principles and standards. These discussions are uniformly valuable in understanding sound practices in all forms of educational and psychological testing. The* Standards *should be read, understood, and periodically reviewed by all individuals involved in testing, whether at the level of test author, test administrator / examiner, interpreting diagnostician, or consumer of test results.*

Dudai, Y. (2002). *Memory from A to Z: Keywords, concepts and beyond.* NY: Oxford University Press.

As the title suggests, this is a reference book that should be useful to newcomers to and experts in the field of memory research. Almost 200 terms related to the domain of memory investigation are included, most with a page or two description of its meaning and what you should know about this term vis-à-vis memory research. Terms range from a priori *to* zeitgeist, *with some being those a newcomer might appreciate (e.g.,* working memory*) and other entries that would likely challenge the experts (e.g.,* palimpsest*). While at times the selections seem a bit idiosyncratic (e.g.,* scoopaphobia*), and there are some surprising omissions (e.g., retrograde and anterograde amnesia), most entries are interesting inclusions* *with enough to clarify the memory context of the term, and sometimes its historical connections. Illustrations are provided (e.g., acetylcholine pathways and cerebellar interconnections), but more impressive is the reference list associated with most entries. No biographical entries are included and the book is no substitute for a neurobiology dictionary. Nonetheless, it probably deserves to be on the shelves of most graduate students and would be a handy reference for the professional receiving a last-minute request to give a presentation on any of a variety of topics related to memory.*

Fletcher-Janzen, E., & Reynolds, C. R. (Eds.). (2002). *Diagnostic reference manual of childhood disorders.* New York: Wiley.

A very large number of neurodevelopmental and genetic disorders have associated memory problems, especially in children and adolescents. This edited work is a compilation of information that is disorder specific and formatted consistently across all disorders represented. For approximately 800 disorders—ranging from obscure problems such as Soto's syndrome to more common disorders like Tourette's syndrome, phenylketonuria, and galactosemia—various experts present the natural history and etiology of each disorder, diagnostic keys, basic treatment approaches, expected outcomes, and implications for special education intervention. Physical, cognitive (including memory and intelligence where such patterns are known), emotional, and behavioral aspects of each disorder are noted and special attention is given to improving diagnostic accuracy.

Haberlandt, K. (1989). *Human memory: Exploration and application.* Needham Heights, MA: Allyn & Bacon.

While in need of updating, this little volume still provides a sound and very readable treatment of what is known about memory. The author is British and so presents a perspective somewhat different than one finds with U.S. neuropsychology writers. This includes discussions of research not typically cited in many U.S. publications. Along with the usual chapters on memory (history, neuroscience, kinds of memory, cognitive psychology, and memory disorders), there are also some intriguing discussions related to developmental memory phenomena (from infancy to old age), autobiographical memory, and memory in every day life. It is a good book to use to form the superstructure of what is known about memory, so that the framework can organize and enrich more in-depth reading. Regardless, it is the kind of book one finds oneself returning to frequently because of its deft handling of details and complex concepts.

Hambleton, R., & Li, S. (2006). Translation and adaptation issues and methods for educational and psychological tests. In C. Frisby & C. R. Reynolds (Eds.), *Comprehensive handbook of multicultural school psychology* (pp. 881–903). New York: Wiley.

Often it seems necessary to translate, adapt, or in some way modify an existing test for application to culturally diverse populations—memory tests are no exception. However, making changes in a way that maximizes or preserves (to the extent possible) the psychometric characteristics of the original test is not simple. Hambleton and Li provide in this chapter a review of many of the potential pitfalls in making such adaptations as well as clear guidelines for day-to-day practice. After a review of the common myths associated with translations and adaptations, Hambleton and Li give a step-by-step guide to best practice in making these changes. This is followed by a presentation and discussion of the Guidelines for Test Adaptation of the International Test Commission. Overall, Hambleton and Li provide an excellent discussion of problems and issues and then give the current state-of-the-art solution to test adaptation.

Kolb, B., & Whishaw, I. Q. (2003). *Fundamentals of human neuropsychology, fifth edition.* NY: Worth Publishers.

This is the classic text in neuropsychology, and its chapter on memory provides a fine overview that expertly interweaves neurological, neuropsychological, and cognitive psychology findings related to memory. Kinds of memory (e.g., implicit versus explicit), neurology of memory, and differentiating brain structures related to memory are all focused on with ample breadth to prepare the reader to progress on to more specialized and technical material. Other chapters include additional sections on memory as appropriate (e.g., a discussion of dementia within a chapter on "Psychiatric and Related Disorders"), and the index includes more than 70 related subtitles under the main entries of "Memory" and "Learning," indicative of the rich supplemental information found in this book related to neuropsychological aspects of memory.

Lee, D., Reynolds, V. L., & Willson. (2003). Standardized test administration: Why bother? *Journal of Forensic Neuropsychology, 3*(3), 55–82.

For a variety of reasons, it is often necessary to make accommodations or alterations in standardized test administration procedures for individuals with disabilities. It has also been documented that examiners will at times make changes in standardized test procedures for their own convenience or simply for the convenience of others. Memory tests seem particularly sensitive to changes in standardized administration procedures. The 1999 Standards (see corresponding previous entry) allow changes when necessary but place the onus of validating interpretations of test performance following such changes squarely on the examiner. In this article, the authors review extant research on changes in performance that occur in accordance with a variety of changes in test administration. The empirical literature on this topic reveals that in some cases very slight changes in test administration can substantially alter how examinees perform, and often the direction of such changes (i.e., making the test easier or harder) is counterintuitive. Changes in score patterns were observed on a variety of both personality and cognitive measures, including a number of memory tests, when standardized test administration procedures were not followed. These authors also conclude that changes in test administration procedures in the absence of data regarding the effects of such changes may lead to misdiagnosis, increased error rates overall in the diagnostic process, failure to meet the Daubert challenge of admissibility of expert testimony based on altered test administration, and strong challenges to the credibility of reports of testing when non-standardized administration procedures have been applied. Specific examples of the dangers of altered test administration and the changes they can produce as well as summaries of this literature in the personality and behavioral domains and in the cognitive domain are provided.

Lezak, M.D., Howieson, D.B., and Loring, D.W. (2004) *Neuropsychological Assessment, Fourth Edition.* New York: Oxford.

While this encyclopedic volume covers many other areas, its two chapters on memory do provide an excellent compilation of various tasks and tests that have been used to measure memory over the last 65 years. One chapter focuses on single-task measures whereas the second features memory batteries. Unfortunately, both the WRAML2 and TOMAL-2 were released too recently to be included. Nonetheless, the discussion by Lezak and her colleagues is extensive and probably the most comprehensive inclusion of memory measures found anywhere. Memory assessment tools evaluating verbal, visual, and tactile sensory areas are covered along with incidental, prospective, and remote memory domains. Fairly comprehensive and clinically relevant literature reviews are included along with extensive descriptions of test contents and procedures.

Neisser, U., & Hyman, I. E. (2000). *Memory observed: Remembering in natural contexts, second edition.* NY: Worth Publishers.

In his lucid, iconoclastic style, Neisser condemned much memory research as being too detached from the real world, and set out to remedy that situation in the first edition of this volume. While the authors in the second edition state that progress has been made over the last 2 decades, there is still a need to conscientiously apply new findings to the real world, and to intentionally choose to investigate ecologically meaningful phenomena when conducting memory research. With such bias, the authors provide a fascinating selection of readings that highlight ways memory impacts everyday life and the varied methodologies that have been used to better understand aspects of everyday memory demands or accomplishments. Within the book there are chapters describing those with prodigious memory capacities, cultural differences in memory usage, recovered and false memory phenomena, the veracity of eye witness memory and other forensic linkages depending on memory, gender differences in memory, and meeting common memory challenges in everyday life. Most every chapter presents interesting and provocative findings anchored in everyday memory phenomena. Accordingly, the book is very readable, yet empirically solid and informative.

Ochoa, H. S. (2003). Assessment of culturally and linguistically diverse children. In C. R. Reynolds & R. W. Kamphaus (Eds.), *Handbook of psychological and educational assessment of children, vol. 1: Intelligence, aptitude and achievement* (pp. 563–583). New York: Guilford.

The number of individuals living and working in the United States who are from outside the mainstream, traditional cultures of the United States continues to grow rapidly. The assessment of all persons who are culturally or linguistically divergent from the standardization samples of tests or the background of the examiner presents us with special challenges. The use of comprehensive memory batteries such as the WRAML2 and the TOMAL-2 with these individuals is no exception and indeed may require even greater care and expertise. In this chapter, Ochoa provides a comprehensive review of the issues and stumbling blocks that surround the proper assessment of culturally and linguistically diverse students. His focus is on critical issues that affect day-to-day practice in conducting such assessments. Solutions are suggested as well as areas for future research where our current level of knowledge is meager.

Reynolds, C. R. (1997). Forward and backward memory span should not be combined for clinical analysis. *Archives of Clinical Neuropsychology, 12*(1), 29–40.

In this paper, the practice of combining forward and backward memory span, as represented so prominently on the various Wechsler Scales and some other memory scales, to arrive at a composite score for clinical interpretation is examined historically and actuarially using a large (N = 1,342) nationally stratified random sample of children from ages 5 years through 19 years. Past clinical literature does not support the additive nature of forward and backward memory span as elements of a common process. Factor analyses of forward and backward recall using both digits and letters indicate that the two memory processes are distinct as well and should not be combined routinely for clinical interpretation. The author concludes that while combining forward and backward memory span may be useful at times (essentially for examining attention span only, and then rather cautiously) the evidence now seems overwhelming that separate scaled scores for forward and for backward memory span tasks should be provided routinely on any standardized assessment. This practice facilitates clinical practice and research applications concerning the differential meaning of performance on the two tasks. Current evidence seems to support forward span tasks as being simpler, perhaps verbally oriented, and strongly sequential while backward memory span invokes more complex processes that require transformations not necessary with for-

ward memory span. Backward recall may also invoke, for many individuals, visuospatial imaging processes even for ostensibly verbal material such as letters. Potential differences in the attentional demands or components of these two types of tasks deserve additional study as well. Forward memory span measures may have a stronger attentional component than backward recall measures, which are more highly correlated with general intelligence and require cognitive transformation, an element missing from rote, forward recall. Surprisingly, much remains to be done to understand the distinction between forward and backward memory span and what it means both clinically and to theories of brain-behavior relationships; but it is clear the tasks are sufficiently different to be assessed separately for clinical purposes.

Riccio, C. A., Reynolds, C. R., & Lowe, P. A. (2001). Clinical applications of continuous performance tests: Measuring attention and impulsive responding in children and adults. New York: Wiley.

Attention is a key precursor to memory, and continuous performance tests (CPTs) have been proffered as strong performance-based means of assessing attention as well as impulsivity (which also may have adverse impact on performance during memory testing). The importance of attention to memory is evident in many venues but clearly in the emphasis attention receives in the WRAML2 and the TOMAL-2. This book-length treatment of the now-enormous 40-year history of CPTs presents a comprehensive perspective on how CPTs should be used. Riccio, Reynolds, and Lowe review information from over 400 studies involving CPTs and various diagnostic groups, reporting that CPTs are highly sensitive performance-based measures of attention problems and impulsive responding. This makes the CPT a useful adjunct to rapid, rote memory tasks and to impressionistic behavior rating scales in the assessment of attention and impulsive responding. The authors begin with a tutorial on the neurobiology of attention, discussing both neurochemistry and neuropsychological models of executive control, all of which are of interest in the interpretation of performance on memory tests as well. Next, they describe the major paradigms surrounding CPTs suggested for clinical use and the differences among them. The volume presents a review of technical adequacy and standardization of each major paradigm, followed by chapters on the sensitivity and specificity of CPTs in the diagnosis of disorders of childhood and adults. The relationship of CPTs to other tests is also reviewed, and the uses of CPTs in diagnosis and in monitoring treatment effects, especially psychopharmacological effects, are noted. This work provides a reference source for everyone who evaluates children and / or adults with behavioral and emotional problems associated with disorders of attention, executive control, or both, in either using CPTs as a component of the diagnostic process or interpreting reports from those who do. As Hynd notes in the foreword, CPTs can vary considerably, and performance can be impaired by a host of disorders, making a comprehensive reference such as this text not simply useful, but necessary.

Romine, C., & Reynolds, C. R. (2005). A model of the development of frontal lobe functioning: Findings from a meta-analysis. *Applied Neuropsychology*, *12*(4), 190–201.

The frontal lobes play a significant role in several aspects of memory, especially working memory and related tasks for which sequence of recall is of particular importance. There is considerable controversy over the developmental path of the frontal lobes, especially with regard to the age of maturation or the achievement of full functional capacity of the frontal lobes. In this article, the authors relate the findings of a meta-analysis of studies examining the course of frontal development from early childhood into the young adult years of the early 20s. The model emerging from these studies revealed a sharp increase in frontal function as measured on various cognitive tasks in the childhood years, especially from ages 5 to 11 or 12 years with continuing but slowing rates of growth and development throughout adolescence, and into early adulthood. Many of the observed developmental curves mimic those seen on a variety of memory tasks when viewed as growth or developmental curves.

Strauss, E., Sherman, E. M., & Spreen O. (2006). *A compendium of neuropsychological tests: Administration, norms and commentary, third edition.* NY: Oxford University Press.

As the title suggests, this volume is a vast resource concerning neuropsychological tests. Of relevance here is the more than 200-page treatment of memory testing. Following a conceptual overview of memory, an impressive gathering of dozens of tests (many commercially available) from Europe and the United States appears, along with useful test descriptions, intended age ranges, administration guidelines, administration times, standardization information, and relevant psychometric properties when available. For measures developed without a true standardization effort, norms have been pooled from supplemental sources, mostly journal articles that provided norms on specific subsamples, many of which have clinical diagnoses. Often, supplemental norms for additional age or educational subgroupings are also among the inclusions. Primarily, tests of visual and verbal memory are included. Evaluative comments are also provided for most of the tests included, especially if the test is commonly used. This is a good source from which to gain an appreciation and knowledge of the breadth of isolated or niche memory tests that exist, in addition to those that are available as batteries of subtests.

Zillmer, E. A., Spiers, M. V., & Culbertson, W. C. (2008). *Principles of neuropsychology, second edition.* Belmont, CA: Thomson.

This updated version of a solid overview text in neuropsychology has a good chapter on memory that nicely integrates attention, emotion, and executive functioning with memory functions. While it is not a comprehensive treatment, it does provide a solid and reasonably complete overview of essential aspects of memory. Empirical human and animal research along with case studies provide a nice balance of clinical applications and their scientific basis. Since this is just one chapter in a general neuropsychology text, the remainder of the book is available for pursuing more in-depth discussions of several topics related to memory functioning.

Index

About the Authors

Wayne Adams, PhD, earned his doctoral degree in developmental/child clinical psychology from Syracuse University. After teaching at Colgate University for several years, he received postdoctoral training in pediatric psychology at Memorial Hospital, the University of North Carolina, Chapel-Hill. Thereafter, he worked at DuPont Hospital for Children (Wilmington, DE), a full-service children's hospital with academic ties to the pediatric residency program of Jefferson Medical College in nearby Philadelphia. He served as the hospital's director of the Division of Pediatric Psychology and was chief psychologist within the Division of Behavioral Medicine; at the same time he was associate clinical professor at Jefferson Medical College. During his 23 years at DuPont Hospital, he participated with several medical services, including an inpatient rehabilitation program, an outpatient Learning Disorders Clinic, and a multidisciplinary Developmental Disabilities clinic. He has had a private practice as well.

Adams' primary research interests include topics related to child memory and its assessment, child/adolescent assessment generally, pediatric (hospital-based) psychology, learning disorders (including ADHD), school consultation, and a variety of childhood/adolescent behavior and developmental disorders. His clinical interests include learning and related behavior disorders, pediatric neuropsychological assessment, and various neuro-developmental disorders. He has published more than 30 articles in various professional outlets, coauthored five nationally used test instruments, and made more than 70 presentations at national conventions of professional organizations. He is a Fellow of APA's Division of Clinical Psychology as well as the National

Academy of Neuropsychology. He also holds diplomate status in clinical psychology within the American Board of Professional Psychology.

Dr. Adams now lives outside of Portland, Oregon, where he moved almost 10 years ago. He serves as tenured professor and chairperson of the APA-accredited Graduate Department of Clinical Psychology at George Fox University. He teaches courses in Cognitive Assessment and Neuropsychological Assessment. He recently served as a Fulbright research scholar assisting Chinese officials adapt and norm the WRAML2 to that culture.

Cecil R. Reynolds, PhD, earned his Doctoral Degree from the University of Georgia in 1978 under the tutelage of Alan Kaufman, with a major in School Psychology and minors in Statistics and in Clinical Neuropsychology. Prior to joining the Texas A&M University faculty in 1981, Dr. Reynolds was a faculty member at the University of Nebraska-Lincoln, where he served as associate director and acting director of the Buros Institute of Mental Measurement, after writing the grants and proposals to move the institute to Nebraska following the death of its founder, Oscar Buros. He is the author of more than 300 scholarly publications and author or editor of more than 45 books, including *The Clinician's Guide to the BASC, Clinical Applications of Continuous Performance Tests, The Handbook of School Psychology,* and the *Handbook of Clinical Child Neuropsychology.* He is the author of several widely used tests of personality and behavior, including the *Behavior Assessment System for Children* and the *Revised Children's Manifest Anxiety Scale.* He is also senior author of the *Test of Memory and Learning–Second Edition,* the *Clinical Assessment Scales for the Elderly,* and coauthor of several computerized test interpretation systems. He is senior author of the *Reynolds Intellectual Assessment Scales* (RIAS). He maintained a clinical practice treating trauma victims and individuals with traumatic brain injury for 25 years before retiring from clinical work at the end of 2003.

Dr. Reynolds holds a diplomate in Clinical Neuropsychology from the American Board of Professional Neuropsychology, of which he is also a past president, and was a diplomate in School Psychology of the American Board of Professional Psychology, prior to retiring his diplomate in 2004. He is a past president of the National Academy of Neuropsychology and APA Divisions 5 (Evaluation, Measurement, and Statistics), 40 (Clinical Neuropsychology), and 16 (School Psychology). He served as editor of *Archives of Clinical Neuropsychology* (1990–2002), the official journal of the National Academy of Neuropsychology, and serves on the editorial boards of 11 other journals. He is the current editor of *Applied Neuropsychology*. Dr. Reynolds received multiple national awards recognizing him for excellence in research, including the Lightner Witmer Award and early career awards from APA Divisions 5 and 15. He is a corecipient of the Society for the Psychological Study of Social Issues Robert Chin Award. In 1999, Dr. Reynolds received the Senior Scientist Award from APA Division 16 (School Psychology). In 2000, he received the National Academy of Neuropsychology's Distinguished Neuropsychologist Award, the Academy's highest award for research accomplishments. He received the NASP 2003 Lifetime Achievement Award in Neuropsychology. His service to the profession and to society has been recognized as well through the President's Gold Medal for Service to the National Academy of Neuropsychology as well as the Academy's Distinguished Service Award, and the University of North Carolina at Wilmington's 50th Anniversary Razor Walker Award for Service to the Youth of North Carolina. He is currently a professor of Educational Psychology, Professor of Neuroscience, and Distinguished Research Scholar at Texas A&M University.